OHIO GENEALOGICAL

RESEARCH

by
George K. Schweitzer, Ph.D., Sc.D.
407 Ascot Court
Knoxville, TN 37923-5807

Word Processing by
Anne M. Smalley

ISBN 0-913857-16-5

TABLE OF CONTENTS

Abbreviations

ACPL	Allen County Public Library
C	1890 Union pension census
CH	County court houses
D	Death or mortality censuses
DAR	Daughters of the American Revolution
F	Farm and ranch censuses
FHC	Family History Center
FHL	Family History Library
LGL	Large genealogical libraries
LL	Local libraries
LR	Local repositories
M	Manufactures censuses
NA	National Archives
NARB	National Archives Regional Branches
OGS	Ohio Genealogical Society
OHS	Ohio Historical Society
ONAHRC	Ohio Network of American History Research Centers
P	1840 Revolutionary War veteran census
PLC	Public Library of Cincinnati
R	Regular censuses
RL	Regional libraries
SLO	State Library of Ohio
T	Tax substitutes for censuses
WPA	Works Progress Administration
WRHS	Western Reserve Historical Society

Chapter 1

OHIO BACKGROUND

1. OH geography

The state of Ohio (hereafter abbreviated OH) is located in the Great Lakes region of the Middle West of the US. In shape, it is almost square (225 miles wide and 215 miles high) with a slightly irregular northern boundary and a considerably irregular southern boundary. See Figure 1. OH is bounded on the north by MI (northwest) and Lake Erie. On the east, its boundaries are defined by PA (northern) and the Ohio River, across which rests WV. The entire southern border is made up by the Ohio River across which rest WV (in the east) and KY. The western boundary is constituted entirely by IN. These borders can be seen in Figure 2, which also shows the major rivers of OH. Reading from left to right along the shore of Lake Erie, three rivers can be seen to flow into the Lake: the Maumee, the Sandusky, and the Cuyahoga Rivers. Then in the northeast area, the Mahoning River flows eastward out of OH into PA where it empties into the OH River. Now, reading from left to right along the OH River, five main rivers flow into the OH River: the Great Miami, the Little Miami, the Scioto, the Hocking, and the Muskingum Rivers. All of the waterways of OH (the lake and the rivers) are of exceptional importance to genealogical researchers because they are the chief transportation routes by which early settlers entered the area. The early settlements were also made along them, because the people needed to be near the transportation routes in order to ship produce out and to receive materials from elsewhere. Please note that the OH River flows westward from PA and northeastern WV (VA until 1863), and that Lake Erie is a water connection to western NY. These geographic characteristics defined major early migration routes into OH.

Figure 3 shows the present-day population centers of OH, which include the cities (with populations in thousands, K) of Columbus (633K), Cleveland (506K), Cincinnati (365K), Toledo (333K), Akron (224K), Dayton (182K), Youngstown (96K), Parma (88K), Canton (85K), Lorain (72K), and Springfield (70K). The four principal land regions of OH are depicted in Figure 4: (1) the Great Lakes Plains, (2) the Till Plains, (3) the Appalachian Plateau, and (4) the Lexington Plain. The Great Lakes Plains are a narrow strip of very flat land running along Lake Erie. It is about 60 miles broad in the west and gradually narrows to about 10 miles in the east. The fertile soil of the region is good for crops. Marshes and swamps were prevalent in the early years of OH, but many have been drained.

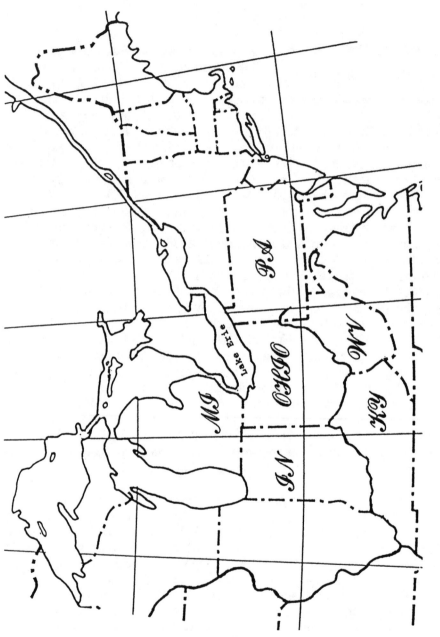

Figure 1. OH in the US

MI   LAKE ERIE   PA

Maumee   Sandusky   Cuyahoga   Mahoning

IN

Great Miami   Little Miami   Scioto   Hocking   Muskingum   WV

OHIO RIVER

KY   OHIO RIVER

WILLIAMS   Bryan
FULTON   Wauseon
LUCAS   Toledo
North Bass   Middle Bass I   South Bass   Kelleys I
OTTAWA   Port Clinton
LAKE   Paines-ville
ASHTABULA   Jefferson

DEFIANCE   Defiance
Napoleon
WOOD   Bowling Green
SANDUSKY   Fremont
Sandusky
ERIE
Cleveland
CUYAHOGA
Chardon
GEAUGA
TRUMBULL   Warren

Paulding
HENRY
Elyria
LORAIN

PAULDING
PUTNAM   Ottawa
HANCOCK   Findlay
SENECA   Tiffin
Norwalk
HURON
Medina
MEDINA
SUMMIT   Akron
PORTAGE   Ravenna
Youngstown
MAHONING

Van Wert
VAN WERT
ALLEN   Lima
WYANDOT   Upper Sandusky
CRAWFORD   Bucyrus
RICH-LAND   Mansfield
ASH-LAND   Ashland
WAYNE   Wooster
STARK   Canton
COLUMBIANA   Lisbon

MERCER   Celina
AUGLAIZE   Wapakoneta
HARDIN   Kenton
MARION   Marion
Mt. Gilead
MORROW
KNOX   Mount Vernon
HOLMES   Millersburg
TUSCARAWAS   New Philadelphia
CARROLL   Carrollton
HARRISON   Cadiz
Steuben-ville
JEFFERSON

SHELBY   Sidney
LOGAN   Bellefontaine
UNION   Marysville
Delaware
DELAWARE
COSHOCTON   Coshocton
GUERNSEY   Cambridge
St. Clairsville
BELMONT

DARKE   Greenville
MIAMI   Troy
CHAMPAIGN   Urbana
CLARK   Springfield
FRANKLIN   Columbus
LICKING   Newark
MUSKINGUM   Zanesville

PREBLE   Eaton
MONT-GOMERY   Dayton
GREENE   Xenia
MADISON   London
FAIRFIELD   Lancaster
New Lexington
PERRY
MORGAN   McConnels-ville
NOBLE   Caldwell
MONROE   Woodsfield

BUTLER   Hamilton
WARREN   Lebanon
FAYETTE   Washington C.H.
PICKAWAY   Circleville
Logan
HOCKING
WASHINGTON   Marietta

HAMILTON   Cincinnati
CLERMONT   Batavia
Wilmington
CLINTON
ROSS   Chillicothe
VINTON   McArthur
ATHENS   Athens

Hillsboro
HIGHLAND
Waverly
PIKE
Jackson
JACKSON
MEIGS   Pomeroy

BROWN   George-town
ADAMS   West Union
SCIOTO   Portsmouth
GALLIA   Gallipolis

LAWRENCE   Ironton

Figure 2.
OH
Rivers

Figure 3. OH Population
Centers

Figure 4.
OH
Land
Regions

The Till Plains make up most of the western half of the remaining part of OH. Its gently rolling terrain and broad river valleys provide some of the best farming country for grains in the US. The area shows a gradual slope down toward the southwestern corner of OH as evidenced by the flows of the Great and Little Miami Rivers. The Appalachian Plateau occupies the eastern part of the state. The northern third of the region has rolling hills and valleys, and the soil is not as fertile as that in the Till Plains. The southern two-thirds is quite rugged with much steeper hills and valleys, and the soil is thin and not very fertile. The area has forests, waterfalls, and mineral deposits of salt, clay, coal, gas, and oil. The very small triangular area in the south is called the Lexington Plain or the Bluegrass Region. As the names indicate, this is an extension of the KY Bluegrass Region which centers on Lexington. The topography is rolling and the soil is not highly fertile.

2. Pre-Revolutionary OH

In 1607, the English began settlement in VA of the eastern coast of what is now the US. Settlement by the English spread to MA (1620), MD (1634), ME (1630s), CT and RI (1636), NH (1638), NC (1670s), SC(1670), and PA (1683). The Dutch planted colonies in NY in 1624, and the Swedes settled DE and NJ in 1638, but England took these three areas (NY, DE, NJ) over in 1664. Therefore, as of 1685, the entire coast from ME to SC was occupied by the English, and they were moving inland toward the Appalachian Mountains. These mountains ran along the back country of the colonies, parallel to the coast, all the way from northern ME to the northwestern tip of SC. They offered a formidable barrier to any further movement because of their height and ruggedness, but there were several passages through them that offered access. These passages, however, were blocked by Indians who resisted English attempts to send settlers through.

At almost the same time that the English settlements were beginning, the French started establishing posts in Canada at Port Royal (1605) on the Atlantic seacoast and at Quebec (1608) on the St. Lawrence River which ran northeastward into the Atlantic Ocean. Their fur-trading activities, managed out of these places, lead them to send explorers, then traders and missionaries up the St. Lawrence River (southwestward), into the area above the Great Lakes (northwestward), into the areas around the Great Lakes (westward), then south from the Lake Michigan into the upper MS River Valley, and onto several of the river's tributaries. As of 1685, they had established fur-trading and/or missionary posts along what is now the US-Canadian border, around the Great Lakes, and in what are now the areas of northern NY, MI, northern IN, IL, and WI. See the top part of Figure 5. French traders

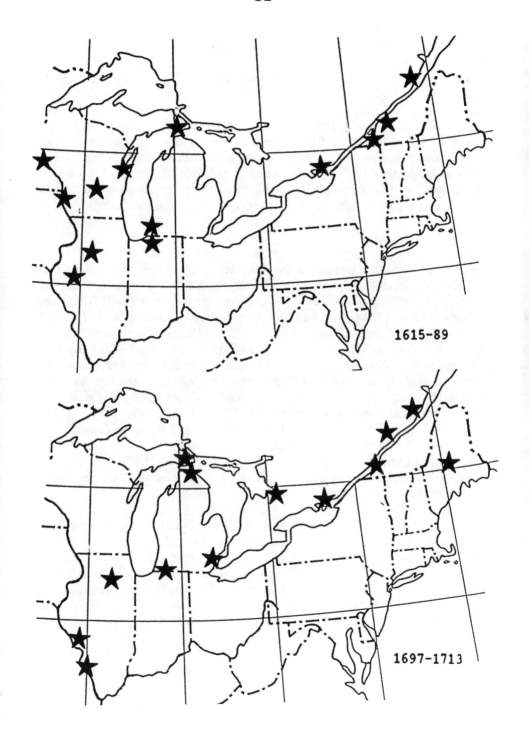

1615-89

1697-1713

Figure 5. French Posts

were beginning to enter OH from the northwest and the west, and English traders were starting to enter from the east.

In general, the Indians were friendly to the fur traders because the trade brought them items they wanted, and it enhanced their economy. However, they tended to strongly oppose the settlers who would take their lands from them. Thus, the Indians usually sided with the French, and against the English, although there are some notable exceptions for some tribes and for some periods of time. The French and their Indian allies wanted to confine the English settlers to the land areas east of the Appalachian Mountains, but the English wanted to penetrate the Appalachians and settle and farm the vast lands west of them.

The conflicting agendas of the French/Indians and the English resulted in constant hostility from 1685 to 1763. These hostilities came to heated encounters in a series of four French/Indian-against-English wars: King William's War (1689-97), Queen Anne's War (1702-13), King George's War (1744-48), and the French and Indian War (1756-63). The first of the wars, King William's War (1689-97) was fought largely on the northern borders of NY, NH, ME, MA, and CT. See the top part of Figure 5. The English failed in a large-scale seaborne assault on Quebec, and no net gain was had by either side. After the war, the French built up their posts and added more. Chief among the new ones were additional forts in southern MI, IL, and especially two near the mouth of the MS River on what is now the MS and AL Gulf Coast. This resulted in a further tightening of the French hold on the trans-Appalachian territory. Both French and English fur traders in the OH country increased, the French chiefly in the west, and the English chiefly in the east.

The second war, Queen Anne's War (1702-13), was fought back and forth across the boundaries between New England and French Canada. See the bottom part of Figure 5. The English took Acadia (Nova Scotia) and Newfoundland, but failed again in an attempt to capture Quebec. Shortly after the war, more English traders from VA and PA began operating in the OH country, gradually expanding their activities westward. They came into frequent contact with French traders who were operating in western OH. Both the French and the English strengthened their frontiers, with the French moving into northeastern and northwestern NY, building more forts in IN and IL, setting up posts in the lower OH Valley, and establishing New Orleans on the MS River Delta in LA. As of 1740, the English were in control of the upper OH Valley, and the French were in control of the lower OH Valley. See the top part of Figure 6.

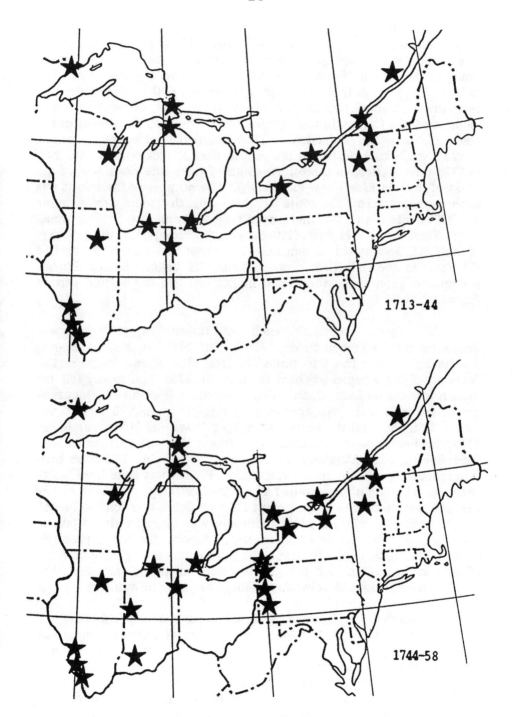

1713-44

1744-58

Figure 6. French Posts

The third war, King George's War (1744-48), was centered along the Canadian interfaces with VT, NH, MA, ME, and NY, with neither side gaining any advantage. The English made a sea attack on Louisbourg at the mouth of the St. Lawrence River, and captured it in 1745. In late 1748, English traders pushed far westward in the OH country and established a trading post at Pickawillany (near what is now the town of Piqua in Miami County in west-central OH). Much to the dismay of the colonists, the peace settlement of 1748 returned Louisbourg to France. In 1752, the French destroyed the English post at Pickawillany, and then in 1753 built a chain of three forts south of Lake Erie down toward the Forks of the OH River (now Pittsburgh). The purpose of these forts was to throw a line across the route by which English traders were entering the OH country. In 1754, the French built a strong fort, Ft. Duquesne, at the Forks in the OH River (Pittsburgh), thus completing the blockage of the English westward movement. They knew that whoever controlled the Forks in the OH River controlled the OH Valley. Several English attempts to capture the fort ended in failure. See the bottom part of Figure 6.

The fourth war, the French and Indian War (1756-63) was dominated by the French during 1756-7, with NY, VA, and PA bearing devastating raids. The tide turned in late 1757 when a new English Secretary of State began to direct the war. In 1758, Louisbourg fell, the French fortress on Lake Ontario (Ft. Frontenac) fell, and Ft. Duquesne was abandoned upon the approach of English troops. The fort was renamed Ft. Pitt, and the settlement around it was called Pittsburgh. In 1759, the French were driven out of northern NY, and Quebec fell. In the following year, Montreal was captured, and during 1761, the forts throughout the west country surrendered. France was gone from North America. The English now owned all the lands making up Canada and all the land east of the MS River, except for New Orleans, which the French gave to Spain. The British government now was saddled with the task of governing this vast newly acquired area. Among the major problems would be the Indians, the fur trade, the large numbers of people desirous of land in the region, and the growing spirit in the colonies that they should have the right to solve these difficulties in their own way.

Upon the conclusion of the French and Indian War in 1763, the Indians knew that their situation would not be as favorable under the English as it had been under the French. As a result, they mounted a rebellion in which they attempted to drive the English out of the back country, which included the OH lands. After overwhelming several English forts in western OH, the successful defense of Detroit and Ft. Pitt foiled the uprising. This incident marked the start of over 30 years of frontier warfare in which the OH Indians were gradually moved west and north. The English, in order to save the fur trade and appease the

Indians, decreed that the territory beyond the Appalachian Moun was to be reserved for Indians and fur traders, and that no settlem ...ts were to be established in the area. However, land-hungry colonists in MA, CT, NY, PA, and VA ignored the decree, and began settling on the land. Moravian missionary activity started up in the region, and several Indian mission settlements were established in eastern OH. In 1774, the English attached the lands west of the Appalachians to Canada in a further effort to protect Indians and to forestall settlement.

The American Revolution (1775-83) began in 1775, and the Indians sided with the English, because they had opposed the colonists' encroachments upon Indian lands, and had attempted to stem violence against them. During the war, OH Indians raided into KY and PA, and frontier American troops retaliated by attacking Indian villages and capturing English forts. The treaty of 1783, which ended the war, ceded to the newly-formed US the land behind the thirteen colonies all the way to the MS River. This cession included the Old Northwest which was approximately made up of the lands in present-day OH, IN, IL, MI, WI, and part of MN.

3. Territorial OH

When the US received the Old Northwest from Britain after the Revolutionary War, four of the former colonies (now the states of NY, VA, MA, and CT) invoked their original grants and claimed all or a portion of the area. As a compromise with the former colonies which had no western-land claims, these four states ceded the US their rights: NY in 1781, VA in 1784, MA in 1785, and CT in 1786. However, VA kept the right to award its Revolutionary War veterans land in an area between the Little Miami and the Scioto Rivers in the southwest, and CT kept the right to sell the land in a strip along the shore of Lake Erie in northeastern OH. VA's area was called the VA Military District, and CT's area was called the Western Reserve. VA continued to award land in the VA Military District until 1852, but CT had granted or sold all its holdings before 1800, most of it to the CT Land Company.

A US congressional act of 1785 formally took charge of the Old Northwest, and provided a plan to survey and sell the lands other than those reserved by VA and CT. The land was to be laid out into townships six miles square with each township being divided into 36 one-square-mile sections. Each township was identified with a RANGE number (such as R1 or R4) which gave its location on an east-to-west axis, and a TOWNSHIP number (such as T2 or T5) which gave its location on a south-to-north axis. The sections in each township were numbered from 1 to 36. So, a complete description of a section within a given township might read like this: R2 T4 Sec27, which would mean Range 2, Township 4, Section 27. This would be followed by a designation of the part of the section that was involved.

A further congressional act of 1787 established the Old Northwest as the Territory Northwest of the Ohio River. This act provided for a representative territorial government and for the formation of states out of the territory. Settlers began to move into the OH Territory, coming in chiefly on the OH River. The first permanent settlement was made by New Englanders in 1788 at Marietta where the Muskingham River entered the OH River. The village occupied part of a large parcel of land which had been purchased by the OH Company from the US government. Shortly after the founding of the small settlement of Columbia, the town of Cincinnati was established nearby on the OH River in 1789 by NJ people who Symmes brought to his purchased land. This Symmes tract rested between the Little and the Great Miami Rivers in southwestern OH. In 1789 Belpre was established just a few miles downstream from Marietta, in 1791 Massieville (Manchester) was set up in the VA Military District, and a group of French refugees started Gallipolis. For two years the territorial capital was at Marietta, but in 1790, it was moved to Cincinnati.

The coming of settlers confirmed the Indians' fears of American encroachment, and they started a continuous series of guerilla raids and violent attacks on the settlements. These activities were supported by the British who were based in Canada and still illegally occupied several frontier forts in the US. Two campaigns were launched to defeat the strong Indian confederation, one in 1790, another in 1791, but they both failed because of leaders inexperienced in frontier warfare. In 1794, Wayne, an experienced leader, led troops into northwest OH where the Indians were defeated and the confederacy was broken up. About the same time, a treaty with Great Britain resulted in the removal of the British from US land. A year later, in 1795, the Treaty of Greenville involved the Indian cession of the southern two-thirds of OH and the entire northeastern area. See Figure 7. All of this was now open for settlement.

With the possibility of Indian hostilities largely removed, OH filled up rapidly. This immigration was enhanced by Zane's Trace, OH's first appreciable road which was completed in 1796-7 to connect Wheeling, VA (now WV), through Zanesville, through Lancaster, through Chillicothe, with Limestone (now Maysville), KY. See Figure 7. South of the treaty line, Hamilton was established in 1795, Chillicothe and Dayton in 1796, Steubenville and Athens and Franklinton (now Columbus) in 1797, and Zanesville in 1799. In the middle of what is now OH (around Columbus) a refugee tract for Canadians who sympathized with the

Figure 7. The Greenville Treaty
Line and Zane's Trace

American Revolution was established in 1796. East of the treaty line, the northeastern section of OH began to be occupied by settlers coming up the Mohawk River Valley in NY, then west to Buffalo, then either by boat on Lake Erie or on foot along the lake shore. Cleveland and Youngstown were founded in 1796, and Mentor and Ravenna in 1799.

A more democratic land law was passed in 1800, reducing the amount of land which could be bought and allowing land to be purchased on credit. To accommodate the great numbers coming in, land sales offices were set up in 1800 at Steubenville, Marietta, Chillicothe, and Cincinnati. Also in 1800, the Northwest Territory was split, the land which is now OH retaining the designation as Northwest Territory, and the land west of OH becoming the Indiana Territory. The Northwest Territory (OH), as it neared the required 60,000 population for statehood, called a convention in 1802 which drew up a state constitution. Approval of the document by the US Congress was given in 1803, OH was declared to have joined the US, and OH began to function as the seventeenth state.

---

4. Early OH statehood

The government of the new state of OH was established at Chillicothe, but in 1810-12 it was at Zanesville, then back to Chillicothe for 1813-16, when it was moved to Columbus. A state college was established in 1804 at Athens. By this time the movement of settlers into OH and the movement of agricultural produce out of OH to southern and eastern markets had resulted in over 1000 miles of crude wagon roads. Boats loaded with settlers and goods were arriving at river and lake ports, and were departing with agricultural produce. The fastest growing town was Cincinnati which was functioning as the major trade center of the area. More land sales offices were opened, Zanesville in 1804, and Canton in 1808.

The population of OH had exceeded 230,000 by 1810, counties were being created rapidly, land sales were booming ($2 per acre with 5 years to pay), schools were being set up, and churches were being built. These churches served as the major social centers in the local areas, although the necessity of hard work left little time for social and recreational activity. In 1811, the first steamboat in the west came down the OH River from Pittsburgh to Cincinnati. This event heralded a rapid multiplication of steamboat traffic, first on the OH River, then later on Lake Erie. Not only was steam power harnessed for boats, but it began to be used in manufacturing, initially to run mills.

5. The War of 1812

The War of 1812 against Great Britain was a result of British blockading and interrupting US trade with France and British support of hostile Indians in what is now IN, MI, and IL and in what is now AL, FL, and MS. The war was fought in these two regions and all along the Canadian border, plus in several places where the British made coastal invasions of the US. The most notable were Washington City, Baltimore, and New Orleans. OH contributed about 25,000 men to the war effort. During the war, the state functioned as the staging area for the northwestern theater (now IN, MI, IL, and Canada just north), and troops and supplies crossed the state. Early in the war, the British-Indian alliance invaded OH following the fall of Detroit. They were successfully resisted and were gradually driven back, even though they won several encounters. Then a naval victory on Lake Erie in 1813, followed by a land victory at the Canadian Thames River ended the British-Indian threat to OH and the areas of IN, MI, and IL. The net result of the war was that the Indians were defeated in the IN-MI-IL and AL-FL-MS areas, which further opened up the western US, but no notable changes in the US-Canadian borders occurred, even though FL, as an indirect result, was eventually added to the US (1821). A few years after the war, the Indians ceded their last substantial lands in OH.

6. Between the wars

The period between the wars (1815-61) was one of almost untrammeled expansion for OH. The population increased, the agricultural economy grew, more efficient transportation facilities spread all over the state, cities prospered, industrial enterprise developed considerably, OH became very important in national politics, and the money flow was large. In and after the War of 1812, immmigrants from states east of OH flooded in, mostly settling along and above the OH River. They expanded the agricultural production (corn, wheat, oats, cattle, hogs, sheep) greatly, most of the large surplus being shipped downstream on the OH River to New Orleans. Shipping produce east was desirable, but Pittsburgh was upstream, and use of the trails was slow, difficult, and expensive.

In 1825, the Erie Canal in NY state was opened. This canal, ran from central NY to Buffalo in western NY (the northeastern tip of Lake Erie). It effectively linked Buffalo with New York City and all the intervening area because the Hudson and Mohawk Valleys led to central NY. It also linked New England with Buffalo, since the Mohawk Valley was easily reached. Hence, in 1825, the route from ME, NH, VT, MA, CT, RI, NY, NJ, and eastern PA was wide open. And once people arrived at Buffalo, two routes accessed northern OH: the water route on

Lake Erie, and the land route along Lake Erie's shore. Settlers took immediate advantage of the canal and its connections, so that by 1850 almost all of OH, north and south, was populated. The main exception was the Black Swamp in the northeast.

The success of NY's Erie Canal so impressed OH that they began construction on an extensive canal system in 1826. The system consisted of two major Lake-Erie-to-OH-River links, plus numerous feeder canals which penetrated most regions of the state. The first major link, the OH and Erie Canal, which connected Cleveland (Lake Erie) with Portsmouth (OH River) in the eastern part of the state was completed in 1830. And the second link, the Miami and Erie Canal, was finished in 1845 to connect Toledo (Lake Erie) with Cincinnati. The southern section of the canal was operational much earlier and served southwestern OH from 1828. Part of the reason the northwestern portion of the second link was delayed was a dispute between OH and the MI Territory over a border strip which included Toledo. This conflict was resolved in 1836 with the US awarding the strip to OH and with the MI Territory receiving statehood and the northern peninsula.

The extensive canal system and the immense increase in steamboats on the OH River and Lake Erie opened up the eastern markets for OH, and produced prosperity. This prosperity, in turn, attracted further settlers who occupied the interior regions of OH. Accompanying the canal construction was turnpike and road improvement and expansion, which produced the same salutary effects. The most noteworthy of these road projects was the National Road (or Turnpike), which came from Cumberland, MD, through Wheeling, VA (now WV), reaching Zanesville in 1826, Columbus in 1833, and the IN border in 1838. See Figure 8. Among the many native American immigrants, there began to appear more and more people from the Germanic states and Ireland. Their numbers rose sharply in the 1840s and 1850s.

The first railroad was built in OH in 1836, but there was not a great deal of expansion until about 1845, when a railroad boom set in. By 1851, practically all of OH's main cities were connected by rail, and by 1856, northern, central, and southern OH were all connected with the eastern seaboard. And by 1860, railroads had overtaken canals as the predominant carrier of people and goods. In this year of 1860, OH boasted more miles of railroad track than any other state in the US. As of 1860, the leading industry of OH was meat packing, which was concentrated in Cincinnati. This city also had sizable activity in the manufacture of cloth, clothing, soap, books, leather, steam engines, and steamboats. Other industries which had undergone considerable development in other areas of the state were the production of salt, ceramics, iron, lumber, and paper, as well as iron working.

Figure 8. The National Road
Through OH

7. The Civil War

After decades of compromise, in 1861 the Southern states declared their independence from the US over issues of state's rights, slavery, and economic policy. A long, devastating war ensued as the Northern states (the Union) invaded the Southern states (the Confederacy) to defeat the secession attempt. Even though the population of southern OH had a large percentage of people with Southern origins, and even though Cincinnati had strong trade connections with the South, OH was mostly anti-slave and strongly Unionist. Abolistionist activity in OH dated back to 1815, and by the 1850s, there was a network of underground railroad stations in the state. These stations functioned to transport runaway slaves to freedom in Canada. Cincinnati was the major underground railroad center along the North-South interface.

In 1861, when Lincoln called for volunteers to suppress the rebellion, OH responded with 30,000 men, well over its quota of 13,000. OH's militia was rapidly reorganized, and in a few months they moved to take western VA, which soon became the Union state of WV. By the time the bloody, traumatic war was over, 346,000 OH participants had been in US service, 34,600 had died, and about 30,000 returned home with severe wounds which would last throughout their lives. The number of deserters was about 18,300. OH men also served the Confederacy, probably several thousand, including seven Confederate generals.

In 1862, a number of Confederate victories, coupled with large numbers of Union deaths, dashed the morale of the North, and strong sentiment arose, both in OH and in the US at large, to abandon the war and let the South go. When Rebel forces threatened Cincinnati and Lincoln issued a preliminary proclamation of slave emancipation, OH elected many peace-desiring representatives to Congress. However, in mid-1863, when the Union began to win battle after battle, starting with Gettysburg and Vicksburg and Chattanooga, this movement slowly subsided. OH troops were involved in almost every major battle of the war, both in the western and in the eastern theaters. The needs of the military operation accelerated the industrial development of OH. Steam power expanded, and the state's mineral resources, coal, clay products, salt, leather, and agricultural produce found ready markets. OH's factories, farms, mines, lumber mills, and transportation network contributed greatly to the war effort.

The Civil War was fought outside OH except for a raid in July 1863 by Confederate General John H. Morgan. Morgan led about 2500 cavalrymen to take over two steamboats in KY, cross over into southeast IN, then sweep eastward into OH. They passed through Cincinnati's northern suburbs, then proceeded across southern OH, doing some looting, foraging, and minor destruction. Morgan tried to cross back over the OH River at Buffinton Island (southeast OH), but Union cavalry were waiting. They captured about 1300 of Morgan's men, then a second attempt to cross 20 miles upsteam was interrupted by Union gunboats. With the remaining 900 men, Morgan headed north. Morgan and his forces were taken prisoner in Columbiana County. In the Spring of 1865, the deadliest war in American history came to a close. OH's contributions had been immense: troops, leaders, arms, supplies, food. This leadership was manifested after the war with seven OH natives occupying the White House during the 54 years 1869-1923.

8. Post-Civil War

In the four decades after the War Between the States, OH continued as a leading producer of grain and livestock, but simultaneously underwent spectacular development in its heavy industry. These developments included iron and steel manufacturing in Cleveland and Youngstown, oil refining in Cleveland and Toledo, glassmaking and ceramic production in Toledo, and rubber manufacturing in Akron. The expanded activity attracted many workers, both native and immigrant, such that by 1900 Cleveland had surpassed Cincinnati as OH's largest city. Native workers came mainly off the farms, and immigrant workers came chiefly from eastern and southern Europe. The industries became so large and powerful that they took over the political scene of OH. They also came to wield tremendous influence nationally. Corruption, graft, and fraudulent elections fluorished in the service of business and often at the expense of public welfare.

A reaction against the vested interests set in during the 1890s, reformers were elected, and many changes were instituted. These included new reform-laden amendments to the state constitution in 1912 and many important reform laws. OH made extensive contributions to the World War I effort (1917-8, with 256,000 serving), which was followed by further industrial expansion and general prosperity. This gave way to a severe economic depression in the 1930s which took a high toll in the industrial centers. Recovery, which had begun in the late 1930s, was assured by the coming of World War II (1941-5, with 839,000 serving). After the war an industrial boom set in, with many new industries such as aluminum and chemicals coming in. Increased automation led to the need for fewer factory workers, and mechanization of agriculture decreased the number of farm laborers. The result was an increase in unemployment. This aggravated the social upheaval of the 1960s which resulted from governmental pressure for racial equality. Since that time, OH has come to face momentous problems in the areas of racial issues, urban decay, government debt, pollution, crime, inflation, recession, and foreign competition. But, if the history of the people of the Buckeye State is any clue, they will overcome these obstacles and OH will continue its development as it looks forward to the year 2003, when it will celebrate its bicentennial.

---

9. OH developmental factors

Many factors influenced the development of the Northwest Territory and the State of OH. Among the strong influences which are pertinent genealogically were the economic, transportation, agricultural, ethnic, and religious factors.

The economic factors were naturally of importance because people must be able to support themselves in order to survive. The early settlers were fortunate in that the trip into OH from the Pittsburgh area was easy (downstream) and led directly to fertile lands along the OH River and its tributaries. The river valleys had rich, black soil, the area was heavily forested (lumber), the waters were filled with fish, and the woods had abundant game. The new inhabitants would soon discover that beneath the surface there were minerals galore: silica, clay, iron ore, salt, and coal. The pioneer or frontier economy was based on the self-sufficiency of family units and/or small settlements. The family or groups of families had to provide food, shelter, and clothing for themselves. The men cleared land, produced lumber, built homes and outbuildings, planted and harvested crops, hunted game, caught fish, cared for livestock, worked leather, and made furniture, utensils, and tools. The women cooked food, preserved fruit, dried meat, cared for livestock, and wove and sewed cloth.

Soon the OH farmers were producing a surplus (grain, livestock, logs), and if it were taken to the OH River towns, it could be traded for manufactured goods which merchants offered there. The difficulties of getting the produce to the OH River brought the farmers to reduce their product in size, whenever possible. Grist mills, distilleries, slaughter houses, tanneries, and saw mills were built to reduce the grain to flour and whiskey, the livestock to meat and leather, and the logs to lumber. The center of the trade activity was Cincinnati, which accordingly prospered. Soon printing, paper making, iron working, firearms production, salt refining, and clothing manufacture arose. Iron mining and smelting followed the discovery of iron ore in the Mahoning Valley in 1804, and soon kettles, ovens, pans, flatirons, and stoves were being made. Steam was harnessed in 1812 in Cincinnati and the power was quickly applied to flour and textile fabric production. During 1814-8, bridge and road building activity exploded, and the iron, timber, livestock, and grain could get to market easier. A period of exuberant prosperity, land speculation, wildcat banking, and currency excesses led to a depression in 1818 which involved widespread unemployment.

A slow recovery set in, and the economy was restored to health as of the mid-1820s, when OH began extensive canal construction. This was done to meet the ever-increasing needs of the farmers for better means of getting their products to market. The ensuing prosperity attracted many immigrants from the eastern states, the British Isles, and the Germanic states. This prosperity ended in 1837 when a nationwide financial panic occurred, in which 30 OH banks failed. Again, a slow recovery came about, things improving from 1840 on. Even though OH was still principally an agricultural state, its factory industry was picking up momentum rapidly. Cincinnati remained the hub of this broad-spread OH enterprise.

Railroad construction had begun in 1837, and by 1846, Cleveland, Columbus, and Cincinnati were connected. By 1860 OH had more railroad than any state, even though its development had been interrupted by a railroad panic (over-speculation) in 1853 and another in 1857. The depression which followed the 1857 event was terminated by the outbreak of the Civil War. The loss of the labor of 340,000 service men in the war was offset by sizable German immigration and by improved labor-saving agricultural machinery. During the war, there was greatly increased industry in and around Cleveland to meet war demands. This industrial expansion continued after the war, with steel production and steel fabrication being the core, but with other industries rising and developing: machine tools, soap, glass, oil refining, coal mining, brick, pottery, tile, and rubber. In 1900, the urban population of OH exceed the rural population, signalling the switch from agriculture to industry as the state's predominant economic activity.

The second set of factors which strongly affected the development of OH were transportation factors. Early OH was settled by means of water routes: the OH River and its tributaries which flowed into it from interior OH, and Lake Erie. The OH River connected with the East (PA, VA, MD, NJ, DE) through Pittsburgh, PA, and Lake Erie connected with the East (NY, MA, CT, NH, VT, RI, NJ) through Buffalo, NY. These water routes were much better than the narrow ridge trails which buffalo herds had probably originally beaten out. The pioneers of OH came by skiffs, large rafts, barges, keel boats, and flat boats down the OH River. Soon river packets were engaged in regularly scheduled 30-day round trips between Cincinnati and Pittsburgh. And there appeared on the river floating general stores, flatboats with all sorts of ironware, cutlery, tinware, cloth, clothes, and sundries.

As settlement proceeded, more people took to the waterways as far as they could, then they struck out on the trails. The trails were terrible: narrow, with fallen trees, boulders, mud, washouts, and steep inclines. In 1805, an improved trail called Zane's Trace was built from Wheeling, WV, to Zanesville, to Lancaster to Chillicothe to Limestone, KY (now Maysville). See Figure 7. The National Road, running from Cumberland, MD, through Wheeling, WV, reached Zanesville in 1826, Columbus in 1833, and Springfield in 1838. See Figure 8. This road became jammed with traffic almost immediately: stagecoaches, freight wagons, mule trains, herds of livestock, and settlers walking and driving all sorts of conveyances.

In 1811, the first steamboat appeared on the OH River, and in 1818, one appeared on Lake Erie. On the River, the steamboat had the novel ability to go easily against the current, and this markedly opened up transport to the East. Within a few years, the River and the Lake had many steamboats. However, there were numerous inland farmers with large surpluses of products who could not get them to market cheaply. So, hearing of the success of canals in NY, they pressed for canals to connect inland areas with the rivers that emptied into Lake Erie and those that emptied into the OH River. They were successful, and in 1825 canal building was begun. These activities led to the OH and Erie Canal (from Cleveland to Portsmouth), the Miami and Erie Canal (from Cincinnati to Toledo), and many branch canals feeding into them. The result was remarkable, with both agriculture and industry getting more markets, and with thousands of immigrants being attracted. The canal system was a major transportation medium for both freight and passengers for over 25 years, at which time the railroads supplanted it.

The first railroad to operate in OH (1836), a 32-mile line, ran from Toledo, OH, to Adrian, MI. By the end of 1846, there were lines from Cincinnati to Sandusky (on Lake Erie), from Cincinnati to Columbus to Cleveland, and from Cleveland to Pittsburgh. The laying of track in OH proceeded rapidly, and by 1857, OH provided a link in the first through connection from the Atlantic Ocean to the MS River: Baltimore to Parkersburg to Marietta to Cincinnati to St. Louis. By 1860, OH had more railroad mileage than any state, with trains replacing most of the movement by stagecoach, freight wagon, pack train, and canal boat. The large steamboats on the OH River and Lake Erie, however, continued to attract large traffic. As of 1900, steamboat shipping and travel were in decline, canal travel was gone, and the 2800 miles of railroad were meeting most of the transportation needs. Soon, automobiles and trucks would slowly enter the picture, along with the greatly improved roads they called for.

The <u>agricultural</u> factors which influenced the development of OH have been mentioned above. Farmers and farming laid the economic foundations of OH, and they continued to be very important. The numerous fertile lands of OH produced heavy crops, and the yields were markedly increased and became less labor-intensive as farm machinery was developed: the iron plow (1819), the corn cultivator (1820s), the reaper (1833), then planting drills, mowing machines, harvesters, threshing machines, and improved cultivators. During the 1820s vineyards were first planted, and better breeds of hogs, cattle, and sheep were brought in. The immigrant canal laborers had to be fed in the 1820s and 1830s, and the railroad builders in the 1850s, all giving farmers a larger market. In 1850, more corn was grown in OH than in any other state. The industrial sector of OH began to increase rapidly after the Civil War, and by 1890/1900 had become more important than farming. Even so, the greatly increased urban population had to be fed, and agriculture remained good business in OH. Because of continued advances in machinery, the number of farmers needed to work the land decreased. By 1930, it had dropped to 15% of the population.

The impact of <u>ethnic</u> factors on OH's development is also notable. Early on the first people to begin to creep into the OH country, even before 1788, were the Scots-Irish (more correctly, the Ulster-Irish). They came from the hill areas of PA, VA(WV), and KY. More and more came, so that they became the predominant ethnic strain in the southern two-thirds of the state. They were joined early by people of English heritage from New England, and people from the Middle Atlantic states who traced their ancestors back to both Scots-Irish and English derivations. The northern part of OH was populated early by native New Englanders (English origins) and New Yorkers of both English and Dutch (Holland) backgrounds. Soon after, PA Dutch (of German origins, not from Holland) moved into the area south of the Western Reserve.

In the years of canal construction in NY, PA, and OH, many settlers from NY, PA, Ireland, and the Germanic states came. In the late 1840s and throughout the 1850s, many more Irish (Catholic) and Germans (both Protestant and Catholic) moved to OH because of economic and political upheavals in the Germanic states, and drought, famine, and oppression in Ireland. So many Germans settled in Cincinnati that it essentially became a German city. After the Civil War, during which immigration slowed, immigration rose once again, many more Germans coming. About 1880, other groups fed OH's need for industrial workers, with Scandinavians, Slavs, Czechs, Magyars, Greeks, and Italians immigrating. During and after World War I, numerous blacks entered OH. They followed the trail of thousands of slaves that the underground railroad had brought through OH to Canada. After

World War II, another sizable wave of blacks seeking industrial employment moved to urban areas of OH from the rural South.

Religious factors were important to the development of OH, many of them following along with ethnic factors, because ethnic groups often represent particular religious propensities. In the pre-territorial period of the OH country, the French sent missionaries to several of the Indian groups beginning as early as 1749. PA Moravians in 1761 also engaged in missionary activity among Indians in what is now eastern OH. The New Englanders who came to Marietta and the Western Reserve brought the Congregational and Presbyterian denominations, the Scots-Irish brought Presbyterianism into south and central OH, and the early PA settlers of German descent brought the pietistic sects such as the Dunkards, the Moravians, the Amish, the Mennonites, and the Shakers. Quakers from PA had preceded them and continued to come in. Not far behind were the PA Lutherans (German). On the frontiers there were few educated clergy, so the Methodist circuit riders, the Baptist farmer-preachers, and itinerant preachers of various evangelistic sects and cults ministered to the pioneers. It is important, however, to recognize that many of the early settlers had no church affiliation at all. Some were merely not interested, but there were some who were actively anti-institutional.

The frontier situation and the multitude of denominations, sects, and cults led to splits in the main-line denominations and to the rapid development of new emotion-based sects and cults, many of them fashioned after ones which had come in from the South. They often specialized in verbal excesses, spectacular emotional display, miracle mongering, and/or belief in the imminent end of the world. Among those which syphoned off many members of the established churches were the New Lights, Holy Rollers, Jerkers, Laughers, Dancers, Stonites, Marshallites, and Millerites. The first Catholic parish priest appeared in Cincinnati in 1817, where he ministered chiefly to German Catholics. In fact, most of the Catholics coming to OH before the middle 1840s were German, but after that increaasing numbers were Irish. Following 1865, Catholics from southern and eastern Europe came in great numbers.

In view of their members defecting to the new emotional cults or splinter groups, some of the main-line denominations (Methodist, Presbyterian, Baptist) began holding camp meetings, which reclaimed many people. These denominations, along with others, started colleges to train ministers to replace the circuit riders, itinerant preachers, and lay preachers: Episcopal (1824), Congregational (1826), Presbyterian (1829), Baptist (1831), Lutheran (1845), Disciples (1850). In 1831, Mormons came into the Western Reserve, and added converts rapidly. However, most of them moved west before 1840. A few Jews were in Cincinnati fairly early, and formed a congregation in 1824. By the time of the Civil War, most other large cities of OH had Jewish congregations. OH was the site of 21 attempts to form utopian religious communities. Among them were the Shakers (Lebanon, North Union), the Zoar German Separatists (Tuscarawas County), Congregationalists (Tallmadge, Oberlin), and United Christians (Berea). After the Civil War, most of the main-line churches of OH became very active in moral instruction, social service, anti-slavery movements, civic reform, temperance, mental health, prison reform, and women's rights.

---

10. OH county formation

The map which makes up Figure 9 depicts the boundaries of the 88 counties of OH as they came to be in 1851, and as they are today. The first county to be organized was Washington (1788), and the last was Noble (1851). Below you will find an alphabetical listing of the 88 counties. Each is followed by an indication of its location on the OH county map of Figure 9. NW stands for the northwestern quarter of the state, NE stands for the northeastern, SW for the southwestern, SE for the southeastern, and C stands for the central portion around the area where all four quarters intersect (at and around Licking County). When you see a hyphenated symbol (such as NW-NE), it means that the county is on the borderline between regions.

Adams SW	Fairfield C	Licking C	Portage NE
Allen NW	Fayette SW	Logan NW	Preble SW
Ashland NE	Franklin C	Lorain NE	Putnam NW
Ashtabula NE	Fulton NW	Lucas NW	Richland NW-NE
Athens SE	Gallia SE	Madison SW	Ross SW-SE
Auglaize NW	Geauga NE	Mahoning NE	Sandusky NW
Belmont SE	Greene SW	Marion C	Scioto SW-SE
Brown SW	Guernsey SE	Medina NE	Seneca NW
Butler SW	Hamilton SW	Meigs SE	Shelby NW-SW
Carroll NE	Hancock NW	Mercer NW	Stark NE
Champaign SW	Hardin NW	Miami SW	Summit NE
Clark SW	Harrison NE	Monroe SE	Trumbull NE
Clermont SW	Henry NW	Montgomery SW	Tuscarawas NE
Clinton SW	Highland SW	Morgan SE	Union NW-SW
Columbiana NE	Hocking SE	Morrow C	Van Wert NW
Coshocton C	Holmes NE	Muskingum SE	Vinton SE
Crawford NW	Huron NW-NE	Noble SE	Warren SW
Cuyahoga NE	Jackson SE	Ottawa NW	Washington SE
Darke NW-SW	Jefferson NE	Paulding NW	Wayne NE
Defiance NW	Knox C	Perry SE	Williams NW
Delaware C	Lake NE	Pickaway SW	Wood NW
Erie NW-NE	Lawrence SE	Pike SW	Wyandot NW

Figure 9. The Counties
of OH, 1851-now

Figures 10-16 show the county boundaries in the years 1790, 1800, 1810, 1820, 1830, 1840, and 1850. Please recall that the map shown as Figure 9 shows the OH counties as they have been from 1851 until now.

Counties, as well as people, have genealogies. The basic genealogies for the 88 counties of OH are as follows in Figures 17-25. The date in parentheses which follows the name of the county indicates the year in which it was organized. The county genealogies are to be read from left-to-right. The counties immediately to the right of a given county are its parents, that is, the counties from which its land came. When you are researching in a county, it is mandatory that you know the parent counties, and it is usually advisable that you know all the ancestral counties, if you are to do a thorough investigation. Counties are abbreviated by the first three letters of their names, except for Monroe (abbreviated Monr) and Montgomery (abbreviated Mont).

11. Recommended reading

For those who are interested in doing further reading on the history of OH, a short well-written, popular, human-interest oriented volume is one prepared as a contribution to the US Bicentennial celebration:

___W. Havighurst, OH: A BICENTENNIAL HISTORY, Norton, New York, NY, 1975.

The most important detailed single volume on OH history is:

___G. W. Knepper, OHIO AND ITS PEOPLE, Kent State University Press, Kent, OH, 1989.

A thorough reading of it will give you an excellent, detailed view of the history of the Buckeye State. Other single-volumed histories include:

___D. W. Bowman, PATHWAY OF PROGRESS, A SHORT HISTORY OF OH, American Book Co., New York, NY, 1943.

___W. R. Collins, OH, THE BUCKEYE STATE, Prentice-Hall, Englewood Cliffs, NJ, 1962.

___W. M. Gregory, HISTORY AND GEOGRAPHY OF OH, Ginn, Boston, MA, 1935.

___H. H. Hatcher, THE BUCKEYE COUNTRY, Kinsey and Co., New York, NY, 1940.

___C. E. Hopkins, OH, THE BEAUTIFUL AND HISTORIC, Page and Co., Boston, MA, 1931.

___D. Lindsey, AN OUTLINE HISTORY OF OH, Allen, Cleveland, OH, 1960.

___E. H. Roseboom, A HISTORY OF OH, Prentice-Hall, New York, NY, 1934.

In addition to the above one–volumed histories of OH, there are some multi-volumed publications which can give you more detail on various events or time periods. The best of these is:

___C. F. Wittke, THE HISTORY OF THE STATE OF OH, OH Archaeological and Historical Society, Columbus, OH, 1941–4, 6 volumes.

Others that you may find useful include:

___C. B. Galbreath, HISTORY OF OH, American Historical Society, Chicago, IL, 1925, 5 volumes.

___O. D. Morrison, OH, THE GATEWAY STATE, Morrison, Athens, OH, 1960–2, 4 volumes.

___E. O. Randall and D. J. Ryan, HISTORY OF OH, Century History Co., New York, NY, 1912–5, 6 volumes.

___H. Howe, HISTORICAL COLLECTIONS OF OH, Howe and Son, Columbus, OH, 1891, 3 volumes.

There are also many regional, county, city, and town histories which either contain genealogical information or will lead you to it. These will be mentioned in section 32 of the next chapter (entitled Regional publications) and under the various OH counties in Chapter 4. A bibliography of such local sources is:

___M. Adams, OH LOCAL AND FAMILY HISTORY SOURCES IN PRINT, Heritage Research, Clarkston, GA, 1984.

The major historical journal published in and about OH is:

___OHIO HISTORY (formerly OHIO HISTORICAL QUARTERLY and OHIO ARCHAEOLOGICAL AND HISTORICAL QUARTERLY), published by the OH Historical Society, 1985 Velma Avenue, Columbus, OH 43211.

This magazine will provide you with an abundance of historical information, much of it pertinent to genealogical research in the state of OH.

Figure 10. OH Counties, 1790

Figure 11. OH Counties, 1800

Figure 12. OH Counties, 1810

Figure 13. OH Counties, 1820

Figure 14. OH Counties, 1830

Figure 15. OH Counties, 1840

Figure 16. OH Counties, 1850

```
Adams(1797)-Hamilton(1790)

Allen(1820)-She(1819)-Mia(1807)-Mont(1803)-Ham(1790)

Ashland(1846)┬Hur(1815)┬Por(1808)-Tru(1800)-Jef(1797)-Was(1788)
             │         └Cuy(1808)-Gea(1806)-Tru(1800)-Jef(1797)-Was(1788)
             ├Lor(1824)┬Hur(1815)┬Por(1808)-Tru(1800)┬Jef(1797)-Was(1788)
             │         │         │                   └Wayne County (MI)
             │         │         └Cuy(1808)-Gea(1806)-Tru(1800)┬Jef(1797)-Was(1788)
             │         │                                       └Wayne County (MI)
             │         ├Cuy(1808)-Gea(1806)-Tru(1800)┬Jef(1797)-Was(1788)
             │         │                              └Wayne County (MI)
             │         └Med(1812)-Por(1808)-Tru(1800)┬Jef(1797)-Was(1788)
             │                                        └Wayne County (MI)
             ├Ric(1808)-Fai(1800)┬Ros(1798)──Ada(1797)-Ham(1790)
             │                    └Was(1788)  └Was(1788)
             └Way(1808)-Col(1803)┬Jef(1797)-Was(1788)
                                 └Was(1788)


Ashtabula(1808)┬Gea(1806)-Tru(1800)-Jef(1797)-Was(1788)
               └Tru(1800)-Jef(1797)-Was(1788)


Athens(1805)-Was(1788)

Auglaize(1848)┬All(1820)-She(1819)-Mia(1807)-Mont(1803)-Ham(1790)
              └Mer(1820)-Dar(1809)-Mia(1807)-Mont(1803)-Ham(1790)

Belmont(1801)┬Jef(1797)-Was(1788)
             └Was(1788)

Brown(1818)┬Ada(1797)-Ham(1790)
           └-Cle(1800)-Ham(1790)

Butler(1803)-Ham(1790)

Carroll┬Col(1810)┬Jef(1797)-Was(1788)
       │         └Was(1788)
       ├Sta(1808)-Col(1810)┬Jef(1797)-Was(1788)
       │                    └Was(1788)
       └Har(1813)┬Jef(1797)-Was(1788)
                 └-Tus(1808)-Mus(1804)┬Was(1788)
                                       └Fai(1800)┬Ros(1798)──Ada(1797)-Ham(1790)
                                                 └Was(1788)  └Was(1788)

Champaign(1805)┬Gre(1803)┬Ham(1790)
               │         └Ros(1798)┬Ada(1797)-Ham(1790)
               │                   └Was(1788)
               └Fra(1803)┬Ros(1798)┬Ada(1797)-Ham(1790)
                         │          └Was(1788)
                         └Wayne County (MI)

Clark(1818)┬Cha(1805)┬Gre(1803)┬Ham(1790)
           │         │         └Ros(1798)┬Ada(1797)-Ham(1790)
           │         │                   └Was(1788)
           │         └Fra(1803)┬Ros(1798)┬Ada(1797)-Ham(1790)
           │                   │          └Was(1788)
           │                   └Wayne County (MI)
           ├Gre(1803)──Ham(1790)
           │         ├Ros(1798)┬Ada(1797)-Ham(1790)
           │                   └Was(1788)
           └Mad(1810)-Fra(1803)┬Ros(1798)┬Ada(1797)-Ham(1790)
                               │          └Was(1788)
                               └Wayne County (MI)
```

Figure 17. OH County Origins

```
Clermont(1800)-Ham(1790)

Clinton(1810)┬Hig(1805)┬Ros(1798)┬Ada(1797)-Ham(1790)
             │         │         └Was(1788)
             │         ├Ada(1797)-Ham(1790)
             │         └Cle(1800)-Ham(1790)
             └War(1803)-Ham(1790)

Columbiana(1810)┬Mus(1804)┬Was(1788)
                │         └Fai(1800)┬Was(1788)
                │                   └Ros(1798)┬Ada(1797)-Ham(1790)
                │                             └Was(1788)
                └Was(1788)

Coshocton(1810)┬Mus(1804)┬Was(1788)
               │         └Fai(1800)┬Was(1788)
               │                   └Ros(1798)┬Ada(1797)-Ham(1790)
               │                             └Was(1788)
               └Tus(1808)-Mus(1804)┬Was(1788)
                                   └Fai(1800)┬Was(1788)
                                             └Ros(1798)┬Ada(1797)-Ham(1790)
                                                       └Was(1788)

Crawford(1820)-Del(1808)-Fra(1803)┬Ros(1798)┬Ada(1797)-Ham(1790)
                                  │         └-Was(1788)
                                  └Wayne County (MI)

Cuyahoga(1808)-Gea(1806)-Tru(1800)┬Jef(1797)-Was(1788)
                                  └-Wayne County (MI)

Darke(1809)-Mia(1807)-Mont(1803)┬Ham(1790)
                                └-Wayne County (MI)

Defiance(1845)--Wil(1820)-Dar(1809)-Mia(1807)-Mont(1803)--Ham(1790)
              ¦                                          ¦-Wayne County (MI)
              ¦-Hen(1820)-She(1819)-Mia(1807)-Mont(1803)--Ham(1790)
              ¦                                          ¦-Wayne County (MI)
              ¦-Pau(1820)-Dar(1809)-Mia(1807)-Mont(1803)--Ham(1790)
              ¦                                          ¦-Wayne County (MI)

Delaware(1808)-Fra(1803)┬Ros(1798)┬Ada(1797)-Ham(1790)
                        │         └-Was(1788)
                        └Wayne County (MI)

Erie(1838)┬Hur(1815)┬Por(1808)-Tru(1800)┬Jef(1797)-Was(1788)
          │         │                   └Wayne County (MI)
          │         └Cuy(1808)-Gea(1806)-Tru(1800)┬Jef(1797)-Was(1788)
          │                                       └Wayne County (MI)
          └San(1820)-Hur(1815)┬Por(1808)-Tru(1800)┬Jef(1797)-Was(1788)
                              │                   └Wayne County (MI)
                              └Cuy(1808)-Gea(1806)-Tru(1800)┬Jef(1797)-Was(1788)
                                                            └Wayne County (MI)

Fairfield(1800)┬Was(1788)
               └Ros(1798)┬Ada(1797)-Ham(1790)
                         └Was(1788)

Fayette(1810)┬Was(1788)
             └Ros(1798)┬Ada(1797)-Ham(1790)
                       └-Was(1788)

Franklin(1803)┬Ros(1798)┬Ada(1797)-Ham(1790)
              │         └Was(1788)
              └Wayne County (MI)
```

Figure 18. OH County Origins

```
Fulton(1850)┬Luc(1835)┬Woo(1820)  Cha(1805)┬Gre(1803)┬Ham(1790)
            │         │   │          │       │        ├Ros(1798)┬Ada(1797)-Ham(1790)
            │         │ Log(1818)    │       │        │         └Was(1788)
            │         │              │       └Fra(1803)┬Ros(1798)┬Ada(1797)-Ham(1790)
            │         │              │                 │         └Was(1788)
            │         │              │                 └Wayne County (MI)
            │         ├San(1820)-Hur(1815)┬Por(1808)-Tru(1800)┬Jef(1797)-Was(1788)
            │         │                   │                   └Wayne County (MI)
            │         │                   └Cuy(1808)-Gea(1806)-Tru(1800)┬Jef(1797)*
            │         │                                                 └Wayne Co (MI)
            │         └Hen(1820)-She(1819)-Mia(1807)-Mont(1803)┬Ham(1790)
            │                                                  └Wayne County (MI)
            ├Hen(1820)-She(1819)-Mia(1807)-Mont(1803)┬Ham(1790)
            │                                         └Wayne County (MI)          *-Was(1788)
            └Wil(1820)-Dar(1809)-Mia(1807)-Mont(1803)┬Ham(1790)
                                                      └Wayne County (MI)


Gallia(1803)┬Was(1788)
            └Ada(1797)-Ham(1790)

Geauga(1806)-Tru(1800)┬Jef(1797)-Was(1788)
                      └Wayne County (MI)

Greene(1803)┬Ham(1790)
            └Ros(1798)┬Was(1788)
                      └Ada(1797)-Ham(1790)

Guernsey(1810)┬Bel(1801)┬Was(1788)
              │         └Jef(1797)-Was(1788)
              └Mus(1804)┬Was(1788)
                        └Fai(1800)┬Was(1788)
                                  └Ros(1798)┬Was(1788)
                                            └Ada(1797)-Ham(1790)

Hamilton(1790)-Original county

Hancock(1820)-Log(1818)-Cha(1805)┬Gre(1803)┬Ham(1790)
                                 │         │-Ros(1798)┬Ada(1797)-Ham(1790)
                                 │         │          └Was(1788)
                                 └Fra(1803)┬Ros(1798)┬Ada(1797)-Ham(1790)
                                           │         └Was(1788)
                                           └Wayne County (MI)

Hardin(1820)-Log(1818)-Cha(1805)┬Gre(1803)┬Ham(1790)
                                │         │-Ros(1798)┬Ada(1797)-Ham(1790)
                                │         │          └Was(1788)
                                └Fra(1803)┬Ros(1798)┬Ada(1797)-Ham(1790)
                                          │         └Was(1788)
                                          └Wayne County (MI)

Harrison(1813)┬Jef(1797)-Was(1788)
              └Tus(1808)-Mus(1804)┬Was(1788)
                                  └Fai(1800)┬Was(1788)
                                            └Ros(1798)┬Ada(1797)-Was(1788)
                                                      └Was(1788)

Henry(1820)-She(1819)-Mia(1807)-Mont(1803)┬Ham(1790)
                                          └Wayne County (MI)

Highland(1805)┬Ada(1797)-Was(1788)
              ├Cle(1800)-Ham(1790)
              └Ros(1798)┬Ada(1797)-Was(1788)
                        └Was(1788)
```

Figure 19. OH County Origins

```
Hocking(1818)┬Ath(1805)-Was(1788)
             ├Ros(1798)┬Ada(1797)-Was(1788)
             │         └Was(1788)
             └Fai(1800)┬Was(1788)
                       └Ros(1798)┬Ada(1797)-Was(1788)
                                 └Was(1788)


Holmes(1824)─Cos(1810)─Mus(1804)┬Was(1788)
             ┊         ┊         └Fai(1800)┬Was(1788)
             ┊         ┊                   └Ros(1798)─Ada(1797)-Was(1788)
             ┊         ┊                              └Was(1788)
             ┊         └Tus(1808)-Mus(1804)┬Was(1788)
             ┊                             └Fai(1800)┬Was(1788)
             ┊                                       └Ros(1798)┬Ada(1797)-Was(1788)
             ┊                                                 └Was(1788)
             ├Way(1808)-Col(1803)┬Was(1788)
             ┊                   └Jef(1797)-Was(1788)
             ┊Tus(1808)-Mus(1804)┬Was(1788)
                                 └Fai(1800)┬Was(1788)
                                           └Ros(1798)┬Ada(1797)-Was(1788)
                                                     └Was(1788)


Huron(1815)─Por(1808)-Tru(1800)─Jef(1797)-Was(1788)
            ┊                   └Wayne County (MI)
            ┊Cuy(1808)-Gea(1806)-Tru(1800)┬Jef(1797)-Was(1788)
                                          └Wayne County (MI)



Jackson(1816)┬Ros(1798)┬Was(1788)
             │         └Ada(1797)-Ham(1790)
             ├Ath(1805)-Was(1788)
             ├Sci(1803)-Ada(1797)-Ham(1790)
             └Gal(1803)┬Was(1788)
                       └Ada(1797)-Ham(1790)


Jefferson(1797)-Was(1788)

Knox(1808)-Fai(1800)┬Was(1788)
                    └Ros(1798)┬Was(1788)
                              └Ada(1797)-Ham(1790)

Lake(1840)┬Gea(1806)-Tru(1800)┬Jef(1797)-Was(178
          │                   └Wayne County (MI)
          └Cuy(1808)-Gea(1806)-Tru(1800)┬Jef(1797)-Was(178
                                        └Wayne County (MI)

Lawrence(1815)┬Sci(1803)-Ada(1797)-Ham(1790)
              └Gal(1803)┬Was(1788)
                        └Ada(1797)-Ham(1790)

Licking(1808)-Fai(1800)──Was(1788)
                        |-Ros(1798)--Ada(1797)-Ham(1790)
                        |-Was(1788)

Logan(1818)-Cha(1805)┬Gre(1803)┬Ham(1790)
                     │         └Ros(1798)┬Ada(1797)-Ham(1790)
                     │                   └Was(1788)
                     └Fra(1803)┬Ros(1798)┬Ada(1797)-Ham(1790)
                               │         └Was(1788)
                               └Wayne County (MI)
```

Figure 20. OH County Origins

```
Lorain(1824)┬Hur(1815)┬Por(1808)-Tru(1800)┬Jef(1797)-Was(1788)
            │         │                   └Wayne County (MI)
            │         └Cuy(1808)-Gea(1806)-Tru(1800)┬Jef(1797)-Was(1788)
            │                                       └Wayne County (MI)
            ├Cuy(1808)-Gea(1806)-Tru(1800)┬Jef(1797)-Was(1788)
            │                             └Wayne County (MI)
            └Med(1812)-Por(1808)-Tru(1800)┬Jef(1797)-Was(1788)
                                          └Wayne County (MI)


Lucas(1835)┬Woo(1820)-Log(1818)-Cha(1805)┬Gre(1803)┬Ham(1790)
           │                             │         └Ros(1798)┬Ada(1797)-Ham(1790)
           │                             │                   └Was(1788)
           │                             └Fra(1803)┬Ros(1798)┬Ada(1797)-Ham(1790)
           │                                       │         └Was(1788)
           │                                       └Wayne County (MI)
           ├San(1820)-Hur(1815)┬Por(1808)-Tru(1800)┬Jef(1797)-Was(1788)
           │                   │                   └Wayne County (MI)
           │                   └Cuy(1808)-Gea(1806)-Tru(1800)┬Jef(1797)-Was(1788)
           │                                                 └Wayne County (MI)
           └Hen(1820)-She(1819)-Mia(1807)-Mont(1803)┬Ham(1790)
                                                    └Wayne County (MI)


Madison(1810)-Fra(1803)┬Ros(1798)┬Ada(1797)-Ham(1790)
                       │         └Was(1788)
                       └Wayne County (MI)


Mahoning(1846)┬Col(1810)┬Mus(1804)┬Was(1788)
              │         │         └Fai(1800)┬Was(1788)
              │         │                   └Ros(1798)┬Ada(1797)-Ham(1790)
              │         │                             └Was(1788)
              │         └Was(1788)
              └Tru(1800)┬Jef(1797)-Was(1788)
                        └Wayne County (MI)


Marion(1820)-Del((1808)-Fra(1803)┬Ros(1798)┬Ada(1797)-Ham(1790)
                                 │         └Was(1788)
                                 └Wayne County (MI)


Medina(1812)-Por(1808)-Tru(1800)┬Jef(1797)-Was(1788)
                                └Wayne County (MI)


Meigs(1819)┬Gal(1803)┬Was(1788)
           │         └Ada(1797)-Ham(1790)
           └Ath((1805)-Was(1788)


Mercer(1820)-Dar(1809)-Mia(1807)-Mont(1803)┬Ham(1790)
                                           └Wayne County (MI)


Miami(1807)-Mont(1803)┬Ham(1790)
                      └Wayne County (MI)


Monroe(1813)┬Bel(Belmont(1801)┬Jef(1797)-Was(1788)
            │                 └Was(1788)
            ├Was(1788)
            └Gue(1810)┬Bel(1801)┬Was(1788)
                      │         └Jef(1797)-Was(1788)
                      └Mus(1804)┬Was(1788)
                                └Fai(1800)┬Was(1788)
                                          └Ros(1798)┬Was(1788)
                                                    └Ada(1797)-Ham(1790)


Montgomery(1803)┬Ham(1790)
                └Wayne County (MI)
```

Figure 21. OH County Origins

45

```
Morgan(1817)┬Was(1788)
            └Gue(1810)┬Bel(1801)┬Was(1788)
            │         │         └Jef(1797)-Was(1788)
            │         └Mus(1804)┬Was(1788)
            │                   └Fai(1800)┬Was(1788)
            │                             └Ros(1798)┬Was(1788)
            │                                       └Ada(1797)-Ham(1790)
            └Mus(1804)┬Was(1788)
                      └Fai(1800)┬Was(1788)
                                └Ros(1798)┬Was(1788)
                                          └Ada(1797)-Ham(1790)

Morrow(1848)┬Kno(1808)-Fai(1800)┬Was(1788)
            │                   └Ros(1798)┬Was(1788)
            │                             └Ada(1797)-Ham(1790)
            ├Mar(1820)-Del((1808)-Fra(1803)┬Ros(1798)┬Ada(1797)-Ham(1790)
            │                              │         └Was(1788)
            │                              └Wayne County (MI)
            ├Del(1808)-Fra(1803)┬Ros(1798)┬Ada(1797)-Ham(1790)
            │                   │         └Was(1788)
            │                   └Wayne County (MI)
            └Ric(1808)-Fai(1800)┬Was(1788)
                                └Ros(1798)┬Ada(1797)-Ham(1790)
                                          └Was(1788)

Muskingum(1804)┬Was(1788)
               └Fai(1800)┬Was(1788)
                         └Ros(1798)┬Was(1788)
                                   └Ada(1797)-Ham(1790)

Noble(1851)┬Mon(1813)┬Bel(Belmont(1801)—Jef(1797)-Was(1788)
           │         │                  └Was(1788)
           │         ├Was(1788)
           │         └Gue(1810)┬Bel(1801)┬Was(1788)
           │                   │         └Jef(1797)-Was(1788)
           │                   └Mus(1804)┬Was(1788)
           │                             └Fai(1800)┬Was(1788)
           │                                       └Ros(1798)┬Was(1788)
           │                                                 └Ada(1797)-Ham(1790)
           ├Was(1788)
           ├Mor(1817)┬Was(1788)
           │         ├Gue(1810)┬Bel(1801)┬Was(1788)
           │         │         │         └Jef(1797)-Was(1788)
           │         │         └Mus(1804)┬Was(1788)
           │         │                   └Fai(1800)┬Was(1788)
           │         │                             └Ros(1798)┬Was(1788)
           │         │                                       └Ada(1797)-Ham(1790)
           │         └Mus(1804)┬Was(1788)
           │                   └Fai(1800)┬Was(1788)
           │                             └Ros(1798)┬Was(1788)
           │                                       └Ada(1797)-Ham(1790)
           └Gue(1810)┬Bel(1801)┬Was(1788)
                     │         └Jef(1797)-Was(1788)
                     └Mus(1804)┬Was(1788)
                               └Fai(1800)┬Was(1788)
                                         └Ros(1798)┬Was(1788)
                                                   └Ada(1797)-Ham(1790)
```

Figure 22. OH County Origins

```
Ottawa(1840)┬Eri(1838)┬Hur(1815)┬Por(1808)-Tru(1800)──Jef(1797)-Was(1788)
            │         │         │                    ├Wayne County (MI)
            │         │         └Cuy(1808)-Gea(1806)-Tru(1800)┬Jef(1797)-Was(1788)
            │         │                                       ├Wayne County (MI)
            │         └San(1820)-Hur(1815)┬Por(1808)-Tru(1800)┬Jef(1797)-Was(1788)
            │                             │                   ├Wayne County (MI)
            │                             └Cuy(1808)-Gea(1806)-Tru(1800)┬Jef(1797)-Was
            │                                                           ├Wayne County
            ├San(1820)-Hur(1815)┬Por(1808)-Tru(1800)┬Jef(1797)-Was(1788)
            │                   │                    ├Wayne County (MI)
            │                   └Cuy(1808)-Gea(1806)-Tru(1800)┬Jef(1797)-Was(1788)
            │                                                 ├Wayne County (MI)
            ├Luc(1835)┬Woo(1820)-Log(1818)-Cha(1805)┬Gre(1803)──Ham(1790)
            │         │                             │          ├Ros(1798)┬Ada(1797)-Ham
            │         │                             │                    ├Was(1788)
            │         │                             └Fra(1803)┬Ros(1798)┬Ada(1797)-Ham
            │         │                                       │         ├Was(1788)
            │         │                                       ├Wayne County (MI)
            │         └San(1820)-Hur(1815)┬Por(1808)-Tru(1800)┬Jef(1797)-Was(1788)
            │                             │                   ├Wayne County (MI)
            │                             └Cuy(1808)-Gea(1806)-Tru(1800)┬Jef(1797)-Was
            │                                                           ├Wayne County
            └Hen(1820)-She(1819)-Mia(1807)-Mont(1803)┬Ham(1790)
                                                     ├Wayne County (MI)

Paulding(1820)-Dar(1809)-Mia(1807)-Mont(1803)┬Ham(1790)
                                             ├Wayne County (MI)

Perry(1818)──Was(1788)
        ├Fai(1800)──Was(1788)
        ┊         ├Ros(1798)┬Ada(1797)-Ham(1790)
        ┊                   ├Was(1788)
        ├Mus(1804)┬Was(1788)
                  └Fai(1800)┬Was(1788)
                            ├Ros(1798)┬Was(1788)
                                      ├Ada(1797)-Ham(1790)

Pickaway(1810)┬Ros(1798)┬Was(1788)
              │         ├Ada(1797)-Ham(1790)
              ├Fai(1800)┬Was(1788)
              │         ├Ros(1798)┬Ada(1797)
              │                   ├Was(1788)
              ├Fra(1803)┬Ros(1798)┬Ada(1797)-Ham(1790)
              │                   ├Was(1788)
              ├Wayne County (MI)

Pike(1815)┬Ros(1798)──Was(1788)
          │         ├Ada(1797)-Ham(1790)
          ├Sci(1803)-Ada(1797)-Ham(1790)
          ├Ada(1797)-Ham(1790)

Portage(1808)-Tru(1800)┬Jef(11797)-Was(1788)
                       ├Wayne County (MI)

Preble(1808)┬Mont(1803)┬Ham(1790)
            │          ├Wayne County (MI)
            ├But(1803)-Ham(1790)

Putnam(1820)-She(1819)-Mia(1807)-Mont(1803)┬Ham(1790)
                                           ├Wayne County (MI)

Richland(1808)-Fai(1800)┬Was(1788)
                        ├Ros(1798)┬Ada(1797)-Ham(1790)
                                  ├Was(1788)
```

Figure 23. OH County Origins

```
Ross(1798)┬Ada(1797)-Ham(1790)
          └Was(1788)

Sandusky(1820)-Hur(1815)—Por(1808)-Tru(1800)—Jef(1797)-Was(1788)
                        ¦                   ├Wayne County (MI)
                        ├Cuy(1808)-Gea(1806)-Tru(1800)—Jef(1797)-Was(1788)
                                                      ├Wayne County (MI)

Scioto(1803)-Ada(1797)-Ham(1790)

Seneca(1820)-Hur(1815)—Por(1808)-Tru(1800)—Jef(1797)-Was(1788)
                      ¦                   ├Wayne County (MI)
                      ├Cuy(1808)-Gea(1806)-Tru(1800)—Jef(1797)-Was(1788)
                                                    ├Wayne County (MI)

Shelby(1819)-Mia(1807)-Mont(1803)┬Ham(1790)
                                 └Wayne County (MI)

Stark(1808)-Col(1810)┬Mus(1804)┬Was(1788)
                     │         └Fai(1800)┬Was(1788)
                     │                   └Ros(1798)┬Ada(1797)-Ham(1790)
                     │                             └Was(1788)
                     └Was(1788)

Summit(1840)┬Por(1808)-Tru(1800)┬Jef(11797)-Was(1788)
            │                   └Wayne County (MI)
            ├Med(1812)-Por(1808)-Tru(1800)┬Jef(1797)-Was(178
            │                             └Wayne County (MI)
            └Sta(Stark(1808)-Col(1810)┬Mus(1804)┬Was(1788)
                                      │         └Fai(1800)┬Was(1788)
                                      │                   └Ros(1798)┬Ada(1797)-Ham
                                      │                             └Was(1788)
                                      └Was(1788)

Trumbull(1800)-Mus(1804)┬Was(1788)
                        └Fai(1800)┬Was(1788)
                                  └Ros(1798)┬Was(1788)
                                            └Ada(1797)-Ham(1790)

Tuscarawas(1808-Mus(1804)┬Was(1788)
                         └Fai(1800)┬Was(1788)
                                   └Ros(1798)┬Was(1788)
                                             └Ada(1797)-Ham(1790)

Union(1820)┬Fra(1803)┬Ros(1798)┬Ada(1797)-Ham(1790)
           │         │         └Was(1788)
           │         └Wayne County (MI)
           ├Mad(1810)-Fra(1803)┬Ros(1798)┬Ada(1797)-Ham(1790
           │                   │         └Was(1788)
           │                   └Wayne County (MI)
           ├Log(1818)-Cha(1805)┬Gre(1803)┬Ham(1790)
           │                   │         └Ros(1798)┬Ada(1797)-Ham(1790)
           │                   │                   └Was(1788)
           │                   └Fra(1803)┬Ros(1798)┬Ada(1797)-Ham(1790)
           │                             │         └Was(1788)
           │                             └Wayne County (MI)
           └Del(1808)-Fra(1803)┬Ros(1798)┬Ada(1797)-Ham(1790)
                               │         └Was(1788)
                               └Wayne County (MI)

Van Wert(1820)-Dar(1809)-Mia(1807)-Mont(1803)┬Ham(1790)
                                             └Wayne County (MI)
```

Figure 24. OH County Origins

```
Vinton(1850)┬Gal(1803)┬Was(1788)
            │         └Ada(1797)-Ham(1790)
            ├Ath(1805)-Was(1788)
            ├Ros(1798)┬Ada(1797)-Ham(1790
            │         └Was(1788)
            ├Jac(1816)┬Ros(1798)┬Was(1788)
            │         │         └Ada(1797)-Ham(1790)
            │         ├Ath(1805)-Was(1788)
            │         ├Sci(1803)-Ada(1797)-Ham(1790)
            │         └Gal(1803)┬Was(1788)
            │                   └Ada(1797)-Ham(1790)
            └Hoc(1818)┬Ath(1805)-Was(1788)
                      ├Ros(1798)┬Ada(1797)-Was(1788)
                      │         └Was(1788)
                      └Fai(1800)┬Was(1788)
                                └Ros(1798)┬Ada(1797)-Was(1788)
                                          └Was(1788)


Warren(1803)-Ham(1790)

Washington(1788)-Original county

Wayne(1808)-Col(1810)┬Mus(1804)┬Was(1788)
                     │         └Fai(1800)┬Was(1788)
                     │                   └Ros(1798)┬Ada(1797)-Ham(1790)
                     │                             └Was(1788)
                     └Was(1788)

Williams(1820)-Dar(1809)-Mia(1807)-Mont(1803)┬Ham(1790)
                                             └Wayne County (MI)

Wood(1820)-Log(1818)-Cha(1805)┬Gre(1803)┬Ham(1790)
                              │         └Ros(1798)┬Ada(1797)-Ham(1790)
                              │                   └Was(1788)
                              └Fra(1803)─Ros(1798)┬Ada(1797)-Ham(1790)
                                                  ├Was(1788)
                                                  └Wayne County (MI)

Wyandot(1845)┬Mar(1820)-Del((1808)-Fra(1803)┬Ros(1798)┬Ada(1797)-Ham(1790)
             │                              │         └Was(1788)
             │                              └Wayne County (MI)
             ├Cra(1820)-Del(1808)-Fra(1803)┬Ros(1798)─Ada(1797)-Ham(1790)
             │                             │          └Was(1788)
             │                             └Wayne County (MI)
             ├Har(1820)-Log(1818)-Cha(1805)┬Gre(1803)┬Ham(1790)
             │                             │         └Ros(1798)┬Ada(1797)-Ham(1790)
             │                             │                   └Was(1788)
             │                             └Fra(1803)┬Ros(1798)┬Ada(1797)-Ham(1790)
             │                                       │         └Was(1788)
             │                                       └Wayne County (MI)
             └Han(1820)-Log(1818)-Cha(1805)┬Gre(1803)┬Ham(1790)
                                           │         └Ros(1798)┬Ada(1797)-Ham(1790)
                                           │                   └Was(1788)
                                           └Fra(1803)┬Ros(1798)┬Ada(1797)-Ham(1790)
                                                     │         └Was(1788)
                                                     └Wayne County (MI)
```

Figure 25. OH County Origins

Chapter 2

TYPES OF RECORDS

1. Introduction

The state of OH is relatively rich in genealogical source materials, although there are some gaps in the early years and there are some problems with the loss of records in court house (CH) fires, which were fairly common in the 19th century. A great deal of work has been done in accumulating, preserving, photocopying, transcribing, and indexing records, and therefore many are readily available. The best collections of OH materials are to be found in the following repositories:

___(OHS) Archives–Library Division, OH Historical Society, 1985 Velma Avenue, Columbus, OH 43211.

___(SLO) Genealogy Division, State Library of OH, 65 South Front Street, Columbus, OH 43266-0334.

___(FHL) Family History Library, Genealogical Library of the Church of Jesus Christ of Latter-day Saints, 35 North West Temple, Salt Lake City, UT 84150.

___(FHC) Family History Center(s), over 1700 of them, located all over the world. They are local branch affiliates of the Family History Library. They can be found in most major US cities, including 10 in OH.

___(ONAHRC) OH Network of American History Research Centers, seven Centers located at University of Akron, Wright State University in Dayton, University of Cincinnati, Western Reserve Historical Society in Cleveland, OH Historical Society in Columbus, Bowling Green State University, and OH University.

___(WRHS) Western Reserve Historical Society Library, 10825 East Boulevard, Cleveland, OH 44106.

___(PLC) Public Library of Cincinnati and Hamilton County, 800 Vine Street, Cincinnati, OH 45202-2071.

___(OGS) OH Genealogical Society Library, 34 Sturges Avenue, Mansfield, OH 44906.

___(ACPL) Allen County Public Library, Genealogical Department, 900 Webster Street, Fort Wayne, IN 46802.

The OHS (OH Historical Society) in Columbus functions in three ways: (1) as the official repository for the preservation of state records (the State Archives), (2) as the official collection center for other records important to the history of OH, (3) and as one of the ONAHRC Centers which stores local records from the region. The original records collection consists of more than 31,000 cubic feet of state and local governmental records. The Society also holds over 130,000 books and pamphlets, over 40,000 reels of microfilm, many manuscripts, and upwards of 20,000 volumes of newspapers. There also numerous large indexes and other finding aids. In the same city is the SLO (State Library of OH). Its Genealogy Division has a wide array of published material (books, journals, pamphlets, microforms), plus extensive holdings of manuscripts and typescripts (especially those put together by the WPA and the DAR).

The collections in Columbus are somewhat matched by that of the FHL (Family History Library) of Salt Lake City, UT. They have by far the largest collection of OH genealogical materials outside of OH. The FHL has microfilmed a vast number of OH documents, which they make available through their numerous branch libraries (called Family History Centers, FHC), located all over the US and in many overseas countries. All these materials can be readily located in the catalog of the FHL, which is available at every FHC.

There are several other very important repositories in OH which must not be overlooked. Included among them are the seven regional centers of the ONAHRC (OH Network of American History Regional Centers). These centers are charged with collecting, preserving, microfilming, cataloging, and indexing materials which are pertinent to the history of the regions of OH which they serve. The regions consist of the county in which the center is located and many surrounding counties. The records they are concerned with are county and township governmental records, as well as newspapers, manuscripts, and other pertinent items.

There is also the WRHS (Western Reserve Historical Society), one of the leading genealogical libraries in the US. Its large collection is strong for northeastern OH, but its coverage of all of OH is outstanding. Its resources include genealogical books, journals, microfilms, records, manuscripts, collections, plus newspapers and maps. Further, the PLC (Public Library of Cincinnati) has an exceptional good collection of genealogical materials. Included are censuses and census indexes, family and local histories, manuscripts, microfilms, indexes, reference works, and periodicals. Not to be neglected are the growing family research resources of the OGS (OH Genealogical Society). Special attention should be paid to their ancestor indexes, genealogical charts, microfilm records, and printed records. And you need to be reminded that just across the border of northwestern OH is another of the largest genealogical libraries in the US, namely, the ACPL (Allen County Public Library) in Fort Wayne, IN.

Finally, it should not be overlooked that there are some fairly well–stocked regional libraries (RL) in the state of OH. These are generally smaller than the large libraries noted above, but considerably larger than most town and county libraries. Of course, local libraries (LL), that is, county, city, town, and private libraries are sources which are very important to the family history researcher.

The above repositories and their collections and other sources will be treated in detail in Chapter 3. In this chapter the many types of records which are available for OH genealogical research are discussed. Those records which are essentially national or state-wide in scope will be treated in detail. Records which are basically county or city records will be discussed only generally, but a detailed listing of them will be delayed to Chapter 4, where the local records available for each of the 88 OH counties will be given.

---

2. Bible records

During the past 200 years it was customary for families with religious affiliations to keep vital statistics on their members in the family Bible. These records vary widely, but among the items that may be found are names, dates, and places of birth, christening, baptism, marriage, death, and sometimes military service. Although most Bibles containing recorded information probably still remain in private hands, some of the information has been submitted for publication and some has been filed in libraries and archives. Bible records may be found in libraries and archives throughout OH. You should inquire about such records at every possible library and archives in and near your ancestor's county or district, especially the regional libraries (RL) and the local libraries (LL). Sometimes there will be indexes or the records will be arranged alphabetically. RL will be listed in Chapter 3, and LL will be listed under the counties in Chapter 4. You should not overlook the possibility that Bible records may be listed in indexes or in files labelled something other than Bible records. The most likely ones are family records, genealogies, manuscripts, names, surnames. Also do not fail to look in the major card index of each library for the names you are seeking.

There are many published compilations of OH Bible records. Among those you should examine are:
___ DAR Chapters in OH, BIBLE RECORDS, or FAMILY AND BIBLE RECORDS, or BIBLE AND CEMETERY RECORDS, and other similar titles, various DAR Chapters, various cities, various dates. Available for these counties: Ada, All, Ash, Cla, Cle, Col, Cuy, Dar, Fai, Fay, Fra, Ful, Gea, Ham, Han, Hoc, Hur, Lak, Lor, Luc, Mad, Mah, Mar, Mia, Mont, Mus, Nob, Pic, Por, Pre, She, Sta, Sum, War, Was, and Way. <Remember that counties are abbreviated with their first three(four) letters.>
___ Mrs. D. R. Short and Mrs. D. Eller, OH BIBLE RECORDS, ACPL, Fort Wayne, IN, 1971.

These and other Bible record compilations for OH are listed in:

___FHL, FAMILY HISTORY LIBRARY CATALOG, LOCALITY SECTION, Salt Lake City, UT, latest microfiche and/or computer edition. Look under OH and then under the county of interest.

___C. W. Bell, OH GUIDE TO GENEALOGICAL SOURCES, Genealogical Publishing Co., Baltimore, MD, 1988. Look under the county.

___P. Khouw, COUNTY BY COUNTY IN OH GENEALOGY, Genealogy Staff, SLO, Columbus, OH, 1992. Look under county.

___E. K. Kirkham, AN INDEX TO SOME OF THE BIBLE AND FAMILY RECORDS OF THE US, Everton Publishers, Logan, UT, 1980/4, volume 2.

___National Society, DAR, DAR LIBRARY CATALOG, VOLUME 2: STATE AND LOCAL HISTORIES AND RECORDS, The Society, Washington, DC, 1986.

___CARD AND COMPUTER CATALOGS in OHS, SLO, WRHS, PLC, OGS, ACPL, RL, and LL.

The Bible record compilations referred to above should be sought in the OHS, SLO, FHL(FHC), WRHS, PLC, OGS, ACPL, RL, and LL, and in the DAR Library in Washington, DC. Do not fail to look for vertical files of Bible records in these repositories. Bible records also appear in genealogical periodical articles and in published family genealogies. These two types of records, as well as details on manuscript sources will be discussed in sections 18, 19, 23, and 32 of this chapter.

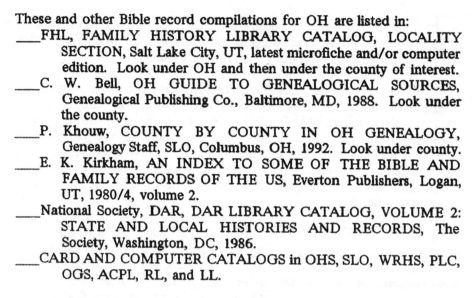

3. Biographies

There are several major national biographical works which contain sketches on nationally-prominent OH personages. There are also numerous good biographical compilations for the state of OH or for sections of it. These volumes list persons who have attained some prominence in the fields of law, agriculture, business, politics, medicine, engineering, science, military, teaching, public service, or philanthropy. There are also many local (county, township, city, town) biographical works, and numerous regional and county histories also contain biographies of leading citizens. In addition, some professional organizations have compiled biographical information on their members. All of these can be of considerable use to genealogical researchers, because they usually carry birth, marriage, and death data, as well as details on children, parents, grandparents, and other ancestors.

Over 500 national biographical compilations have been indexed in a large microfilm/computer set which contains over 6 million entries. This set is available in large libraries, and is added to annually:

___BIOBASE, Gale Research Co., Detroit, MI, latest edition. This database is the successor to M. C. Herbert and B. McNeil, BIOGRAPHY AND GENEALOGY MASTER INDEX, Gale Research Co., Detroit, MI, various dates.

In the OHS, there is a very sizable surname index which covers many biographical sketches in local histories, atlases, and biographical volumes:

___OH COUNTY HISTORY SURNAME INDEX, OHS, Columbus, OH. Also on microfilm at FHL and therefore available through FHC.

Over the years, almost 100 regional and state biographical compilations have been published for OH or sections of it. Among the most useful of these for your investigations are:

___BIOGRAPHICAL HISTORY OF NORTHEASTERN OH, Lewis Publishing Co., Chicago, IL, 1893, 2 volumes. Counties: Ash, Gea, Lak, Mah, Tru.

___HISTORY OF THE UPPER OH VALLEY, Brant and Fuller, Madison, WI, 1890-1, 4 volumes. Counties: Bel, Col, Jef.

___J. F. Brennan, BIOGRAPHICAL CYCLOPEDIA AND PORTRAIT GALLERY AND AN HISTORICAL SKETCH OF THE STATE OF OH, Western Biographical Publishing Co., Cincinnati, OH, 1883, 6 volumes. Statewide.

___J. F. Brennan, A BIOGRAPHICAL CYCLOPEDIA AND POR-TRAIT GALLERY OF DISTINGUISHED MEN, Yorston and Co., Cincinnati, OH, 1879. Statewide.

___W. J. Comley, OH: THE FUTURE GREAT STATE, Comley Brothers, Cincinnati, OH, 1875. Early settlers.

___Cleveland Centennial Commission, INFORMATION ON PIONEER WOMEN OF THE WESTERN RESERVE, Western Reserve Historical Society, Cleveland, OH, microfilmed records. Also available at FHL(FHC).

___COMMEMORATIVE BIOGRAPHICAL RECORD OF NORTH-WESTERN OH, Beers and Co., Chicago, IL, 1899. Counties: Ful, Hen, Wil.

___J. P. Cutler, THE FOUNDERS OF OH, 48 PIONEERS OF THE FIRST WHITE SETTLEMENT OF THE NORTHWEST TERRITORY, Allen County Public Library, Fort Wayne, IN, 1983.

___W. J. Duff, HISTORY OF NORTH CENTRAL OH, Historical Publishing Co., Topeka, IN, 1931. Counties: Ash, Hur, Kno, Lor, Med, Way.

___S. D. Fess, OH HISTORY, GAZETTEER, AND BIOGRAPHIES, Lewis Publishing Co., Chicago, IL, 1937, 5 volumes. Statewide.

___C. B. Galbreath, HISTORY OF OH, American Historical Society, Chicago, IL, 1925, 5 volumes. To be used with R. Lent, CROSS INDEX TO HISTORY OF OH, Genealogical Reference Builders,

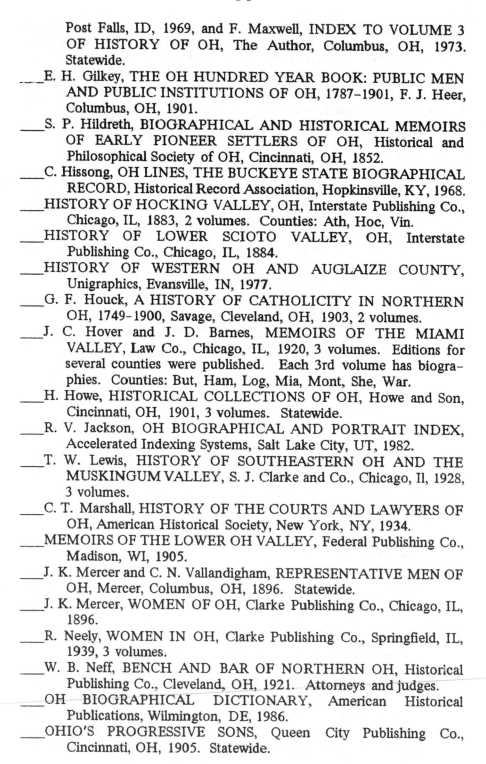

Post Falls, ID, 1969, and F. Maxwell, INDEX TO VOLUME 3 OF HISTORY OF OH, The Author, Columbus, OH, 1973. Statewide.

___E. H. Gilkey, THE OH HUNDRED YEAR BOOK: PUBLIC MEN AND PUBLIC INSTITUTIONS OF OH, 1787–1901, F. J. Heer, Columbus, OH, 1901.

___S. P. Hildreth, BIOGRAPHICAL AND HISTORICAL MEMOIRS OF EARLY PIONEER SETTLERS OF OH, Historical and Philosophical Society of OH, Cincinnati, OH, 1852.

___C. Hissong, OH LINES, THE BUCKEYE STATE BIOGRAPHICAL RECORD, Historical Record Association, Hopkinsville, KY, 1968.

___HISTORY OF HOCKING VALLEY, OH, Interstate Publishing Co., Chicago, IL, 1883, 2 volumes. Counties: Ath, Hoc, Vin.

___HISTORY OF LOWER SCIOTO VALLEY, OH, Interstate Publishing Co., Chicago, IL, 1884.

___HISTORY OF WESTERN OH AND AUGLAIZE COUNTY, Unigraphics, Evansville, IN, 1977.

___G. F. Houck, A HISTORY OF CATHOLICITY IN NORTHERN OH, 1749–1900, Savage, Cleveland, OH, 1903, 2 volumes.

___J. C. Hover and J. D. Barnes, MEMOIRS OF THE MIAMI VALLEY, Law Co., Chicago, IL, 1920, 3 volumes. Editions for several counties were published. Each 3rd volume has biographies. Counties: But, Ham, Log, Mia, Mont, She, War.

___H. Howe, HISTORICAL COLLECTIONS OF OH, Howe and Son, Cincinnati, OH, 1901, 3 volumes. Statewide.

___R. V. Jackson, OH BIOGRAPHICAL AND PORTRAIT INDEX, Accelerated Indexing Systems, Salt Lake City, UT, 1982.

___T. W. Lewis, HISTORY OF SOUTHEASTERN OH AND THE MUSKINGUM VALLEY, S. J. Clarke and Co., Chicago, Il, 1928, 3 volumes.

___C. T. Marshall, HISTORY OF THE COURTS AND LAWYERS OF OH, American Historical Society, New York, NY, 1934.

___MEMOIRS OF THE LOWER OH VALLEY, Federal Publishing Co., Madison, WI, 1905.

___J. K. Mercer and C. N. Vallandigham, REPRESENTATIVE MEN OF OH, Mercer, Columbus, OH, 1896. Statewide.

___J. K. Mercer, WOMEN OF OH, Clarke Publishing Co., Chicago, IL, 1896.

___R. Neely, WOMEN IN OH, Clarke Publishing Co., Springfield, IL, 1939, 3 volumes.

___W. B. Neff, BENCH AND BAR OF NORTHERN OH, Historical Publishing Co., Cleveland, OH, 1921. Attorneys and judges.

___OH BIOGRAPHICAL DICTIONARY, American Historical Publications, Wilmington, DE, 1986.

___OHIO'S PROGRESSIVE SONS, Queen City Publishing Co., Cincinnati, OH, 1905. Statewide.

___PORTRAIT AND BIOGRAPHICAL RECORD OF AUGLAIZE, LOGAN, AND SHELBY COUNTIES, Shelby County Genealogical Society, Sidney, OH, 1976.

___PORTRAIT AND BIOGRAPHICAL RECORD OF THE SCIOTO VALLEY, Lewis Publishing Co., Chicago, IL, 1894.

___PROGRESSIVE MEN OF NORTHERN OH, Plain Dealer Publishing Co., Cleveland, OH, 1906.

___E. O. Randall, BENCH AND BAR OF OH, Century Publishing Co., Chicago, IL, 1897.

___C. Robson, BIOGRAPHICAL CYCLOPEDIA OF OH IN THE 19TH CENTURY, Galaxy Publishing Co., Cincinnati, OH, 1876. Statewide.

___O. G. Rust, HISTORY OF WEST CENTRAL OH, Historical Publishing Co., Indianapolis, IN, 1934, 3 volumes.

___J. V. Sanner, WHO'S WHO IN OH, Biographical Publishing Co., Cleveland, OH, 1930.

___M. P. Sargent, PIONEER SKETCHES, Herald Printing and Publishing Co., Erie, PA, 1891.

___F. E. Scobey and B. L. McElroy, BIOGRAPHICAL ANNALS OF OH, A HANDBOOK OF GOVERNMENTAL INSTITUTIONS OF OH, Clerks of the State Senate and House, Columbus, OH, 1902.

___W. E. Smith, HISTORY OF SOUTHWESTERN OH, THE MIAMI VALLEY, Lewis Historical Publishing Co., West Palm Beach, FL, 1964, 3 volumes.

___SOUTHERN OH AND ITS BUILDERS, A BIOGRAPHICAL RECORD, 20TH CENTURY, Southern OH Biographical Assn., Cincinnati, OH, 1927.

___J. S. Stewart, HISTORY OF NORTHEASTERN OH, Historical Publishing Co., Indianapolis, IN, 1935, 3 volumes.

___S. H. Stille, OH BUILDS A NATION, A MEMOIR TO THE PIONEERS AND CELEBRATED SONS OF THE BUCKEYE STATE, Arlendale, Chicago, IL, 1962.

___E. Summers, GENEALOGICAL AND FAMILY HISTORY OF EASTERN OH, Lewis Publishing Co., New York, NY, 1903.

___W. A. Taylor, OH IN CONGRESS, 1803-1901, WITH NOTES OF SENATORS AND REPRESENTATIVES, Twentieth Century Publishing Co., Columbus, Oh, 1900.

___D. H. Tolzmann, OH VALLEY GERMAN BIOGRAPHICAL INDEX, Heritage, Bowie, MD, 1992. About 4000 Germans listed.

___H. T. Upton, HISTORY OF THE WESTERN RESERVE, Lewis Publishing Co., Chicago, IL, 1910, 3 volumes.

___C. S. Van Tassel, FAMILIAR FACES OF OH, Van Tassel, Bowling Green, OH, 1896.

____C. S. Van Tassel, STORY OF THE MAUMEE VALLEY, TOLEDO, AND THE SANDUSKY REGION, Clarke Publishing Co., Chicago, IL, 1929, 4 volumes.

____C. S. Van Tassel, THE OH BLUE BOOK, WHO'S WHO IN THE BUCKEYE STATE, The Compiler, Toledo, OH, 1917. Statewide.

____M. Whitlock, WOMEN IN OH HISTORY, OHS, Columbus, OH, 1976.

____C. W. Williamson, HISTORY OF WESTERN OH AND AUGLAIZE COUNTY, Linn, Columbus, OH, 1905.

____WHO IS WHO IN AND FROM OH, Queen City Publishing Co., Cincinnati, OH, 1910, 2 volumes.

____WHO'S WHO IN OH, Larkin, Chicago, IL, 1947.

____WHO'S WHO IN OH, US Public Relations Service, Atlanta, GA, 1974.

____N. O. Winter, A HISTORY OF NORTHWEST OH, Lewis Publishing Co., Chicago, IL, 1917, 3 volumes.

____G. F. Wright, REPRESENTATIVE CITIZENS OF OH, MEMORIAL-GENEALOGICAL, Memorial Publishing Co., Cleveland, OH, 1913. Statewide.

Most of these volumes will be found in OHS, SLO, WRHS, PLC, ACPL, and FHL(FHC). Many are at OGS, and those pertinent to various regions will be found in RL and larger LL in the area.

In addition to the above national, state, and regional biographical works, there are many local (county, township, district, city, and town) biographical volumes. Further, biographical sketches are more often than not included in county histories. Listings of many of the biographical volumes and county histories are provided in:

____P. Khouw, COUNTY BY COUNTY IN OH GENEALOGY, SLO, Columbus, OH, 1992.

____S. Harter, OH GENEALOGY AND LOCAL HISTORY SOURCES INDEX, The Author, Columbus, OH, 1986.

____FAMILY HISTORY LIBRARY CATALOG, LOCALITY SECTION, on microfiche and computer, FHL, Salt Lake City, UT, and at every FHC.

When volumes containing biographical information are available in the various OH counties, this fact will be noted under the county listings in Chapter 4. Such volumes will be found in OHS, SLO, WRHS, PLC, ACPL, and FHL(FHC). Some are at OGS, and those pertinent to various counties will be found in RL and LL in the counties. There are also some special biographical collections and some unpublished compilations in several OH libraries. Do not fail to inquire in libraries near your ancestor's homeplace. Care should be exercised in taking the data in biographical sketches too literally. Remember that your ancestor or some family member supplied the information quite often from memory and/or family tradition.

4. Birth records

The state of OH passed a law in 1856 requiring birth, and death records to be kept in OH counties. This law was largely ignored, but some records were kept during 1856/7, and some of those that were kept have survived. They are, however, quite incomplete. When such records are available for the various OH counties, they will be indicated in the county listing in Chapter 4. A law mandating that the Probate Court in OH counties keep birth and death records was legislated in 1867. Again, the law was not adhered to in many places, but more records were produced and many are extant. They are, however, incomplete. The records include the names of the parents and their place of residence. They are available at county Probate Courts, ONAHRC, OHS, and FHL(FHC). Counties for which these records are available will be indicated in Chapter 4.

In December 1908 the state of OH passed a law requiring state-wide birth registration in addition to the county registration. By 1914 the registrations were running at least 90% complete. These records are in the county or city health departments as well as in the central state repository at Columbus:
_____State Department of Health, Room G-20, 65 South Front Street, Columbus, OH 43215. They have indexes.
These records usually contain name, place and date of birth, sex, color, name and birthplace of father, and maiden name and birthplace of mother. In many counties, there were delayed and amended birth registrations, so be sure and seek them out, if you do not find what you want in the regular records.

Prior to the time when OH required birth reports (1908), other records may yield dates and places of birth: biographical, cemetery, census, church, death, divorce, marriage, military, mortuary, newspaper, pension, and published. These are all discussed in other sections of this chapter. The finding of birth record articles in genealogical periodicals is also described separately in this chapter.

5. Cemetery records

If you know or suspect that your ancestor was buried in a certain cemetery, the best thing to do is to write to the caretaker of the cemetery, enclose an SASE and $5, and ask if the records show your ancestor. If this fails, other cemeteries in the region can be investigated. A very convenient listing of many OH cemeteries is provided in:
_____M. H. Smith, OH CEMETERIES, OGS, Mansfield, OH, 1978, with its supplement T. L. M. Klaiber, OH CEMETERIES ADDEN-

DUM, Gateway Press, Baltimore, OH, 1990. Locations of cemeteries and locations of records.

Should this prove unsuccessful, then the next step is to look into cemetery record collections for your ancestor's county. These have been made by the DAR, the WPA's OH Historical Records Survey, local genealogical and historical societies, and individuals. Much work has been done, and at least some cemeteries in every county have been read and the data published. Listings of many of the available records will be found in:

___FAMILY HISTORY LIBRARY CATALOG, LOCALITY SECTION, FHL, Salt Lake City, UT, latest edition, on both microfiche and computer. Look under OH and its counties.

___National Society, DAR, DAR LIBRARY CATALOG, VOLUME TWO: STATE AND LOCAL HISTORIES AND RECORDS, The Society, Washington, DC, 1986.

___C. W. Bell, MASTER INDEX, OH DAR GENEALOGICAL AND HISTORICAL RECORDS, OH Society, DAR, Westlake, OH, 1985. Listing of records and their locations. Many names indexed, but by no means all.

___P. Khouw, COUNTY BY COUNTY IN OH GENEALOGY, SLO, Columbus, OH, 1992.

When you consult these, you will find that the main sources of OH cemetery records are the OHS, SLO, WRHS, and FHL(FHC). In addition, local libraries (LL) in the OH counties often have records of their own cemeteries. OH regional libraries (RL) and large genealogical libraries (LGL) outside of OH may also have records.

Several of the larger genealogical periodicals published in OH contain cemetery listings quite frequently (especially Gateway to the West, OH Records and Pioneer Families now known as OH: The Crossroads of our Nation, The Report of the OGS, The Fireland Pioneer). In addition, many of the local genealogical publications carry cemetery records from time to time. A useful index which covers over 100 periodicals and which will locate many of these articles for you is:

___C. W. Bell, OH GENEALOGICAL PERIODICAL INDEX, A COUNTY GUIDE, The Author, Columbus, OH, latest edition.

There are also some cemetery record compilations which could be of value to you:

___E. P. Bentley, OH CEMETERY RECORDS EXTRACTED FROM THE OLD NORTHWEST GENEALOGICAL QUARTERLY, Genealogical Publishing Co., Baltimore, OH, 1984. About 20,000 persons chiefly from these counties: Ath, Del, Fai, Fra, Gea, Gue, Jac, Kno, Lic, Lor, Mad, Pic, Port, Ros, Tru, and Vin.

___Franklin County Chapter of the OGS, CONFEDERATE CEMETERIES IN OH, The Chapter, Columbus, OH, 1980.

____P. B. Miller, INDEX TO THE GRAVE RECORDS OF SERVICE-
MEN OF THE WAR OF 1812, STATE OF OH, US Daughters of
the War of 1812 of OH, Lima, OH, 1988. To be used to refer to
the many volumes of grave records compiled by the Daughters.

____Trumbull County Chapter of the OGS, OFFICIAL ROSTER OF
THE SOLDIERS OF THE REVOLUTION BURIED IN OH, The
Chapter, Warren, OH, 1982, 2 volumes.

____WPA, VETERANS' GRAVE INDEX, INDEX FILE, OHS, Colum-
bus, OH. Covers soldiers who fought in wars from the Revolution through World War II.

There are files of veterans' graves in the County Recorders Offices in
almost all OH counties. And in some of them, you will also find one or
more grave registration books.

In Chapter 4, those counties for which extensive cemetery records
exist in printed or microfilmed form are indicated. Instructions regarding
locating the above reference volumes and the records themselves will be
presented in Chapter 3. More detailed instructions regarding the finding
of cemetery records in genealogical periodical articles are given in a
section of this chapter devoted to such periodicals.

6. Census records

Excellent ancestor information is available in six types of census reports
which have been accumulated for OH:
tax substitutes for lost censuses (T),
regular (R), farm and ranch (F),
manufactures (M), mortality (D for death), the special 1840 Revolutionary War Pension Census (P), and the special Civil War Union veterans
census (C).

Tax records have been put together in order to provide substitute
records (T) for the 1800 and 1810 OH census records which were almost
completely destroyed. These records list the names of land owners along
with their counties of residence. They are available in published form,
which are indexed:

____R. D. Craig, RESIDENT PROPRIETORS OF THE CT WESTERN
RESERVE, AN OH TAX LIST OF 1804, The Author, Cincinnati,
OH, 1963.

____R. V. Jackson, INDEX TO OH TAX LISTS, 1800–1810, Accelerated
Indexing Systems, Salt Lake City, UT, 1977. About 45,000
entries.

____G. M. Petty, OH 1810 TAX DUPLICATE, The Compiler, Columbus,
OH, 1976.

____E. W. Powell, EARLY OH TAX RECORDS, The Compiler, Akron,
OH, 1971, use with C. W. Bell, INDEX, The Compiler, Akron,

OH, 1973. About 130 tax lists included, some from every existing county, about 1800-1825.

Chapter 4 lists the tax-substitute censuses (T) available for each of the OH counties in existence during the period of few regular censuses, namely, 1800-1819. Also see the later section entitled tax records. There are a few surviving census records during this period. Those for Washington County in 1800, 1803, and 1810 and a few others have been published in:

___R. V. Jackson, EARLY OH CENSUS RECORDS, 1800-1810, Accelerated Indexing Systems, Salt Lake City, UT, 1974. About 4000 entries.

Regular census records (R) are available for almost all OH counties in 1820, 1830, 1840, 1850, 1860, 1870, 1880, 1900, 1910, and 1920. The major exception is that the data for Franklin and Wood Counties in the 1820 census are missing. Please note also that the 1890 census did not survive. Only fragments of it are available for OH, these fragments being for Cincinnati in Hamilton County and Wayne Township in Clinton County. The 1840 census and all before it listed the head of the household plus a breakdown of the number of persons in the household according to age and sex brackets. Beginning in 1850 the names of all persons were recorded along with age, sex, real estate, marital, and other information, including the state of birth. With the 1880 census and thereafter, the birthplaces of the mother and father of each person are also shown. Chapter 4 lists the regular census records (R) available for each of the 88 OH counties.

State-wide indexes have been compiled and most have been printed for the 1820, 1830, 1840, 1850, 1860, and 1880 OH regular census records. These volumes are:

___OH Family Historians, 1820 FEDERAL POPULATION CENSUS, OH INDEX, OH Library Foundation, Columbus, OH, 1976. Over 92,000 heads of household listed.

___R. V. Jackson, OHIO 1820 CENSUS INDEX, Accelerated Indexing Systems, Bountiful, UT, 1977. About 90,000 entries.

___OH Family Historians, 1830 FEDERAL POPULATION CENSUS, OH INDEX, OH Library Foundation, 1976. About 150,000 entries.

___R. V. Jackson, OH 1830 CENSUS INDEX, Accelerated Indexing Systems, Bountiful, UT, 1976. About 160,000 entries.

___C. G. Wilkens, INDEX TO THE 1840 POPULATION CENSUS OF OH, The Compiler, Fort Wayne, IN, 1969-72, 4 volumes.

___R. V. Jackson, OH 1840 CENSUS INDEX, Accelerated Indexing Systems, Bountiful, UT, 1978.

___OH Family Historians, 1850 FEDERAL POPULATION CENSUS, OH INDEX, Edwards Brothers, Ann Arbor, MI, 1972.

___R. V. Jackson, OH 1850 CENSUS INDEX, Accelerated Indexing Systems, Bountiful, UT, 1978.

___L. F. Harshman, INDEX TO THE 1850 CENSUS OF OH, OH Family Historians, Mineral Ridge, OH, 1972.   Over 500,000 entries.

___L. F. Harshman, INDEX TO THE 1860 CENSUS OF OH, Edwards Brothers, Ann Arbor, MI, 1979.   Over 650,000 names.

___OH Genealogical Society, INDEX TO THE 1880 OH CENSUS, The Society, Mansfield, OH.   Contact the Society.

___Automated Archives, 1880 OH CENSUS INDEX, CD-ROM 20, GeneSys, Provo, UT, 1993.

No state-wide index is available for the 1870 OH Census, but a number of county-wide and city-wide indexes are in print.   These include ones for Akron, Canton, Cincinnati, Cleveland, Toledo, Columbiana County, Hancock County, Lucas County, and Summit County.

In addition to the above indexes, there is a National Archives microfilm index which contains only families with a child 10 or under in the 1880 census.   There is a microfilm index to the surviving fragments of the 1890 census.   There are also complete National Archives microfilm indexes to the 1900, 1910, and 1920 OH censuses.   The 1910 index is by Miracode, and the others are arranged by Soundex.   Librarians or archivists can show you how to use these indexing methods.   These microfilm indexes are:

___US Bureau of the Census, INDEX (SOUNDEX) TO THE 1880 POPULATION SCHEDULES, OH, Microfilm T767, Rolls 1-143, National Archives, Washington, DC.

___US Bureau of the Census, INDEX TO THE ELEVENTH CENSUS OF THE US, 1890, Microfilm M496, 2 Rolls, National Archives, Washington, DC.

___US Bureau of the Census, INDEX (SOUNDEX) TO THE 1900 POPULATION SCHEDULES, OH, Microfilm T1065, Rolls 1-395, National Archives, Washington, DC.

___US Bureau of the Census, INDEX (MIRACODE) TO THE 1910 POPULATION SCHEDULES, OH, Microfilm T1272, Rolls 1-418, National Archives, Washington, DC.

___US Bureau of the Census, INDEX (SOUNDEX) TO THE 1920 POPULATION SCHEDULES, OH, Microfilm M1581, Rolls 1-476, National Archives, Washington, DC.

Once you have located an ancestor in the indexes, you can then go directly to the reference in the census microfilms and read the entry. When indexes are not available (1870), it may be necessary for you to go through the census listings entry-by-entry.   This can be essentially prohibitive for the entire state, so it is necessary to know the county in order to limit your search.   The census record microfilms are as follows:

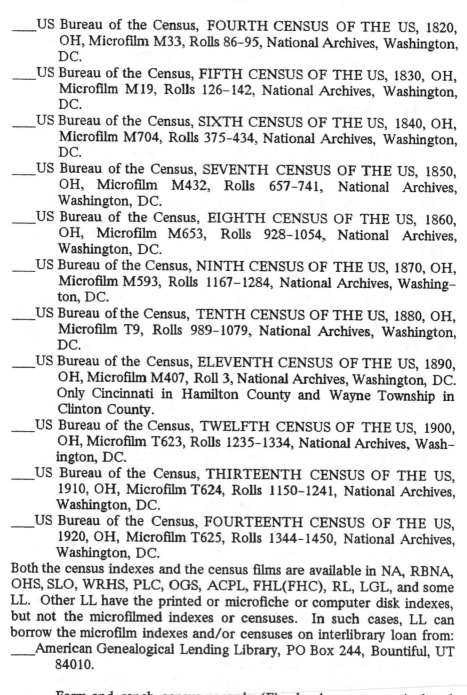

____US Bureau of the Census, FOURTH CENSUS OF THE US, 1820, OH, Microfilm M33, Rolls 86–95, National Archives, Washington, DC.

____US Bureau of the Census, FIFTH CENSUS OF THE US, 1830, OH, Microfilm M19, Rolls 126–142, National Archives, Washington, DC.

____US Bureau of the Census, SIXTH CENSUS OF THE US, 1840, OH, Microfilm M704, Rolls 375–434, National Archives, Washington, DC.

____US Bureau of the Census, SEVENTH CENSUS OF THE US, 1850, OH, Microfilm M432, Rolls 657–741, National Archives, Washington, DC.

____US Bureau of the Census, EIGHTH CENSUS OF THE US, 1860, OH, Microfilm M653, Rolls 928–1054, National Archives, Washington, DC.

____US Bureau of the Census, NINTH CENSUS OF THE US, 1870, OH, Microfilm M593, Rolls 1167–1284, National Archives, Washington, DC.

____US Bureau of the Census, TENTH CENSUS OF THE US, 1880, OH, Microfilm T9, Rolls 989–1079, National Archives, Washington, DC.

____US Bureau of the Census, ELEVENTH CENSUS OF THE US, 1890, OH, Microfilm M407, Roll 3, National Archives, Washington, DC. Only Cincinnati in Hamilton County and Wayne Township in Clinton County.

____US Bureau of the Census, TWELFTH CENSUS OF THE US, 1900, OH, Microfilm T623, Rolls 1235–1334, National Archives, Washington, DC.

____US Bureau of the Census, THIRTEENTH CENSUS OF THE US, 1910, OH, Microfilm T624, Rolls 1150–1241, National Archives, Washington, DC.

____US Bureau of the Census, FOURTEENTH CENSUS OF THE US, 1920, OH, Microfilm T625, Rolls 1344–1450, National Archives, Washington, DC.

Both the census indexes and the census films are available in NA, RBNA, OHS, SLO, WRHS, PLC, OGS, ACPL, FHL(FHC), RL, LGL, and some LL. Other LL have the printed or microfiche or computer disk indexes, but not the microfilmed indexes or censuses. In such cases, LL can borrow the microfilm indexes and/or censuses on interlibrary loan from:
____American Genealogical Lending Library, PO Box 244, Bountiful, UT 84010.

____Farm and ranch census records (F), also known as agricultural census records, are available for 1850, 1860, 1870, and 1880 for OH. These records list the name of the owner, size of the farm or ranch, value of the property, and other details. If your ancestor was a farmer (many were), it will be worthwhile to seek him in these records. No indexes are available, so it helps to know the county. The records or microfilm copies are available at OHS, SLO, and from the National Archives. The records appear in:

____US Bureau of the Census, NON-POPULATION CENSUS SCHED-ULES FOR OH, Microfilm T1159, 104 Rolls, National Archives, Washington, DC. Numerous counties missing each year.

Manufactures census records (M) are available for 1820, 1850, 1860, 1870, and 1880. The 1820 records list manufacturing businesses in the various counties. The later records list manufacturing firms which produced articles having an annual value of $500 or more. Given in these later records are the name of the firm, the owner, the product, the machinery used, and the number of employees. There is an index to the 1820 records, but no other indexes are available, so a knowledge of the county is helpful. The records or microfilmed copies are at OHS, SLO, and in the National Archives. The records appear in:

____US Bureau of the Census, RECORDS OF THE 1820 CENSUS OF MANUFACTURES, Microfilm M653, 27 Rolls, National Archives, Washington, DC.

____US Bureau of the Census, NON-POPULATION CENSUS SCHED-ULES FOR OH, Microfilm T1159, 104 Rolls, National Archives, Washington, DC. Numerous counties missing for 1860, 1870, and 1880.

An index to the 1820 records is:

____INDEXES TO MANUFACTURES CENSUS OF 1820, OH, Bookmark, Knightstown, IN, 1977.

Mortality census records (D for death) are available for the periods June 01-May 31, 1850, 1860, 1870, and 1880. Those for 1850 cover only the counties Huron through Wyandot, for 1860 all counties are represented, for 1870 only Seneca County is available, and for 1880 only the counties Adams through Geauga are covered. These records give information on persons who died in the year preceding the 1st of June of each of the above census dates (1850, 1860, 1870, 1880). The data contained in the compilations include name, age, sex, occupation, place of birth and other such information. The 1850, 1860, and 1880 records have been copied on microfilm by the National Archives:

____US Bureau of the Census, NON-POPULATION CENSUS SCHED-ULES FOR OH, Microfilm T1159, 104 Rolls, National Archives, Washington, DC. Numerous counties missing in 1850 and 1880. All counties except Seneca missing 1870.

And the 1870 records for Seneca County have been published as follows:

____SENECA COUNTY, OH, 1870 MORTALITY CENSUS RECORDS, OH Records and Pioneer Families, volume 24, number 1, page 25.

The 1850, 1860, and 1880 records have been printed in alphabetical order or indexed which makes searching them easy:

____R. V. Jackson, OH MORTALITY SCHEDULE 1850, Accelerated Indexing Systems, Salt Lake City, UT, 1979. Huron through Wyandot Counties only.

____B. Carmean, 1860 MORTALITY SCHEDULE, OH, Southern OH Genealogical Society, Hillsboro, OH, 1980.

____J. B. Workman, 1880 OH MORTALITY RECORDS, Workman, North Olmstead, OH, 1991. Adams through Geauga Counties only.

These indexes will be found in OHS, SLO, WRHS, PLC, OGS, ACPL, FHL(FHC), and some RL and LL.

In 1840 a special census of <u>Revolutionary</u> War <u>Pensioners</u> (P) was taken. This compilation was an attempt to list all pension holders, however, there are some omissions and some false entries. The list and an index have been published:

____CENSUS OF PENSIONERS, A GENERAL INDEX FOR REVO- LUTIONARY OR MILITARY SERVICE (1840), Genealogical Publishing Co., Baltimore, MD, 1965.

This volume may be found at OHS, SLO, WRHS, PLC, OGS, ACPL, FHL(FHC), and in some RL and LL.

In 1890, a special census of <u>Civil</u> War <u>Union</u> <u>Veterans</u> (C) was taken. These records are as follows:

____US Bureau of the Census, SPECIAL SCHEDULES OF THE ELEVENTH CENSUS, 1890, ENUMERATING UNION VETERANS AND WIDOWS, Microfilm M123, Rolls 60-75, National Archives, Washington, DC.

Microfilm copies of the records are available at OHS, SLO, WRHS, PLC, OGS, ACPL, FHL(FHC), and some RL and LGL, as well as the National Archives. They may be borrowed on interlibrary loan from:

____American Genealogical Lending library, PO Box 244, Bountiful, UT 84010.

These records show the veteran's name, widow (if applicable), rank, company, regiment or ship and other pertinent military data.

One final set of censuses which you must not overlook are the <u>quadrennial enumerations</u> (Q). These were taken every four years and are arranged alphabetically by township within the various OH counties. The enumerations list the males over 21 and indicate the age, race, occupation, and if he is a landowner. They are located in court houses, ONAHRC, and as microfilms in OHS. Relatively few of them survive, especially during the early years, but later on, records during a few years for most counties exist.

7. Church records

Many early OH families were affiliated with a church, many denominations being represented by 1850: Amish, Baptist, Brethren, Church of Christ, Congregationalist, Disciples, Episcopal, German Methodist, Jewish, Lutheran, Methodist, Mennonite, Moravian, Mormon, Presbyterian, Quaker, Roman Catholic, Shaker, and Universalist-Unitarian. The arrival of these church groups in OH is chronicled in the following useful work:

___F. R. Lubbers and M. Dieringer, ADVENT OF RELIGIOUS GROUPS INTO OH, OGS, Mansfield, OH, 1978.

The records of these churches often prove to be very valuable since they frequently contain information on births, baptisms, marriages, deaths, admissions, dismissals, and reprimands. The data are particularly important for the years before county or state vital records were kept. Some of these church records have been copied into books or micro-filmed, some have been sent to denominational archives, but many still remain in the individual churches. Several major works and collections list sizable numbers of available church records:

___SURVEY FORMS OF HISTORIES AND LOCATIONS OF ABOUT 7000 OH CHURCHES, OHS, Columbus, OH.

___FAMILY HISTORY LIBRARY CATALOG, LOCALITY SECTION, FHL, Salt Lake City, UT, latest edition. Look under OH and its counties.

___P. Khouw, COUNTY BY COUNTY IN OH GENEALOGY, SLO, Columbus, OH, 1992. Many published church records.

___S. Harter, OH GENEALOGY AND LOCAL HISTORY SOURCES, The Author, Columbus, OH, 1986. Many published church records.

___C. W. Bell, OH GUIDE TO GENEALOGICAL SOURCES, Genealogical Publishing Co., Baltimore, MD, 1988.

___Mrs. Carl Main, OH GENEALOGICAL RECORDS, The Author, Cleveland, OH, 1968. Manuscript church records in WRHS.

___MANUSCRIPT AND LOCALITY CARD AND COMPUTER CATALOGS, at OHS, SLO, WRHS, OGS, ACPL, ONAHRC, and RL.

Use of the above works will convince you that the major sources of church records are the individual churches, OHS, SLO, WRHS, OGS, ACPL, ONAHRC, RL, and special denominational archives. If you have the good fortune to know your ancestor's church, then you can write directly to the proper church official, enclosing a $5 donation and an SASE, and requesting a search of the records. If you don't know the church and therefore need to look at records of several churches in the county, the collections at the aforementioned repositories should be consulted. LL may have some local records, as is the case for LGL. The

RL usually have some records for the area. In Chapter 4, counties which have church records in published or microfilmed form are indicated. Instructions regarding the above referenced volumes and locating the records will be given in Chapter 3. Church records are often published in genealogical periodicals, so instructions for finding these will be given in a section to follow.

If, as is often the case, after exploring the resources mentioned above, you have not located your ancestor's church, you will need to dig deeper. This further searching should involve writing letters (with an SASE) to the LL, the local genealogical society, and/or the local historical society. Names and addresses of these organizations are given under the various counties in Chapter 4. If these procedures still do not yield data, then it might be well for you to contact the headquarters of the denomination you think your ancestor may have belonged to. It is well to remember that English immigrants were usually Episcopalian, Methodist, Quaker, or Congregational, Germans and Swiss were usually Lutheran or Reformed or German Methodist (although those from southern Germany were often Catholic), the Scots-Irish were generally Presbyterian or Quaker, the Dutch were Reformed, the Swedes Lutheran, and the Irish ordinarily Roman Catholic. The denominational headquarters can usually give you a list of the churches of their denomination in a given county, and the dates of their origin. Often they can also direct you to collections of church records.

Some of the major denominations of OH are listed below along with brief historical notes, their denominational and/or historical headquarters, and books which deal with their histories and/or genealogical records.

____(Amish) Broke away from Swiss Mennonites in 1693 under leadership of Jakob Ammann. First came to America in 1727, settling in PA. The largest numbers came into the OH counties of Holmes and Wayne. Contact: Der Neue Amerikanische Calendar, 2467 C R 600, Baltic, OH 43804. Books: J. A. Hostetler, AMISH SOCIETY, Johns Hopkins Press, Baltimore, MD, 1980; J. A. Hostetler, ANNOTATED BIBLIOGRAPHY OF THE AMISH, Mennonite Publishing House, Scottsdale, PA, 1951; W. I. Schreiber, OUR AMISH NEIGHBORS, THE STORY OF THE OH AMISH, University of Chicago Press, Chicago, IL, 1962; H. E. Cross, OH AMISH GENEALOGY, HOLMES COUNTY AND VICINITY, Johns Hopkins University Press, Baltimore, MD, 1967; E. Gingerich, OH AMISH DIRECTORY, Johns Hopkins Press, Baltimore, MD, 1965.

____(Baptist) Originated under leadership of John Smyth, who organized a Baptist Church among English exiles in Holland about 1607. Some of these exiles returned to England and started a Baptist Church there in 1611. The first Baptist Church in the American colonies was formed in Providence, RI, by Roger Williams in 1639. The first Baptist Church in

OH was formed in 1790 five miles east of Cincinnati. There are four major Baptist groups today: American Baptist Churches, Southern Baptist Convention (separated in 1845), National Baptist Convention USA, and National Baptist Convention of America (separated in 1880), the latter two being predominantly black. Contacts: American Baptist Churches, PO Box 851, Valley Forge, PA 19482; Cleveland Baptist Association, 1737 Euclid Avenue, Cleveland, OH 44115; OH Baptist Convention, PO Box 376, Granville, OH 43023; American Baptist Historical Society, 1100 South Goodman Street, Rochester, NY 14620; Southern Baptist Historical Commission, 901 Commerce Street, Nashville, TN 37203; OH Southern Baptist Convention, 1680 East Broad Street, Columbus, OH 43203; National Baptist Convention USA Headquarters, 1620 Whites Creek Pike, Nashville, TN 37207. Books: W. W. Sweet, RELIGION ON THE AMERICAN FRONTIER, VOL. 1, BAPTISTS, Harper, New York, NY, 1931; R. H. Clossman, THE HISTORY OF THE OH BAPTIST CONVENTION, University Microfilms, Ann Arbor, MI, 1971; L. H. Moore, THE HISTORY OF SOUTHERN BAPTISTS IN OH, State Convention of Baptist in OH, Columbus, OH, 1979; R. G. Torbet, A HISTORY OF THE BAPTISTS, Judson Press, Valley Forge, PA, 1973; H. L. McBeth, THE BAPTIST HERITAGE, Broadman Press, Nashville, TN, 1983; S. M. Eltscher, A BASIC GUIDE TO REGIONAL BAPTIST ARCHIVES AND HISTORICAL RESOURCES FOR OH, American Baptist Historical Society, Rochester, NY, 1981; ENCYCLOPEDIA OF SOUTHERN BAPTISTS, Broadman Press, Nashville, TN, 1958, 3 volumes.

_____(Brethren) German pietistic anabaptist sect founded in 1709 by Alexander Mack in Schwarzenau, Germany. First came to American colonies in 1719, settling at Germantown, PA. Their first OH settlements were in the Miami Valley shortly before 1800 and in the northwest shortly after. Headquarters: Church of the Brethren, 1451 Dundee Avenue, Elgin, IL 60120; also contact Fellowship of Brethren Genealogists at the same address. Books: T. S. Moherman, HISTORY OF THE BRETHREN IN NORTHEASTERN OH, Brethren Publishing House, Elgin, IL, 1914; C. Denlinger, EVERY NAME INDEX FOR HISTORY OF THE BRETHREN OF THE SOUTHERN DISTRICT OF OH, Brethren Historical Committee, Elgin, IL, 1982; H. Holsinger, HISTORY OF THE TUNKERS AND THE BRETHREN CHURCH, Pacific Press, Lathrop, CA, 1901; M. G. Brumbaugh, A HISTORY OF THE GERMAN BAPTIST BRETHREN IN EUROPE AND AMERICA, AMS Press, New York, NY, 1909; L. M. Brien, ABSTRACTS FROM THE HISTORY OF THE BRETHREN IN OH, Allen County Public Library, Ft. Wayne, IN, 1983.

_____(Christian Church-Disciples of Christ) Established largely from a melding of movements started by three Presbyterians, Barton W. Stone (1804) in KY and Thomas and Alexander Campbell (1809) in PA. Contact: Disciples of Christ Historical Society, 1101 Nineteenth Avenue,

Nashville, TN 37212; The Christian Church (Disciples of Christ) in OH, 38007 Butternut Ridge Road, Elyria, OH 44035. Book: W. E. Garrison and A. T. DeGroot, THE DISCIPLES OF CHRIST, A HISTORY, Bethany Press, St. Louis, MO, 1948; A. S. Hayden, EARLY HISTORY OF THE DISCIPLES IN THE WESTERN RESERVE, Unigraphic, Evansville, IN, 1977.

____(Churches of Christ) Individual churches began to split off from the Christian Church (Disciples) after the 1860s, the movement being essentially complete by about 1900. The Christian Church had been established from a melding of movements started by Barton W. Stone (1804) of KY and by Thomas and Alexander Campbell (1809) of PA. Contact: Harding Graduate School of Religion Library, 1000 Cherry Road, Memphis, TN 38117. Books: W. E. Garrison and A. T. DeGroot, THE DISCIPLES OF CHRIST, A HISTORY, Bethany Press, St. Louis, MO, 1948; A. T. DeGroot, THE GROUNDS OF DIVISIONS AMONG THE DISCIPLES OF CHRIST, The Author, St. Louis, MO, 1940.

____(Congregationalists) Started in England in the early 1600s as a branch of Puritanism, called Separatists. First settled in the colonies in MA in 1620, where they merged with non-Separatist Puritan settlers to form the Congregational Church. Their first OH church was constituted at Marietta in 1796, and the second was at Austinburg in the Western Reserve in 1801. In 1931, they merged with other groups to form the Congregational Christian Churches. This group, in turn, merged with the Evangelical and Reformed Church in 1957 to form the United Church of Christ. Contact: Congregational Library, 14 Beacon Street, Boston, MA 02108. Books: W. W. Sweet, RELIGION ON THE AMERICAN FRON-TIER, VOL. 3, THE CONGREGATIONALISTS, Harper, New York, NY, 1939-40; G. G. Atkins and F. L. Fagley, HISTORY OF AMERICAN CONGREGATIONALISM, Pilgrim Press, Boston, MA, 1942; W. Walker, THE HISTORY OF THE CONGREGATIONAL CHURCHES IN THE US, American Congregational Historical Society, New York, NY, 1894.

____(Episcopal Church) Developed from the Church of England which split from the Roman Catholic Church in 1534. First brought to the American colonies by English settlers of VA in 1607. Contact: Archives of the Episcopal Church, 815 Second Avenue, New York, NY 10017; Library and Archives of the Church Historical Society, 606 Rathervue Place, Austin, TX 78767; OH Diocese, Episcopal Church, 2230 Euclid Avenue, Cleveland, OH 44115: Southern OH Diocese, 412 Sycamore Street, Cincinnati, OH 45202; OH Episcopalian Archives, Gambier College. Gambier, OH 43022. Books: THE EPISCOPAL CHURCH ANNUAL, Morehouse, Wilton, CT, latest issue; W. S. Perry, HISTORY OF THE AMERICAN EPISCOPAL CHURCH, 1587-1883, Osgood, Boston, MA, 1885, 2 volumes; R. W. Albright, A HISTORY OF THE PROTESTANT EPISCOPAL CHURCH, Macmillan, New York, NY, 1964.

___(German Methodists) There were two predominant groups of German people who adopted Methodist polity. The first was the United Brethren established by Philip W. Otterbein and Martin Boehm in PA in 1800. The second was the Evangelical Church formed by Jacob Albright in PA in 1803. These two united in 1946 to form the Evangelical United Brethren, which in turn, united with the Methodist Church in 1968 to form the United Methodist Church. Contact: Center for Evangelical United Brethren Studies, 1810 Harvard Boulevard, Dayton, OH 45406; German Methodist Collection, Cincinnati Historical Society, Eden Park, Cincinnati, OH 45402. Books: J. M. Overton, MINISTERS AND CHURCHES OF THE CENTRAL OH GERMAN CONFERENCE (METHODISTS), 1835-1907, The Author, Yellow Springs, OH, 1975; J. R. Sinnema, GERMAN METHODISM IN OH, ITS LEADERS AND INSTITUTIONS, American-German Institute, Berea, OH, 1983; C. Wittke, WILLIAM NAST, PATRIARCH OF GERMAN METHODISM, Wayne State University Press, Detroit, MI, 1959.

___(Jewish) Jewish congregations stem back to the Old Testament patriarch Abraham at about 1900 BC. The first established religious community was formed in 1654 in New York, NY. The first Jewish congregation in OH was established at Cincinnati in 1824. Contact: American Jewish Archives, 3101 Clifton Avenue, Cincinnati, OH 45220; American Jewish Historical Society, 2 Thornton Road, Waltham, MA 02154. Books: JEWISH ENCYCLOPEDIA, Funk and Wagnalls, New York, NY, 1901-6, 12 volumes; D. Rottenberg, FINDING YOUR FATHERS, Random House, New York, NY, 1977; M. H. Stern, FIRST AMERICAN JEWISH FAMILIES, American Jewish Archives, Cincinnati, OH, 1991. Periodical article: THE JEWS OF COLUMBUS, OH, American Jewish Historical Quarterly 65:1, September, 1975.

___(Lutheran) Lutheran church bodies derive from the controversy of Martin Luther with the Roman Catholic Church in the Germanic area in 1521. A Dutch Lutheran Church was formed in New Amsterdam (New York, NY) in the middle 1600s, but most of the early Lutherans came from Germanic areas into Philadelphia and New York, and then moved north, west, and south. The earliest OH Lutheran Church dates back to 1803 in Columbiana County. Today there are several Lutheran groups, so it may be necessary to contact several agencies. Contact: Lutheran Church MO Synod Archives and Library, 801 De Mun Avenue, St. Louis, MO 63105; Archives of the Lutheran Church in America, 333 Wartburg Place, Dubuque, IA 52001; Lutheran Archives Center, 7301 Germantown Avenue, Philadelphia, PA 19119; Archives of Cooperative Lutheranism, Evangelical Lutheran Church in America, 8765 West Higgins Road, Chicago, IL 60631; OH Lutheran Archives, Wittenberg University Library, Springfield, OH 45501. Books: W. D. Albeck, A CENTURY OF LUTHERANS IN OH, Antioch Press, Yellow Springs, OH, 1966; J. Bodensieck, THE ENCYCLOPEDIA OF THE LUTHERAN CHURCH, Augsburg Publishing House, Minneapolis, MN, 1965; E. L. Luecker, LU-

THERAN CYCLOPEDIA, Concordia Press, St. Louis, MO, 1975.
Microfilm: WPA, LUTHERAN CHURCH SURVEY FORMS, 1937–40,
2 rolls of microfilm, OHS, Columbus, OH.

___(Mennonite) This denomination originated in Switzerland under the
leadership of Conrad Grebel and Georg Blaurock in 1525. They were
originally known as Anabaptists, but took the name Mennonites after
their leader Menno Simons who joined them in 1536. Their first
settlement in the American colonies was at Germantown, PA, in 1683.
Contact: Mennonite Historical Committee, 1700 South Main, Goshen IN
46526; Mennonite General Office, 421 South Second Street, Elkhart, IN
46516; Mennonite Historical Library, Bluffton College, Bluffton, OH
45817. Books: H. S. Bender and C. H. Smith, THE MENNONITE
ENCYCLOPEDIA, Mennonite Brethren Publishing House, Hillsboro, KS,
1955–9, 4 volumes; C. J. Dyck, AN INTRODUCTION TO MENNONITE
HISTORY, Herald Press, Scottsdale, PA, 1967; G. M. Stoltzfus,
MENNONITES OF THE OH AND EASTERN CONFERENCE, Herald
Press, Scottsdale, PA, 1969.

___(Methodist) The Methodist movement began in the Church of
England in the late 1720s under the leadership of John Wesley. In 1784,
the group formally separated from the Church of England. Contact:
United Methodist Historical Library, Beghley Library, OH Wesleyan
University, Delaware, OH 43105; General Commission on Archives and
History, The United Methodist Church, P.O. Box 127, Madison, NJ
07940; Methodist Archives, Library, Baldwin-Wallace College, Berea, OH
44017. Books: W. W. Sweet, CIRCUIT RIDER DAYS ALONG THE
OH, 1812–26, Methodist Book Concern, New York, NY, 1923; H. C.
Luccock, THE STORY OF METHODISM, Abingdon Press, New York
NY, 1949: J. M. Barker, THE HISTORY OF OH METHODISM, Courts
and Jennings, Cincinnati, OH, 1898; W. W. Sweet, RELIGION ON THE
AMERICAN FRONTIER, VOL. 4, THE METHODISTS, Harper, New
York, NY, 1946; F. D. Harter, GUIDE TO MANUSCRIPTS COLLEC-
TION OF EARLY OH METHODISM, United Methodist Archives
Center, Delaware, OH, 1980; B. R. Little, METHODIST UNION
CATALOG OF HISTORY, BIOGRAPHY, DISCIPLINES, AND
HYMNALS, Association of Methodist Historical Societies, Lake
Junaluska, NC, 1967; J. B. Finley, SKETCHES OF WESTERN
METHODISM, Arno Press, New York, NY, 1969; S. Gregg, THE
HISTORY OF METHODISM WITHIN THE ERIE ANNUAL
CONFERENCE, Carlton and Porter, New York, NY, 1865, 2 volumes.
Microfilm: METHODIST MINISTERS' CARD INDEX, OH CONFER-
ENCES, 1797–1981, 4 rolls of microfilm, OHS, Columbus, OH.

___(Moravian) Moravians had their origins as a community of followers
of the Reformer John Hus about 1410 in Bohemia (now the Czech
Republic). The faith spread into neighboring Moravia (now the western
section of the Slovak Republic), but the members were almost annihilated
in the Thirty Years War (1618-48). They first came to the American

colonies in 1735, settling in GA, then moving to PA in 1740. Contact: Archives of the Moravian Church, 41 West Locust Street, Bethlehem, PA 18018; Moravian Historical Society, Nazareth, PA 18064. Books: J. E. Hutton, HISTORY OF THE MORAVIAN CHURCH, Moravian Publication Office, London, England, 1909; E. Langton, HISTORY OF THE MORAVIAN CHURCH, Allen and Unwin, London, England, 1955.

___(Mormon or Church of Jesus Christ of Latter-day Saints) Organized in 1830 at Fayette, NY, by Joseph Smith. Contact: Library and Historical Department, CJCLDS, both at 50 East North Temple, Salt Lake City, UT 84150. Books: L. J. Arrington and D. Bitton, THE MORMON EXPERIENCE, A HISTORY OF THE LATTER DAY-SAINTS, Random House, New York, NY, 1979; T. F. O'Dea, THE MORMONS, University of Chicago Press, Chicago, IL, 1957; J. Shipps, MORMONISM, THE STORY OF A NEW RELIGIOUS TRADITION, Harper, New York, NY, 1985.

___(Presbyterian) The churches of the Presbyterian or Reformed tradition (as they were and are called in Europe) are Protestant churches governed by boards of ministers and lay persons called elders (presbyters). These churches had their origin by John Calvin in Zurich, Switzerland, during the Reformation in the year 1523. The doctrines and church organization were introduced into Scotland in 1557-60 by John Knox. Although there were some similar churches before, the first clearly Presbyterian congregation in the colonies was probably the one on the Elizabeth River near Norfolk, VA, about 1675. A church was definitely formed at Rehoboth, MD, in 1683, and the first presbytery (association) dates back to 1706 in Philadelphia. The first Presbyterian Church in OH was one organized in 1790 in Cincinnati. Contact: Presbyterian Historical Association, Presbyterian Church USA, 425 Lombard Street, Philadelphia, PA 19147; Historical Center, Presbyterian Church in America, 12330 Conway Road, St. Louis, MO 63141. Books: W. W. Sweet, RELIGION ON THE AMERICAN FRONTIER, VOL. 2, THE PRESBYTERIANS, Harper, New York, NY, 1936; ONE HUNDRED FIFTY YEARS OF PRESBYTERIANISM IN THE OH VALLEY, 1790-1940, Presbyterian Churches of Cincinnati, Cincinnati, OH, 1941; E. B. Welsh, BUCKEYE PRESBYTERIANISM, United Presbyterian Synod of OH, Columbus, OH, 1968; L. A. Loetscher, A BRIEF HISTORY OF THE PRESBYTERIANS, Westminster Press, Philadelphia, PA, 1978; W. L. Lingle, PRESBYTERIANS, THEIR HISTORY AND BELIEFS, John Knox Press, Richmond, VA, 1960; UNION CATALOG OF PRESBYTERIAN MANUSCRIPTS, Presbyterian Library Association, Philadelphia, PA, 1964; T. W. Marshall, INVENTORY OF THE CHURCH ARCHIVES OF OH PRESBYTERIAN CHURCHES, OH Historical Record Survey, WPA, Columbus, OH, 1940.

___(Quakers or Religious Society of Friends) These people trace their origin back to George Fox who began making converts in 1647 in the midlands of England. Quakers soon began showing up in the American colonies. The first Quaker yearly meeting in the colonies was organized in 1661 in Newport, RI, by the many Friends who had come to RI. The first Monthly Quaker meeting in OH came together at Concord (close to Colerain) in 1801. Contact: Friends Historical Library, Swarthmore College, Swarthmore, PA 19081; Quaker Collection, Haverford College, Magill Library, Haverford, PA 19041; Historical Committee of the Yearly Meeting, Route 2, Barnesville, OH 43713. Books: W. W. Hinshaw, ENCYCLOPEDIA OF AMERICAN QUAKER GENEALOGY, OHIO QUAKER RECORDS, Genealogical Publishing Co., Baltimore, MD, 1973, volumes 4-5; E. A. Davis, QUAKER RECORDS OF THE MIAMI VALLEY OF OH, The Author, Piqua, OH, 1981; E. T. Elliott, QUAKERS IN THE AMERICAN FRONTIER, Friends United Press, Richmond, IN, 1969; W. Heiss and L. S. Mote, EARLY SETTLEMENT OF FRIENDS IN THE MIAMI VALLEY, Woolman Press, Indianapolis, IN, 1961.

____(Roman Catholic) The Roman Catholic Church traces its origins back to Peter, an apostle of Jesus and traditionally the first Bishop of Rome, approximately 55-64 AD. The first coming of Catholics to the American English colonies was to St. Marys, MD, in 1634. Their first church to be established in OH was in 1808 at Somerset. Contact the Catholic dioceses of OH: Cincinnati, Columbus, Cleveland, Steubenville, Toledo, Youngstown. Addresses in the telephone books. Books: J. P. Dolan, THE AMERICAN CATHOLIC EXPERIENCE, A HISTORY FROM COLONIAL TIMES TO THE PRESENT, Doubleday, New York, NY, 1985; THE NEW CATHOLIC ENCYCLOPEDIA, McGraw-Hill, New York, NY, 1967, 15 volumes, with supplementary volumes published after; G. F. Houck, A HISTORY OF CATHOLICITY IN NORTHERN OH, 1749-1900, Savage, Cleveland, OH, 1903, 2 volumes; Historical Records Survey, INVENTORY OF RECORDS OF ROMAN CATHOLIC CHURCH, DIOCESE OF CLEVELAND, WPA, Columbus, OH, 1942.

____(Shakers) This fellowship, more correctly the United Society of Believers in Christ's second coming, was founded in 1772 in Manchester, England, by Ann Lee. She and some of her followers came to Watervliet, NY, in 1776. Contact: Western Reserve Historical Society Library, 10825 East Boulevard, Cleveland, OH 44106. Books: E. A. Andrews, THE PEOPLE CALLED SHAKERS, Dover Publications, New York, NY, 1953; M. F. Melcher, THE SHAKER ADVENTURE, Oxford University Press, London, England, 1960; J. P. Maclean, SHAKERS OF OH, Heer, Columbus, OH, 1907.

____(Unitarian-Universalist) In 1779, John Murray became the pastor of the first Universalist Church in the US at Gloucester, MA. Many other churches in New England and PA soon joined them. The first Unitarian Church in the US was established by Joseph Priestly in 1796 in Philadelphia. By the early 1800s, many Congregational churches were joining the movement, and in 1825 a separate denomination was formed. In 1961, the Unitarians and the Universalists united to form the

Unitarian-Universalist Association. Contact: Archives of the Unitarian-Universalist Association, 25 Beacon Street, Boston, MA 02108. Books: C. L. Scott, THE UNIVERSALIST CHURCH OF AMERICA, A SHORT HISTORY, Universalist Historical Society, Boston, MA, 1957; G. W. Cooke, UNITARIANISM IN AMERICA, American Unitarian Association, Boston, MA, 1906.

Many OH city and county histories contain histories of churches. These city and county histories are discussed in section 9 of this chapter. Numerous church records have also been published in genealogical periodicals. Indexes are generally available for these periodicals, which makes searching them for church records very convenient. The periodicals and their indexes will be treated in a later section. The books referred to above can be located at OHS, SLO, WRHS, PLC, OGS, ACPL, FHL(FHC), and in some RL and LL. Look up the county, the church name, and the denominational name in the card and/or computer catalogs in these repositories.

8. City directories

During the 19th century many larger cities in the US began publishing city directories. These volumes usually appeared erratically at first, but then began to come out annually a little later on. They list heads of households and workers plus their addresses and occupations. The earliest series of directories (starting before 1860) in OH are:

____Akron: 1859/60
____Canton: 1856, 1860
____Chillicothe: 1855/6, 1858/9, 1860/1
____Cincinnati: 1819, 1825, 1829, 1831, 1834, 1836/7, 1840, 1842, 1843, 1846-53, 1855-60
____Circleville: 1859
____Cleveland: 1837/8, 1845/6, 1848/9-53, 1856-60
____Columbus: 1843/4, 1845/6, 1848, 1850/1, 1855-62
____Dayton: 1850, 1856/7-61
____Delaware: 1859/60
____Hamilton: 1858/9
____Mansfield: 1858/9
____Marietta: 1860/1
____Mt. Vernon: 1858/9
____OH Regional Directories (cover several counties each, most only listing businesses): 1853/4, 1857, 1859/60, 1860/1
____Portsmouth: 1859/60
____Sandusky: 1855, 1858
____Springfield: 1852, 1859/60
____Steubenville: 1856/7

___Toledo: 1858, 1860
___Western Reserve Area (businesses): 1852
___Zanesville: 1851, 1856, 1860/1

After about 1865, many of these towns and cities published a city directory each year. In general, the smaller cities and towns of OH did not begin regular publication until later in the 19th or in the 20th century. Many of the directories are available in OHS, SLO, WRHS, PLC, OGS, ACPL, FHL(FHC), and ONAHRC. RL and LL also usually have collections pertaining to their own cities. The holdings in OHS are listed in:
___W. L. Phillips, CITY AND COUNTY DIRECTORIES AT THE OHS, Heritage Books, Bowie, MD, 1985.

The telephone was invented in 1876-7, underwent rapid development, and became widespread fairly quickly. By the late years of the century telephone directories were coming into existence. Older issues can often be found in LL, and as the years go on, they have proved to be ever more valuable genealogical sources.

9. City and county histories

Histories for many OH counties and numerous cities have been published. These volumes usually contain biographical data on leading citizens, details about early settlers, histories of organizations, businesses, trades, and churches, and often list clergymen, lawyers, physicians, teachers, governmental officials, farmers, military men, and other groups. Six works which list many of these histories are:
___P. Khouw, COUNTY BY COUNTY IN OH GENEALOGY, SLO, Columbus, OH, 1992.
___S. Harter, OH GENEALOGY AND LOCAL HISTORY SOURCES INDEX, The Author, Columbus, OH, 1986.
___C. W. Bell, OH GUIDE TO GENEALOGICAL SOURCES, Genealogical Publishing Co., Baltimore, MD, 1988.
___M. J. Kaminkow, US LOCAL HISTORIES IN THE LIBRARY OF CONGRESS, Magna Carta, Baltimore, MD, 1975, 5 volumes, index in the 5th volume.
___P. W. Filby, A BIBLIOGRAPHY OF COUNTY HISTORIES IN 50 STATES, Genealogical Publishing Co., Baltimore, MD, 1985.
___FAMILY HISTORY LIBRARY CATALOG, LOCALITY SECTION, in either microform or computer, FHL, Salt Lake City, UT, latest edition. Look under state, then under county, then city or town. Also at every FHC.

Most of the OH volumes in these bibliographies can be found in OHS, SLO, WRHS, PLC, and ACPL. Many are available at FHL or through

FHC, and some are usually in LGL. RL and LL are likely to have those relating to their particular areas.

A useful index to many of the county histories of OH is found in OHS and FHL(FHC):
___OHS, OH COUNTY HISTORY SURNAME INDEX, 64 rolls of microfilm, The Society, Columbus, OH, 1936.
A special OH history volume contains brief county histories for all the OH counties which existed in 1901:
___H. Howe, HISTORICAL COLLECTIONS OF OH, Howe and Son, Cincinnati, OH, 1901, 3 volumes.
In Chapter 4 you will find listed under the counties various recommended county histories. Also there will be an indication under each county for which city histories are available.

10. Court records

Among the most unexplored genealogical source materials are the court records of the state of OH and of the OH counties. They are often exceptionally valuable, giving information that is obtainable no where else. It is, therefore, of great importance that you carefully examine all available court documents. Several good treatments of the court system of OH are available:
___C. T. Marshall, A HISTORY OF THE COURTS AND LAWYERS OF OH, American Historical Society, New York, NY, 1934, 4 volumes.
___DEVELOPMENT OF THE JUDICIAL SYSTEM OF OH, OH State Archaeological and Historical Quarterly 41, 195.
___D. Levine, OH's COURT SYSTEM, The Report, OGS, 20 (Winter 1980) 171-4.

There are two minor difficulties that need to be recognized if you are not to miss court data. The first is that there were several types of courts, some no longer exist, some replaced others, some had their names changed, often their jurisdictions overlapped, and further, the exact court situation sometimes varies from county to county. You are likely to find records of the following courts:
___County Courts of Common Pleas (1787-present)
___County Probate Courts (1787-1802, 1852-present)
___County Courts (1800-present)
___Municipal, Mayor, Police, and Justice of the Peace Courts (1800-present)
___County District Courts (1851-83)
___County Circuit Courts (1883-1912)
___State Supreme Court (1787-present), early it was the appeals court, now the state court of final resort. The early State Supreme Court

travelled from county to county where it held court, causing the records to be generated in each county.

___State Courts of Appeal (1912–present)

___Northwest Territorial Court (1787–1803)

___US Federal District Courts (approximately 1803–present)

___US Federal Circuit Courts (approximately 1807–1911)

The second difficulty is that the records of the different courts appear in record books, file cabinets, and filing boxes with various titles and labels. These titles and labels do not always describe everything in the volumes, and records of various types may be mixed up or they may all appear in a single set of books. This latter is especially true in earlier years. Fortunately, there is a simple rule that avoids all these difficulties: look for your ancestor in all available court records, regardless of what the label-lings on the books, cabinets, files, and boxes happen to be.

In certain kinds of court matters (such as trials, estates, wills, and others), the record books will refer to folders which contain detailed documents concerning the matters. The folders are usually filed in the court house (CH) and must not be overlooked because they are often gold mines of information. In the county of your interest, you may find records dealing with proceedings of the various courts (records, minutes, dockets, enrollments, registers, orders), with land (deeds, entries, land grants, mortgages, trust deeds, surveys, ranges, plats, roads), with probate matters (wills, estate, administrators, executors, inventories, settlements, sales, guardians, orphans, insolvent estates, bastardy, apprentices, insanity), with vital records (birth, death, marriage, divorce), and with taxation (tax, bonds, appropriations, delinquent taxes). In most cases there will not be records with all these titles, but several of these items will appear in one type of book, cabinet, file, or box. If all of this seems complicated, do not worry. All you need to do is to remember the rules: examine all court records, be on the lookout for references to folders, ask about them and then examine them also.

First, we will discuss the county records. The original record books, boxes, cabinets, files, and folders are in the county court houses (CH) and/or in the ONAHRC (regional centers). Microfilms and tran-scripts (published and manuscript) of many of the books have been made, but only a very few of the boxes, files, folders, and cabinet contents have been copied. Many of the microfilmed and transcribed records are available at OHS, SLO, WRHS, PLC, and ACPL. Many are in FHL and are available through FHC. Some of the transcribed materials are to be found in RL but only a few of the microfilms. A few LGL have some of the transcribed records. LL may have transcribed records for the local area. Listings of many of the microfilms available at OHS, SLO, WRHS, PLC, ACPL, and FHL(FHC) are shown in:

___FAMILY HISTORY LIBRARY CATALOG, LOCALITY SECTION, FHL, Salt Lake City, UT, latest microfiche and computer editions. Look under OH and its counties.

___P. Khouw, COUNTY BY COUNTY IN OH GENEALOGY, SLO, Columbus, OH, 1992.

___S. Harter, OH GENEALOGY AND LOCAL HISTORY SOURCES INDEX, The Author, Columbus, OH, 1986.

___C. W. Bell, OH GUIDE TO GENEALOGICAL SOURCES, Genealogical Publishing Co., Baltimore, MD, 1988.

Please recall that early OH State Supreme Court records were recorded in the counties. Thus, these records will be located under the counties. Chapter 3 discusses the process of obtaining these records, and Chapter 4 lists those available for each of the 88 OH counties.

Not only were there county-based courts, there were ones with regional and state-wide jurisdiction. The records of many of these are available in original, microfilm, or published form. Included among the most promising of these sources for genealogists are:

___GENEALOGICAL NAME INDEX TO OH SUPREME COURT RECORDS, 1783-1839, Franklin County Genealogical Society, Columbus, OH, 1983.

___MICROFILM COPIES OF OH STATE SUPREME COURT RECORDS, OHS, Columbus, OH, and FHL(FHC), Salt Lake City, UT. See listings in Chapter 4 under the various counties.

Further, there is a name index to cases which were appealed from a lower OH court to a higher one:

___W. H. Page, OH DIGEST, Anderson, Cincinnati, OH, 1958-, 16 volumes, with numerous supplements.

Finally, the federal and territorial court records must not be overlooked. Many of the records of the US Federal District and Circuit Courts for OH (approximately 1803-1962) are available at the Chicago Branch of the National Archives, 7358 South Pulaski Road, Chicago, IL 60629 [Phone 1-(312)-581-7816]. The territorial records of the Northwest Territory, including some court records, are available at the National Archives in Washington, DC in Record Group 59.

---

11. DAR records

The Daughters of the American Revolution (DAR), in their quest for the lines linking them to their Revolutionary War ancestors, have gathered and published many volumes of records of genealogical pertinence. The OH chapters of the organization have been quite prolific and have provided many volumes of county records (chiefly court, deed, marriage, probate, tax, will), Bible records, cemetery records, and family records. Copies of most of the books or microfilms of most of them are available at the DAR Library in Washington, OHS, SLO, WRHS, PLC, OGS, ACPL, FHL, and through FHC. Copies of some are in RL and LGL, and materials of local interest will often be found in LL. Chapter 3 tells you how to locate these records, and in Chapter 4, these records are included in the listings for the various OH counties.

There are several excellent catalog volumes to the many records that the DAR members have compiled:

___National Society, DAR, DAR LIBRARY CATALOG, VOLUME 1: FAMILY HISTORIES AND GENEALOGIES, VOLUME 2: STATE AND LOCAL HISTORIES AND RECORDS, The Society, Washington, DC, 1982/6.

___P. Khouw, COUNTY BY COUNTY IN OH GENEALOGY, SLO, Columbus, OH, 1992.

___C. W. Bell, OH GUIDE TO GENEALOGICAL SOURCES, Genealogical Publishing Co., Baltimore, MD, 1988.

___C. W. Bell, MASTER INDEX, OH DAR GENEALOGICAL AND HISTORICAL RECORDS, OH Society, DAR, Westlake, OH, 1985. Listing of records and their locations. Many names indexed, but by no means all.

___Western Reserve Chapter, DAR, BIBLE AND FAMILY RECORDS IN THE WESTERN RESERVE HISTORICAL SOCIETY, The Society, Westlake, OH, 1967, 2 volumes.

Those counties for which there are DAR compilations will be so indicated in Chapter 4. Look into these DAR volumes for materials on your OH ancestor(s).

---

12. Death records

The state of OH passed a law in 1856 requiring birth, and death records to be kept in OH counties. This law was largely ignored, but some records were kept during 1856/7, and some of those that were kept have survived. They are, however, quite incomplete. When such records are available for the various OH counties, they will be indicated in the county listing in Chapter 4. A law mandating that the Probate Court in OH counties keep birth and death records was legislated in 1867. Again, the law was not adhered to in many places, but more records were produced and many are extant. They are, however, incomplete. They are available at county Probate Courts, ONAHRC, OHS, and FHL(FHC). Counties for which these records exist will be indicated in Chapter 4.

In December 1908 the state of OH passed a law requiring state-wide death registration in addition to the county registration. By 1914 the registrations were running at least 90% complete. These records are in the county or city health departments as well as in central state repositories at Columbus. OH death records for 1908–36 are in the OHS, along with indexes for 1908–38. The records for the period 1937–present are in:

_____State Department of Health, Room G-20, 65 South Front Street, Columbus, OH 43215. They have indexes.

These records usually contain name, place and date of death, sex, age, marital state, place of birth, parents, occupation, cause of death, and last residence. Valuable sources of death information for war veterans are to be found in the following:

_____OH Adjutant General's Office, GRAVE REGISTRATIONS OF SOLDIERS BURIED IN OH (from the Revolution up through World War I), card file available at OHS, Columbus, OH, microfilm copy at FHL, Salt Lake City, UT, can be obtained from FHC.

_____County Recorder's Office, GRAVE REGISTRATIONS OF SOLDIERS BURIED IN THE COUNTY, in each OH county, some files more complete than others, all somewhat incomplete.

And a rich source of death records for eastern OH, although quite incomplete, is:

_____Public Library of Youngstown Staff, INDEX TO THE BALDWIN GENEALOGICAL RECORDS, ACPL, Ft. Wayne, IN, 1983, 8 volumes.

Prior to the time when OH required state death reports (1908), other records may yield dates and places of death: Bible, biographical, cemetery, census, church, DAR, military, mortuary, newspaper, pension, and published. The DAR compilations are especially important. These are all discussed in other sections of this chapter. The locating of death record articles in genealogical periodicals is also described separately in this chapter.

13. Divorce records

From 1795–1803 divorces in the area which is now OH are by the general court and the circuit court of the Northwest Territory. From 1804–52, OH divorces were granted by the Supreme Court when it sat in the different counties. The Legislature, acting quasi-legally, also gave divorces during the period 1804–47. From 1853–forward divorces have been handled in each county by the Court of Common Pleas. The records of the Supreme Court (1804–52) are to be found in the various counties. These records have usually been filed with the records of the Court of Common Pleas (1853–). A listing of the 102 divorces granted by the Legislature (1800–47) is given in:

_____D. G. Null, OH DIVORCES, National Genealogical Society Quarterly 69 (1981) 109–14.

In chapter 4, the various divorce records available for the OH counties are given.

---

14. Emigration and immigration records

Early settlement in OH (1787–90) involved the Scots-Irish who left from VA, KY, and PA, and came first to the area around Marietta. At about the same time, people of English derivation came to the same area from MA and CT, while NJ people moved into the area around Cincinnati. Quakers from PA and VA went into practically all early settlement areas of OH. French immigrants entered the area of Gallipolis in 1790–1.

Beginning about 1796, CT settlers entered northeastern OH (the CT Western Reserve area), with people from VT coming in 1799–1800. The year 1796 also saw settlers from northern-most MA (now ME) come to the land just east of Cincinnati, immigrants from Scotland to the area north of Cincinnati, and Canadians who had supported the American Revolution were given land in central OH (around Columbus). The influx was so great that in 1800 land offices were placed in Marietta (southeast OH), Steubenville (central-eastern OH), Chillicothe (south-central OH), and Cincinnati (southwestern OH). Please recall that the land in the northeast was being sold by CT at an almost matching pace. Germans entered OH very early from PA, MD, and the Shenandoah Valley of VA, some Swiss coming also. They came to constitute sizable portions of the populations in Toledo, Cincinnati, and Columbus. Sizable numbers of people from southern and eastern Europe (Italians, Russian Jews, Czechs, Slovenes, Hungarians, Poles, Greeks) did not come to early OH, but after 1880, large numbers immigrated. OH had ports on Lake Erie, but no passenger lists for them are available. The majority of OH immigrants (both early and late) entered the country through eastern ports, principally New York and Philadelphia.

The movement of population into OH can be readily seen by examination of the statistics provided by the censuses of the latter half of the 19th century. Numbers of people are expressed in thousands (K). In 1850, the birth places of OH people born outside of OH were as follows:

201K(PA), 111K(Germany), 86K(VA), 84K(NY),
52K(Ireland)

In 1860:
>175K(PA), 168K(Germany), 77K(Ireland), 76K(VA),
>>76K(NY)

In 1870:
>183K(Germany), 149K(PA), 140K(Irish/British),
>>67K(NY), 59K(VA)

In 1880:
>193K(Germany), 137K(PA), 79K(Ireland), 64K(NY),
>>42K(England)

In 1890:
>236K(Germany), 121K(PA), 70K(Ireland), 57K(NY),
>>51K(England)

In 1900:
>204K(Germany), 131K(PA), 56K(NY), 55K(Ireland),
>>53K(KY)

Now, let us turn to view those living in other states which were born in OH. This will show you the pattern of migration out of OH in 1850:
>120K(IN), 64K(IL), 30K(IA), 15K(MI), 11K(WI)

In 1860:
>171K(IN), 131K(IL), 99K(IA), 34K(MI), 24K(WI)

In 1870:
>189K(IN), 163K(IL), 126K(IA), 76K(MO), 61K(MI),
>>38K(KS)

In 1880:
>185K(IN), 136K(IL), 120K(IA), 93K(KS), 78K(MO),
>>76K(MI)

In 1890:
>164K(IN), 126K(IL), 117K(KS), 103K(IA), 85K(MO),
>>80K(MI), 60K(NE)

In 1900:
>178K(IN), 137K(IL), 88K(IA), 88K(MI), 88K(KS),
>>81K(MO), 41K(NE)

In addition to OH histories which have been previously mentioned, there are several other books which will give you information on the above topics:

___Mrs. P. A. Dolle, GEOGRAPHICAL ORIGINS OF EARLY OHIOANS AS SHOWN IN LAND OFFICE RECORDS, Dolle, Columbus, OH, 1963.

___F. Maxwell, OH INDIAN TRAILS, REVOLUTIONARY TRAILS, AND THE ESTABLISHMENT OF OH COUNTIES, The Author, Columbus, OH, 1973.

___C. N. Smith, EARLY 19TH CENTURY GERMAN SETTLERS IN OH AND KY, Westland Publications, McNeal, AZ, 1984.

____S. S. Sprague, KENTUCKIANS IN OH AND IN, Genealogical Publishing Co., Baltimore, MD, 1986.

____F. P. Weisenberger, HISTORY OF IMMIGRANT GROUPS INTO OH, in O. F. Ander, IN THE TREK OF THE IMMIGRANTS, Augustana College Library, Rock Island, IL, 1964.

____H. G. H. Wilhelm, THE ORIGIN AND DISTRIBUTION OF SETTLEMENT GROUPS, OHIO, 1850, OH University Press, Athens, OH, 1982.

There are also some valuable articles in genealogical journals (OGR = The Report of the OH Genealogical Society, OHR = OH Records and Pioneer Families, OSA = OH State Archaeological and Historical Quarterly, WRM = Western Reserve Magazine) Among the most notable are:

____EARLY MIGRATION TO THE WESTERN RESERVE, WRM 5 (1977) 37.

____EMIGRANTS TO WI, OHR 18 (1977) 84.

____FINNISH SETTLEMENTS IN OH, OSA 43 (1934) 452, OSA 49 (1940) 151.

____GERMAN PIONEERS, OSA 2 (1888) 55.

____INTERSTATE MIGRATION, OSA 32 (1923) 395.

____OH FOLKS WHO WENT TO CO, OHR 19 (1978) 173.

____OH PEOPLE WHO WENT TO NE, OHR 20 (1979) 23.

____OH PIONEERS WHO MIGRATED TO IL, OHR 1 (1960) 69, 107, 2 (1961) 17, 82, 140, 179.

____OHIOANS IN CA 1856, OGS 15 (1975) 22.

____SCOTCH-IRISH IN CENTRAL OH, OSA 57 (1948) 111.

____SETTLEMENT PATTERNS IN THE GREAT LAKES REGION, OSA 60 (1951) 48.

____WELSH SETTLEMENTS IN OH, OSA 16 (1907) 194.

15. Ethnic records

The various ethnic groups of OH tended to each be largely affiliated with a particular religious persuasion. The English tended to be Congregational, Episcopalian, and Quaker. Many of these turned Methodist or Baptist or Christian later. Blacks tended to be Baptist or Methodist. Early Germans were Lutheran, Brethren, Mennonite, Moravian, and Reformed, with many later Germans being Catholic. The Scots-Irish and the Scots were chiefly Presbyterian, and the Irish were usually Catholic. The immigrants from eastern and southern Europe tended to be Catholic if they were from the western parts of these areas and Orthodox if they were from the eastern parts. Hence, for many of these groups, ethic information and connections are closely allied with their religious affiliations. Therefore, for all but the blacks, please see the previous section on church records.

83

Among the historical, reference, and source materials for blacks in OH are the following volumes which will get you started if you have interest in this ethnic group.

___BLACK HISTORY ARCHIVES, WRHS, Cleveland, OH.

___L. G. Davis, BLACKS IN THE STATE OF OH, 1800-1976, A PRELIMINARY SURVEY, OH State University, Columbus, OH, 1976.

___S. S. Fuller, THE OH BLACK HISTORY GUIDE, OHS, Columbus, OH, 1975.

___D. A. Gerber, BLACK OH AND THE COLOR LINE, 1860-1915, University of IL Press, Urbana, IL, 1976.

___S. E. Haller and R. H. Smith, REGISTERS OF BLACKS IN THE MIAMI VALLEY, A NAME ABSTRACT, 1804-57, Wright State University, Dayton, OH, 1977.

___C. T. Hickock, THE NEGRO IN OH, 1802-70, AMS Press, New York, NY, 1896.

___P. E. Nitchman, BLACKS IN OH, 1880, The Author, Decorah, IA, and Ft. Meade, MD, 1985-, several volumes.

___OH State Auditor, SPECIAL ENUMERATION OF BLACKS IMMIGRATING TO OH, 1861-3, microfilm, State Archives Series 2261, OHS, Columbus, OH.

___J. Turpin, REGISTER OF BLACK, MULATTO, AND POOR PERSONS IN FOUR OH COUNTIES, 1791-1861, Heritage Books, Bowie, MD, 1985.

___C. H. Wesley, OH NEGROES IN THE CIVIL WAR, OHS, Columbus, OH, 1962.

___R. F. Weston, BLACKS IN OH HISTORY, OHS, Columbus, OH, 1976.

___L. R. Wynar, ETHNIC GROUPS IN OH, Cleveland State University, Cleveland, OH, 1975. Emphasis on Cleveland.

The last of the native Americans to leave OH, namely those in the northwestern region, left in 1833. For investigations of this group in OH, a beginning can be made by the use of the following volumes:

___W. Moorhead, THE INDIAN TRIBES OF OH, OH Archaeological and Historical Society, Columbus, OH, 1899.

___S. Rafert, AMERICAN INDIAN GENEALOGICAL RESEARCH IN THE MIDWEST, RESOURCES AND PERSPECTIVES, National Genealogical Society Quarterly 76 (1988) 212.

16. Gazetteers, atlases, and maps

A gazetteer is a volume which lists geographical names (towns, settlements, rivers, streams, hills, mountains, crossroads, villages, districts), locates them, and sometimes gives a few details concerning them. Several such volumes or similar volumes which list OH place names which could be of help to you include:

___J. Kilbourne, THE OH GAZETTEER, 1828/33, Bookmark, Knightstown, IN, 1978.

___W. Jenkins, THE OH GAZETTEER AND TRAVELER'S GUIDE, Whiting, Columbus, OH, 1841.

___G. W. Hawes, OH STATE GAZETTEER AND BUSINESS DIRECTORY, Hawes, Columbus, OH, 1859–60, and 1860–1, 2 volumes.

___J. R. Armstrong, A TABLE OF POST OFFICES IN OH, Nevins, Columbus, OH, 1851 and 1861, 2 volumes.

___S. D. Fess, OH HISTORY, GAZETTEER, AND BIOGRAPHIES, Lewis Publishing Co., Chicago, IL, 1937, 5 volumes.

___W. D. Overman, OH PLACE NAMES, The Author, Akron, OH, 1951.

___W. D. Overman, OH TOWN NAMES, Atlantic Press, Akron, OH, 1958.

___NEW TOPOGRAPHICAL ATLAS AND GAZETTEER OF OH, Unigraphics, Evansville, IN, 1976.

___M. R. Fitak, PLACE NAMES DIRECTORIES, NORTHEAST OH, SOUTHEAST OH, AND SOUTHERN OH, OH Department of Natural Resources, Columbus, OH, 1976/82, 3 volumes.

___J. S. Gallagher and A Patera, THE POST OFFICES OF OH, The Depot, Burtonsville, MD, 1979.

___J. C. Gioe, OH, HER COUNTIES, HER TOWNSHIPS, AND HER TOWNS, The Researchers, Indianapolis, IN, 1979.

___F. R. Abate, editor, OMNI GAZETTEER OF THE USA, Omnigraphics, Detroit, MI, 1991, OH listings, volume 6, pages 525–645.

Numerous atlases (collections of maps) are available for OH, for its counties, and for some of its larger cities. Many of these are listed in:

___C. E. LeGear, US ATLASES, Library of Congress, Washington, DC, 1950–3, 2 volumes.

Among the state volumes and the county/state compilations are:

___L. A. Brown, EARLY MAPS OF THE OH VALLEY, 1673–1783, University of Pittsburgh Press, Pittsburgh, PA, 1959.

___J. H. Long and S. L. Hansen, HISTORICAL ATLAS AND CHRONOLOGY OF COUNTY BOUNDARIES, 1788–1980, Newberry Library, Chicago, IL, 1984.

___W. Thorndale and W. Dollarhide, MAP GUIDE TO THE US FEDERAL CENSUSES, OH, 1790–1910, Bellingham, WA, 1984.

___H. F. Walling, ATLAS OF THE STATE OF OH, 1868, The Bookmark, Knightstown, OH, 1976.

___D. J. Lake, ATLASES OF OH COUNTIES, Lake and Co., Philadelphia, PA, 1870-91, 25 volumes. For counties of Ash, Ath, Bro, Cla, Cle, Col, Coc, Cuy, Dar, Gue, Hig,, Hoc, Hur, Jac, Lak/Gea, Law, Lor, Mah, Mia, Mor, Per, Pic, Pre, Vin, and Was.

___H. F. Walling and O. W. Gray, NEW TOPOGRAPHICAL ATLAS OF THE STATE OF OH, 1872, Stebbins, New York, NY, 1872.

___L. H. Everts, COMBINATION ATLAS MAPS OF SOME OH COUNTIES, Everts, Philadelphia, PA, 1874-5, numerous volumes. For counties of Fai, Lic, Mus, Tru, War, Gre, Por, Sta, Tus, Cla, Del, Fay, Mia, and Med.

___S. E. Clagg, OH ATLAS, The Author, Huntington, WV, 1959. Early settlements, land divisions, Indian areas, rivers.

___OH Department of Transportation, INDIVIDUAL MAPS OF OHIO'S 88 COUNTIES, The Department, Columbus, OH, latest editions.

___OH COUNTY MAP BOOK, County Maps, Appleton, WI, 1989.

Those counties for which atlases are available are indicated in Chapter 4. OHS, SLO, WRHS, PLC, ACPL, and FHL(FHC) have most of the above materials. Some RL have some of them, and LL are likely to have those of the counties in which they are located.

There are good to excellent OH map collections in OHS, CPL, and at Kent State University. The special indexes in each of these places should be consulted. These collections contain state maps for about half the years following 1800, county maps for practically every county (some quite early), considerable numbers of city maps, and a few for towns. Some volumes relating to OH maps include:

___C. C. Baldwin, EARLY MAPS OF OH AND THE WEST, A BIBLIOGRAPHY, Western Reserve and Northern OH Historical Society, Cleveland, OH, 1875.

___T. H. Smith, THE MAPPING OF OH, Kent State University Press, Kent, OH, 1977.

Especially valuable are landowner maps. These are maps which show the lands of a county with the names of the owners written on them. Most of these maps date between 1860-1900 and are available for 69 OH counties. Such maps are listed in:

___R. W. Stephenson, LAND OWNERSHIP MAPS, Library of Congress, Washington, DC, 1967. [69 OH counties have such maps.]

Very good detail maps of OH are available at reasonable prices from the US Geological Survey. Each of these maps shows only a portion of a county and therefore a great deal of detail can be shown. Write to the address below and request the Index to Topographic Maps of OH. Then order the maps pertaining to your ancestor's area. These maps show roads, streams, cemeteries, settlements, and churches. Such maps will aid you greatly if your ancestor lived in a rural area and you desire to visit the property and the surrounding region.

____Branch of Distribution, Eastern Region, US Geological Survey, 1200 South Eads Street, Arlington, VA 22202.

Another source of detailed county maps is the OH Department of Transportation. They can provide you with individual maps of the 88 OH counties showing roads, cities, streams, railroads, and other features.Order them from:

____OH Department of Transportation, 63 South Front St., Columbus, OH 43215.

---

17. Genealogical compilations and indexes

For the state of OH there are a number of books which are essentially compilations and/or indexes of state-wide or regional genealogical information. Some of the volumes are mentioned under other headings in this chapter: Biographies, County histories, DAR records, Regional publications. Others of this general sort which can possibly be useful to you include:

____H. R. Baldwin, THE BALDWIN COLLECTION, Public Library of Youngstown and Mahoning County, Youngstown, OH. 67 volumes of genealogical information from eastern OH with index. Also available at ACPL and FHL(FHC).

____C. W. Bell, editor, FIRST FAMILIES OF OH, OFFICIAL ROSTER, OGS, Mansfield, OH, 1988. Over 2500 settlers before 1820. Additions are given in the OGS journal THE REPORT, 1988-.

____R. Bowers and A. Short, GATEWAY TO THE WEST, 1967-1978, Genealogical Publishing Co., Baltimore, MD, 1989, 2 volumes, indexed.

____L. M. Brien, A GENEALOGICAL INDEX OF PIONEERS IN THE MIAMI VALLEY, OH, Mayhill Publ., Knightstown, IN, 1970. Chiefly counties of Mia, Mont, Pre, and War.

____Columbus Genealogical Society, OH SOURCE RECORDS FROM THE OH GENEALOGICAL QUARTERLY, Genealogical Publishing Co., Baltimore, MD, 1986.

____M. L. Cunningham, EVERY NAME INDEX, TOGETHER WITH ABSTRACTED ITEMS OF GENEALOGICAL INTEREST, FOUND IN THE OH LEGISLATURE, 1787-1806, Cunningham, Columbus, OH, 1980.

____Franklin County Chapter, OGS, ANCESTRAL SURNAME INDEX, The Chapter, Columbus, OH, 1980-2, 3 volumes.

____B. Fernow, THE OH VALLEY IN COLONIAL DAYS, Polyanthos, New Orleans, LA, 1978. Early migrations and people in the OH Valley.

___Firelands Historical Society, INDEX, 1858-1927, OBITUARY INDEX, 1858-1909, and EVERY NAME INDEX TO THE FIRELANDS PIONEER, The Society, Norwalk, OH, 1939/75., The Firelands Historical Society, Norwalk, OH, 1939.

___C. A. Hanna, OH VALLEY GENEALOGIES, Genealogical Publishing Co., Baltimore, MD, 1975. Early settlers in Bel, Har, and Jef Counties. Use with care.

___R. V. Jackson, EARLY OH, 1779-89, 1800-10, Accelerated Indexing Systems, Bountiful, UT, 1980, 2 volumes.

___C. L. Maskey, SOME EARLY OH AND PA FAMILIES, Maskey, Los Angeles, CA, 1945.

___MEMOIRS OF THE LOWER OH VALLEY, PERSONAL AND GENEALOGICAL, Federal Publ., Madison, WI, 1905.

___OH Genealogical Society, ANCESTOR CHARTS OF MEMBERS OF THE OGS, The Society, Mansfield, OH, 1987. Over 1100 members submitted material.

___OH SOURCE RECORDS, FROM THE OH GENEALOGICAL QUARTERLY, 1937-44, Genealogical Publishing Co., Baltimore, MD, 1986. About 45,000 people indexed.

___M. Smith, OH MARRIAGES AND OH CEMETERY RECORDS ABSTRACTED FROM THE OLD NORTHWEST GENEALOGICAL QUARTERLY, Genealogical Publishing Co., Baltimore, MD, 1980, 2 volumes.

___E. Summers, GENEALOGICAL AND FAMILY HISTORY OF EASTERN OH, Lewis Publ. Co., New York, NY, New York, NY, 1903.

___D. H. Tolzmann, OH VALLEY GERMAN BIOGRAPHICAL INDEX, Heritage, Bowie, MD, 1992.

___G. F. Wright, REPRESENTATIVE CITIZENS OF OH, MEMORIAL-GENEALOGICAL, Memorial Publishing Co., Cleveland, OH, 1913.

18. Genealogical periodicals

Many genealogical periodicals have been or are being published in OH. These journals or newsletters contain genealogies, local histories, genealogical records, family queries and answers, book reviews, and other pertinent local information. If you had an OH ancestor, you will find it of great value to subscribe to one or more of the state-wide periodicals, as well as to any periodicals published in the region or county where he/she lived. Among the more important previous or present OH statewide and regional periodicals are:

___Allstates Research Co., OH RESEARCHER, Allstates, Murray, UT, 1962-.

___Columbus Genealogical Society, OH GENEALOGICAL QUARTERLY, The Society, Columbus, OH, 1937-44, volumes 1-8. See the book OH SOURCE RECORDS FROM THE OH GENEALOGICAL QUARTERLY, Genealogical Publishing Co., Baltimore, MD, 1986.

___Firelands Historical Society, THE FIRELANDS PIONEER, The Society, Norwalk, OH, volumes 1-13 (1858-78), new series volumes 1-25 (1882-1927). Use with INDEX, 1858-1927, and OBITUARY INDEX, 1858-1909, The Society, Norwalk, OH, 1939. Also see EVERY NAME INDEX, The Society, Norwalk, OH, 1975.

___Maxwell Publications, THE OH GENEALOGICAL HELPER, Maxwell, Columbus, OH, 1975-, volume 1-.

___OH Genealogical Society, OH, THE CROSSROADS OF OUR NATION, formerly OH RECORDS AND PIONEER FAMILIES, The Society, Mansfield, OH, 1960-, volume 1-.

___OH Genealogical Society, OH GENEALOGICAL SOCIETY NEWSLETTER, The Society, Mansfield, OH, 1970-.

___OH Genealogical Society, THE REPORT OF THE OH GENEALOGICAL SOCIETY, The Society, Mansfield, OH, 1970-, volume 1-.

___OH Historical Society, OH HISTORY, formerly OH HISTORICAL QUARTERLY, formerly OH ARCHAEOLOGICAL AND HISTORICAL QUARTERLY, The Society, Columbus, OH, 1887-

___The Old Northwest Genealogical Society, THE OLD NORTHWEST GENEALOGICAL QUARTERLY, The Society, Columbus, OH, 1898-1912, volumes 1-15. For marriage and cemetery records abstracted from this journal, consult M. Smith, OH MARRIAGES AND OH CEMETERY RECORDS ABSTRACTED FROM THE OLD NORTHWEST GENEALOGICAL QUARTERLY, Genealogical Publishing Co., Baltimore, MD, 1980, 2 volumes.

___A. Short and R. Bowers, GATEWAY TO THE WEST, The Editors, Arcana, OH, 1967-78, volumes 1-11. See book by R. Bowers and A. Short, GATEWAY TO THE WEST, 1967-1978, Genealogical Publishing Co., Baltimore, MD, 1989, 2 volumes, indexed.

A very helpful index to the major OH periodicals has been published. You should by no means overlook this very important time saver. Look up all counties you are interested in.

___C. W. Bell, OH GENEALOGICAL PERIODICAL INDEX, A COUNTY GUIDE, The Author, Columbus, OH, latest edition. Over 100 journals indexed by subject and by name referring to family records.

In addition to the above statewide periodicals, many regional, county, and some city and private historical and genealogical organizations publish periodicals (newsletters, quarterlies, monthlies, journals, yearbooks) which can be of exceptional value to you if you are forebear hunting in their areas. Those societies which issue periodicals and/or record compilations are indicated in the county listings of Chapter 4. Most of these publications are in the OHS, SLO, and OGS. Many are available at WRHS, PLC, ACPL, FHL(FHC), and RL, some are in LGL, and those of various local regions are likely to be found in LL.

Not only do articles pertaining to OH genealogy appear in these OH publications, they also are printed in other genealogical periodicals. Fortunately, indexes to the major genealogical periodicals (including those from OH) are available:
___For periodicals published 1847-1985, then annually 1986-present, consult Allen County Public Library Foundation, PERIODICAL SOURCE INDEX, The Foundation, Fort Wayne, In, 1986-.
These index volumes will be found in OHS, SLO, WRHS, PLC, OGS, ACPL, and FHL(FHC), most RL, most LGL, and a few LL. In them you should consult all OH listings under the county names which concern you and all listings under the family names you are seeking.

---

19. Genealogical and historical societies

In the state of OH various societies for the study of genealogy, the accumulation of data, and the publication of the materials have been organized. These societies are listed in Chapter 4 under the names of the OH counties in which they have their headquarters. Most of them publish regular journals and/or newsletters containing the data which they have gathered, queries from their members, and book reviews. They are indicated in Chapter 4. The local members of such societies are generally well informed about the genealogical resources of their regions, and often can offer considerable help to non-residents who had ancestors in the area. It is thus advisable for you to join the societies in your ancestor's county as well as the OH Genealogical Society, 34 Sturges Avenue, Mansfield, OH 44906. The large majority of county and local genealogical societies in OH are chapters of the OH Genealogical Society (OGS). There are also numerous independent local and special societies. All correspondence with societies should be accompanied by an SASE. Detailed listings of them are provided by
___OH Genealogical Society, THE REPORT OF THE OH GENEALOGICAL SOCIETY, The Society, Mansfield, OH, recent issue. Addresses of local societies often change. This will give you up-to-date information.
___E. P. Bentley, THE GENEALOGIST'S ADDRESS BOOK, Genealogical Publishing Co., Baltimore, MD, 1991.

Historical societies are often also of interest to genealogists. In addition to the OH Historical Society (Interstate 71 at 17th Avenue,

Columbus, OH 43211), there are many city, county, and regional historical societies in OH. These organizations along with their addresses are listed in the reference volumes named below. Some of these societies have strong genealogical interests (as does the OHS), some deal with genealogical interests in addition to their historical pursuits, and some have essentially no interest in genealogy. Even if they do not carry out much genealogy as such, their work will be of considerable interest to you since it deals with the historical circumstances through which your ancestor lived. It is often well for you to dispatch an SASE and an inquiry to one or more asking about membership, genealogical interest, and publications. Most of these valuable organizations are named in these very detailed compilations:

___DIRECTORY OF HISTORICAL SOCIETIES AND AGENCIES IN THE US AND CANADA, American Association for State and Local History, Nashville, TN, latest edition.

____DIRECTORY OF MUSEUMS, HISTORICAL SOCIETIES, AND ASSOCIATED ORGANIZATIONS IN OH, OH Association of Historical Societies and Museums, Granville,OH, latest edition.

20. Land records

One of the most important types of genealogical records are those which deal with land. This is because OH for many years was predominantly an agricultural state. In addition, land was up until the 20th century (the 1900s) widely available and quite inexpensive. These factors meant that the vast majority of Ohio people owned land, and therefore their names appear in land records. The land was first granted by the government to private individuals or groups, and thereafter the land records were locally kept. These latter records (deed, entry, mortgage, settler, survey, tax) for the 88 OH counties are indicated in Chapter 4 along with the dates of availability. In most cases, the originals are in the CH or the ONAHRC, but transcripts and/or microfilm copies of many of them are to be found in OHS, WRHS, PLC, OGS, ACPL, and FHL, and are available through FHC. Some transcribed land records are available in RL and LGL, and transcribed copies and some microfilms for individual counties are often available in the LL of the counties.

In addition to the county records, there were a large number of early land grants made to the first settlers in various areas of the state. To understand the granting of lands by the government to its first owners, it is necessary to recognize that the area which makes up OH was divided into 12 major regions for the original granting of land. These regions are depicted in Figure 26. Notice that they are the VA Military District (VMD, 1784), the CT Western Reserve (CWR, 1786), The Seven Ranges (SR, 1787), the OH Company Purchase (OCP, 1787/92), the Donation Tract (DT, 1792), the CT Firelands (CF, 1792), the Symmes Purchase

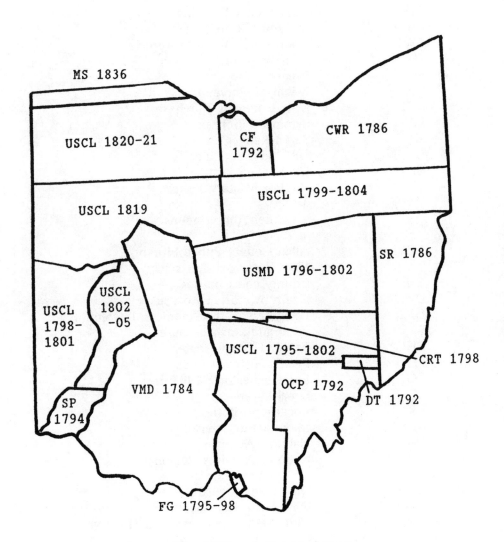

Figure 26. OH Land Grant Areas

Map Abbreviations

CF	Connecticut Firelands
CRT	Canadian Refugee Tract
CWR	Connecticut Western Reserve
DT	Donation Tract
FG	French Grants
MS	Michigan Survey
OCP	Ohio Company Purchase
SP	Symmes Purchase
SR	Seven Ranges
USCL	US Congress Lands
USMD	US Military District
VMD	Virginia Military District

Other Abbreviations

ACPL	Allen County Public Library
C	1890 Union pension census
CH	County court houses
D	Death or mortality censuses
DAR	Daughters of the American Revolution
F	Farm and ranch censuses
FHC	Family History Center
FHL	Family History Library
LGL	Large genealogical libraries
LL	Local libraries
LR	Local repositories
M	Manufactures censuses
NA	National Archives
NARB	National Archives Regional Branches
OGS	Ohio Genealogical Society
OHS	Ohio Historical Society
ONAHRC	Ohio Network of American History Research Centers
P	1840 Revolutionary War veteran census
PLC	Public Library of Cincinnati
R	Regular censuses
RL	Regional libraries
SLO	State Library of Ohio
T	Tax substitutes for censuses
WPA	Works Progress Administration
WRHS	Western Reserve Historical Society

(SP, 1794), the French Grants (FG, 1795/8), the US Congress Lands (USCL, 1795), the US Military District (USMD, 1796), the Canadian Refugee Tract (CRT, 1798), and the MI Survey (MS, 1836). Remember that land grants are for the first disposition of the land from the colonial or state or federal government to an individual owner. Thereafter the county records (see above paragraph) must be consulted for changes in land ownership. Your first step in seeking the land grant of an ancestor is to use the three major indexes which lead to most of the original grantees in OH, except for those in the CT Western Reserve (CWR), the CT Firelands (CF), and the Symmes Purchase (SP).

____Auditor of State Land Office of OH, CARD INDEX OF ENTRY-MEN, PLATS, AND WITHDRAWN ENTRIES, The Office, PO Box 1140, Columbus, OH 43266. A surname index with over 175,000 cards. Send SASE to have the index searched.

____Bureau of Land Management, GLO AUTOMATED RECORDS AND INDEX TO PATENTS, GRANTS, AND WARRANTS IN OH, The Bureau, 7450 Boston Blvd., Springfield, VA 22153. Almost 98,000 documents. Write to have the index searched.

____C. N. Smith, FEDERAL LAND SERIES, American Library Association, Chicago, IL, 1972/73/80/82, 4 volumes. Many grantees in the Congress Lands, US Military District, and the VA Military District.

The information obtained from these indexes will permit records to be obtained from one or more of the following repositories: Auditor of State Land Office of OH, Federal Bureau of Land Management, National Archives. Details will be given below. Now let us consider the conditions and procedures in each of the 12 regions.

At the conclusion of the Revolutionary War, the US took possession of the lands that are now OH. The states of NY, VA, MA, and CT all laid claim to parts of the area. NY gave its claim up in 1781, VA in 1784, MA in 1785, and CT in 1786 and 1800. However, CT reserved the CT Western Reserve (CWR) and the CT Firelands (CF) for itself, and VA reserved the VA Military District (VMD) to award to its Revolutionary War and French and Indian War veterans. Over 16,000 parcels of land with indiscriminant surveys (metes and bounds) are found in the VA Military District. VA issued its veteran a warrant for land. This warrant could be sold or redeemed for land in the VA Military District after a survey had been made by a VA state surveyor. The US issued the final land awarding document, which was called a US patent. Those who redeemed warrants (not necessarily the person who first received the warrant) for land in the VA Military District may be located in:

____Auditor of State Land Office, CARD INDEX OF VA MILITARY DISTRICT RECORDS, indexed by surname, warrant number, and survey number, The Office, 1272 South Front Street, Columbus,

OH 43266. These references lead to entry books and survey books.

A listing of the original warrantees is given in the following volume. This information will permit you to request the applications for these warrants and the warrants themselves from the VA State Archives (11th and Capitol Streets, Richmond, VA 23219).

___ G. M. Brumbaugh, REVOLUTIONARY WAR RECORDS OF VA, Lancaster Press, Lancaster, PA, 1936.

The files of entry papers for those who redeemed the warrants may be obtained from the National Archives (PA Avenue between 7th and 9th Streets, Washington, DC 20408). They have the following indexes to assist them in locating the file:

___ National Archives, NAMES OF WARRANTEES IN THE VA MILITARY DISTRICT, VA MILITARY WARRANTS- NUMERICAL-CONTINENTAL AND STATE LINES, SURVEYS FOR LAND IN THE VA MILITARY DISTRICT OF OH, The Archives, Washington, DC.

These files will give a volume and page number to the recorded copy of the warrant, which can then be obtained from the Bureau of Land Management (7450 Boston Boulevard, Springfield, VA 22153).

The CT Western Reserve (CWR) [including the CT Firelands (CF)] was reserved by CT in 1786 when it gave up its other claims to land in the OH area. The area labelled CWR (excluding CF) was sold by CT in 1795 to the CT Land Company. The Company surveyed the land into townships, each of which was five miles square. A township is identified by a range number (R 1 through 24) and a township number (T 1 through 13), and townships are subdivided into quarters (given numbers 1 through 4). The records of the lands in the CT Western Reserve (CWR) are in the CT State Library (231 Capitol Street, Hartford, CT 06115):

___ CT State Library, CT LAND COMPANY, WESTERN RESERVE DEEDS, 1800-07, The Library, Hartford, CT.

___ CT State Library, CT LAND COMPANY, REGISTRAR OF CERTIFICATES, MORTGAGES, 1796-1800, The Library, Hartford, CT.

___ CT State Library, CT LAND COMPANY, REGISTER OF DEED TRANSFER, 1795-1807, The Library, Hartford, CT.

___ CT State Library, CT LAND COMPANY, PROCEEDING, VOTES, AND STOCK LEDGERS, The Library, Hartford, CT.

Other sources of records for the CT Western Reserve are the WRHS, the Litchfield Historical Society in Litchfield (CT 06759), and the county records in the CT Western Reserve.

The first federal lands to be surveyed in the OH country were those in the Seven Ranges (SR). The land was surveyed into six mile square townships. These townships were identified by a range number (R 1 through 7) and a township number (T 1 through 16). Townships were subdivided into sections one mile square, which were numbered from 1 through 36. (Different numbering systems were used before and after 1796.) The sections were subsequently divided into quarter sections which could be further subdivided. Land in the Seven Ranges was sold in New York, NY, in 1787, and in Pittsburgh and Philadelphia in 1796. In order to obtain the most records for the original grantee (the person who first took up the land), you should use the two major indexes:

____Auditor of State Land Office of OH, CARD INDEX OF ENTRY- MEN, PLATS, AND WITHDRAWN ENTRIES, The Office, PO Box 1140, Columbus, OH 43266. A surname index with over 175,000 cards. Write to have the index searched.

____Bureau of Land Management, GLO AUTOMATED RECORDS AND INDEX TO PATENTS, GRANTS, AND WARRANTS IN OH, The Bureau, 7450 Boston Blvd., Springfield, VA 22153. Almost 98,000 documents. Write to have the index searched.

These will give you access to the Tract and Entry books in the Auditor's Office, and will then permit you to obtain the Land Entry File Number from the Bureau of Land Management. With this further information you can request the Entry Files (and/or the Bounty Warrants) from the National Archives (their Record Group 49). And you can obtain a copy of the Patent (or grant) from the Bureau of Land Management or the OH county. The tract and entry books often tell the state or county of residence of the grantee at the time the land was entered. This informa- tion is usually of genealogical significance.

The OH Company Purchase (OCP) was a tract of land sold by the Continental Congress in 1787 to a company which wished to develop settlements in the OH country. The area was surveyed in six mile square townships with numbered sections. Small strips of land on the west and north were bought and added to the area in 1792. There are two good sources of records:

____Auditor of State Land Office of OH, CARD INDEX OF ENTRY- MEN, PLATS, AND WITHDRAWN ENTRIES, The Office, PO Box 1140, Columbus, OH 43266. A surname index with over 175,000 cards. Write to have the index searched for plats which show the original owners.

____Marietta College Library, RECORDS OF THE OH COMPANY, The Library, Marietta College, Marietta, OH 45750.

The Donation Tract (DT) was given in 1792 to agents of the OH Company to distribute free to settlers who would settle on the land and act as a buffer toward the Indians. The OH Company was the original grantee. They issued deeds to the settlers. Any land which remained vacant in 1818 was returned to the US Government. The US then sold it through the Marietta Land Office. The procedure for obtaining grant records for these post-1818 sales is the same as that given at the end of the section on the Seven Ranges.

In 1792, the state of CT set the western portion of the CT Western Reserve apart for some CT townspeople who had been burned out by the British in the Revolutionary War. The area was called the CT Firelands (CF). The area was surveyed into five mile square townships, each of which was subdivided into quarters. See the section above on the CT Western Reserve for information on obtaining the records.

The Symmes Purchase (SP), also called the Miami Purchase, was sold to Symmes and his associates in 1794. The tract of land was privately surveyed, which resulted in an odd order for the ranges (R) and townships (T). Most of the records of the disposition of land in the Symmes Purchase were lost in a fire. The Auditor of State Land Office has some surviving tract books, with a few names in them. A helpful reference work is:
_____C. McHenry, SYMMES PURCHASE RECORDS, The Author, Lawrenceburg, IN, 1979.

In 1795 and again in 1798 the French Grants (FG) were made along the OH River in what was to be Scioto County. These lands were granted to French immigrants who had been defrauded by a land agency called the Scioto Company. The procedure for obtaining grant records for these lands is the same as that given at the end of the section on the Seven Ranges.

The areas on the map in Figure 26 which are labelled Congress Lands, and land remaining in the Seven Ranges, US Military District, and the VA Military District after 1852 were granted federally. In 1800, federal offices for land sales were set up in Steubenville, Cincinnati, Chillicothe, and Marietta. Each land office could sell any of the available federal land in its region. As the years went on, more land offices were added. The offices and their periods of operation were as follows: Steubenville (1800-40), Marietta (1800-40), Cincinnati (1801-40), Chillicothe (1801-76), Zanesville (1804-40), Canton (1808-16), Wooster (1816-40), Delaware (1820-28), Piqua (1820-33), Tiffin (1828-32), Bucyrus (1832-42), Wapakoneta (1833-5), Lima (1835-43), Marion (1837-45), Upper Sandusky (1843-8), Defiance (1848-55). The procedure for obtaining grant records for this area is the same as that given at the end of the section on the Seven Ranges.

In 1796, the United States Military District (USMD) was established to provide land for federal bounty land grants to veterans of the Continental Army in the Revolutionary War. The area was surveyed into townships five miles square, with each township being subdivided into quarters. Townships are identified with a Range Number (R 1 through 20) and a Township Number (T 1 through 10), with the 4 quarters being labelled 1 through 4. Bounty land warrants which were exchanged for land in the USMD, along with indexes, are in:

 National Archives, US REVOLUTIONARY WAR BOUNTY LAND WARRANTS USED IN THE US MILITARY DISTRICT OF OH AND RELATED PAPERS (ACTS OF 1788, 1803, 1806), Microfilm M829, 16 rolls, The Archives, Washington, DC.

Applications for bounty land warrants give much information on the veterans who made the applications. These are indexed in:

 National Genealogical Society, INDEX OF REVOLUTIONARY WAR PENSION [AND BOUNTY LAND] APPLICATIONS IN THE NATIONAL ARCHIVES, The Society, Washington, DC, 1976.

The applications themselves are reproduced in:

 National Archives, REVOLUTIONARY WAR PENSION AND BOUNTY LAND APPLICATION FILES, Microfilm M804, 2670 rolls, The Archives, Washington, DC.

After bounty land warrants had been surrendered for land for most of the land, the remaining land was opened for sale to anyone. The procedure for obtaining grant records for this area is the same as that given at the end of the section on the Seven Ranges.

The narrow strip of land called the Canadian Refugee Tract (CRT) was granted to refugees who had fled from Canada because of their support for the Americans in the Revolutionary War. After all refugees desiring land were satisfied, the remainder was opened for sale to anyone. The procedure for obtaining grant records for this area is the same as that given at the end of the section on the Seven Ranges.

In 1836, MI ceded to OH the disputed strip of land on their mutual border, the MI Survey. Grants before this should be sought at the Library of MI (717 Allegan Street, Lansing, MI 48909) and through the OH route as described above. For grant records after 1835, follow the procedure given in the last half of the paragraph on the Seven Ranges.

The federal government made a number of other grants, most quite small, including Moravian Indian Grants (1772–80 until 1823) in Tuscawaras County, the Zane Tracts (1796/1802/06) in southeast OH, and the Dohrman Grant (1787) in Harrison and Tuscawaras Counties. The US also made a number of grants to the state of OH. These included school lands, ministerial lands, turnpike lands, salt reservations, swamp lands, and land to support the establishing of universities. Details on all these may be found in:

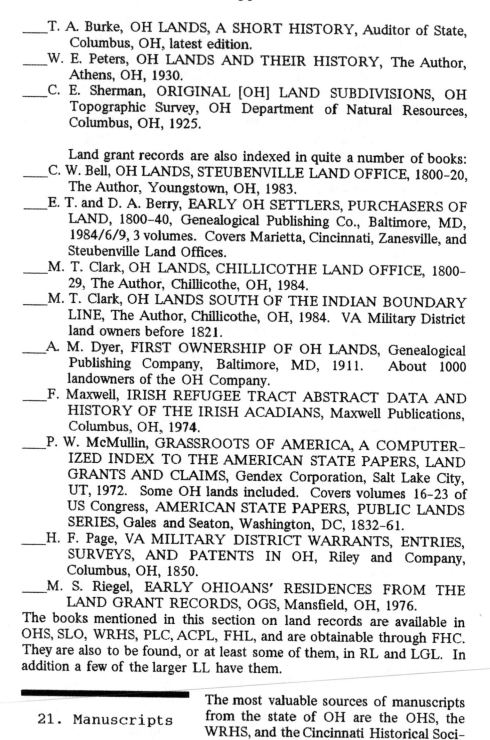

____T. A. Burke, OH LANDS, A SHORT HISTORY, Auditor of State, Columbus, OH, latest edition.

____W. E. Peters, OH LANDS AND THEIR HISTORY, The Author, Athens, OH, 1930.

____C. E. Sherman, ORIGINAL [OH] LAND SUBDIVISIONS, OH Topographic Survey, OH Department of Natural Resources, Columbus, OH, 1925.

Land grant records are also indexed in quite a number of books:

____C. W. Bell, OH LANDS, STEUBENVILLE LAND OFFICE, 1800–20, The Author, Youngstown, OH, 1983.

____E. T. and D. A. Berry, EARLY OH SETTLERS, PURCHASERS OF LAND, 1800–40, Genealogical Publishing Co., Baltimore, MD, 1984/6/9, 3 volumes. Covers Marietta, Cincinnati, Zanesville, and Steubenville Land Offices.

____M. T. Clark, OH LANDS, CHILLICOTHE LAND OFFICE, 1800–29, The Author, Chillicothe, OH, 1984.

____M. T. Clark, OH LANDS SOUTH OF THE INDIAN BOUNDARY LINE, The Author, Chillicothe, OH, 1984. VA Military District land owners before 1821.

____A. M. Dyer, FIRST OWNERSHIP OF OH LANDS, Genealogical Publishing Company, Baltimore, MD, 1911. About 1000 landowners of the OH Company.

____F. Maxwell, IRISH REFUGEE TRACT ABSTRACT DATA AND HISTORY OF THE IRISH ACADIANS, Maxwell Publications, Columbus, OH, 1974.

____P. W. McMullin, GRASSROOTS OF AMERICA, A COMPUTER-IZED INDEX TO THE AMERICAN STATE PAPERS, LAND GRANTS AND CLAIMS, Gendex Corporation, Salt Lake City, UT, 1972. Some OH lands included. Covers volumes 16–23 of US Congress, AMERICAN STATE PAPERS, PUBLIC LANDS SERIES, Gales and Seaton, Washington, DC, 1832–61.

____H. F. Page, VA MILITARY DISTRICT WARRANTS, ENTRIES, SURVEYS, AND PATENTS IN OH, Riley and Company, Columbus, OH, 1850.

____M. S. Riegel, EARLY OHIOANS' RESIDENCES FROM THE LAND GRANT RECORDS, OGS, Mansfield, OH, 1976.

The books mentioned in this section on land records are available in OHS, SLO, WRHS, PLC, ACPL, FHL, and are obtainable through FHC. They are also to be found, or at least some of them, in RL and LGL. In addition a few of the larger LL have them.

---

21. Manuscripts

The most valuable sources of manuscripts from the state of OH are the OHS, the WRHS, and the Cincinnati Historical Society. There are also collections, some small, some moderate sized, in LL, local museums, and local historical societies. Their holdings can include records of religious, educational, patriotic, business, social, civil, professional, governmental, and political organizations; documents, letters, memoirs, notes, and papers of early settlers, politicians, ministers, business men, educators, physicians, dentists, lawyers, judges, and farmers; records of churches, cemeteries, mortuaries, schools, corporations, and industries; works of artists, musicians, writers, sculptors, photographers, and architects; and records, papers, letters, and reminiscences of participants in the various wars, as well as records of various military organizations and campaigns.

Many of these repositories are listed in the following volumes, some of which give brief descriptions of their holdings:

___US Library of Congress, THE NATIONAL UNION CATALOG OF MANUSCRIPT COLLECTIONS, The Library, Washington, DC, issued annually 1959-. Both cumulative indexes and annual indexes. Check your ancestor's county, and then under the heading Genealogy.

___E. Altman and others, INDEX TO PERSONAL NAMES IN THE NATIONAL UNION CATALOG OF MANUSCRIPT COLLECTIONS, 1959-84, Chadwyck-Healey, Arlington, VA, 1988, 2 volumes. Check your ancestor's name.

___US National Historical Publications and Records Commission, DIRECTORY OF ARCHIVES AND MANUSCRIPT REPOSITORIES IN THE US, The Commission, Oryx Press, New York, NY, 1988.

___D. R. Larson, GUIDE TO MANUSCRIPT COLLECTIONS AND INSTITUTIONAL RECORDS IN OH, Society of OH Archivists, Bowling Green, OH, 1974. Also details on many small repositories.

There are also some special volumes which describe and/or catalog the manuscript holdings in various important OH repositories.

___A. D. Lentz, A GUIDE TO MANUSCRIPTS OF THE OH HISTORICAL SOCIETY, OHS, Columbus, OH, 1972.

___K. J. Pike, A GUIDE TO THE MANUSCRIPTS AND ARCHIVES OF THE WESTERN RESERVE HISTORICAL SOCIETY, WRHS, Cleveland, OH, 1972.

___K. J. Pike, A GUIDE TO MAJOR MANUSCRIPT COLLECTIONS ACCESSIONED AND PROCESSED BY THE LIBRARY OF THE WESTERN RESERVE HISTORICAL SOCIETY, WRHS, Cleveland, OH, 1987.

___J. L. Harper, A GUIDE TO THE DRAPER MANUSCRIPTS, WI State Historical Society, Madison, WI, 1982. See OH references on page 285.

Numerous other manuscripts are listed in the manuscript card catalogs and in special indexes provided at OHS, WRHS, and other archives, libraries, and museums in OH. There are also good manuscript collections in some RL and in some of the college and other university libraries of OH. Especially helpful are the manuscripts of the Bierce Library at the University of Akron (Akron, OH 44325), the Library of OH University (Athens, OH 45701), the Library at Bowling Green State University (Bowling Green, OH 43403), the American Jewish Archives (3101 Clifton Avenue, Cincinnati, OH 45220), the Blegan Library at the University of Cincinnati (Cincinnati, OH 45221), the Library of Case Western Reserve University (Cleveland, OH 44106), the Cuyahoga County Archives (2905 Franklin Boulevard, Cleveland, OH 44113), the Library of Wright State University (Dayton, OH 45435), the Library at Kent State University (Kent, OH 44242), the Dawes Library at Marietta College (Marietta, OH 45750), the Archives at Oberlin College (Oberlin, OH 44074), and the Great Lakes Historical Society (480 Main Street, Vermilion, OH 44089).

22. Marriage records

From its beginning, each OH county has kept marriage records. Since 1949, copies of these marriage records have been filed in Columbus on a statewide basis. The state office has a overall state index for the period from 1949 on. For a copy of a given record, write to:

___Division of Vital Statistics, OH Department of Health, 65 South Front Street, Columbus, OH 43216.

Prior to 1949 marriage records were collected by the counties, where the originals remain in the Probate Court. These records generally show the names of the bride and groom, the date of the marriage, the county, and the officiating individual. Sometimes there is information about the ages and residences of the bride and groom, but parents are not usually named until after 1900. The records generally consist of a marriage license application and the returned and witnessed license after the ceremony. There is an overall index for almost all OH marriages up to 1865, and for some of them 1865–80.

___Family History Library, INTERNATIONAL GENEALOGICAL INDEX, OH SECTION, FHL, Salt Lake City, UT. Available on microfiche and/or computer at every FHC, and at several LGL. Microfilm copies of many of these marriage records are available at FHL, and are therefore obtainable through FHC. Some of the records are on microfilm at OHS. Some microfilms are available for individual counties in their LL. Lists of records and microfilms available for the various counties are given in:

___Family History Library, FAMILY HISTORY LIBRARY CATALOG,
   LOCALITY SECTION, FHL, Salt Lake City, UT, latest edition.
   On microfiche and/or computer in each FHC. Look under the
   relevant county.
Those that are available for the various OH counties will be listed under
the counties in Chapter 4. Instructions for locating the records and
microfilms will be given in Chapter 3.

There are also some published county compilations of marriages
which are likely to prove useful. They are listed in:
___C. W. Bell, OH GUIDE TO GENEALOGICAL SOURCES,
   Genealogical Publishing Company, Baltimore, MD, 1988.
___S. Harter, OH GENEALOGY AND LOCAL HISTORY SOURCES
   INDEX, The Author, Columbus, OH, 1986.
___P. Khouw, COUNTY BY COUNTY IN OH GENEALOGY, SLO,
   Columbus, OH, 1992.
They will also be noted in Chapter 4, where each county will be treated
individually. A notable compilation which will be useful for northwestern
OH is:
___M. Smith, OH MARRIAGES EXTRACTED FROM THE OLD
   NORTHWEST GENEALOGICAL QUARTERLY, 1790-1897,
   Genealogical Publishing Company, Baltimore, MD, 1986. About
   7000 marriages from nine counties.

Other records which often yield marriage dates and places include
biographical, cemetery, church, mortuary, newspaper, obituary, pension,
and published. All of these are discussed in other sections of this
chapter. In addition, the location of marriage data in genealogical
periodicals has been described in section 16.

23. Military records: Revolutionary War

The Revolutionary War was fought before OH became a state, that is, in the years 1775-83. During this time parts of what is now OH were claimed by VA, NY, CT, and MA. Since the area was quite sparsely populated during these years, very few, if any, Ohioans actually fought in the Revolution. Shortly after the War, however, many veterans came into the OH country because they were awarded land in OH (actually the Northwest Territory first) for their service. There are three sets of records relating to this War in which data on your ancestor could appear: service records, pension records, and bounty land records. To search out all these records, write the following address and request copies of NATF Form 80:
___Military Service records (NNCC), Washington, DC 20408.

When the forms come, fill them out with as much information on your ancestor as you know, check the record request box on one for military service, the pension box on another, and the bounty land record box on another, attach a note asking for all records, and mail the forms off. The Military Service Records staff will examine their indexes to Revolutionary War soldiers and naval personnel, will try to find your ancestor, then, if they do, will copy and send you his records, along with a bill for their services. The staff is very busy and your reply may take a month or longer. If you live in certain areas of the US, there are quicker alternatives than this route to the military service records, but and the pension or bounty land records. The next paragraph will detail these.

Microfilms of the Revolutionary War indexes (M860, 58 rolls, M879, 1 roll), microfilms of Revolutionary War records (M881, 1097 rolls, M880, 4 rolls), and microfilms of pension and bounty land applications (M804, 2670 rolls) are available at the National Archives (Washington, DC), Regional Branches of the National Archives (Waltham, MA; New York, NY; Philadelphia, PA; East Point, GA; Chicago, IL; Kansas City, MO; Ft. Worth, TX; Denver, CO; San Bruno, CA; Laguna Niguel, CA; Seattle, WA), ACPL, and FHL (Salt Lake City, UT). You may look at the indexes in these locations and also read the records. The indexes and the record microfilms may also be ordered through FHC and by your local library from AGLL (PO Box 329, Bountiful, UT 84011).

There are also several printed national sources which you should consult regarding your Revolutionary War ancestor:
____F. J. Metcalf et al., INDEX TO REVOLUTIONARY WAR PEN-
SION [AND BOUNTY LAND] APPLICATIONS, National
Genealogical Society, Washington, DC, 1966.
____National Society of the DAR, DAR PATRIOT INDEX, The Society,
Washington, DC, 1967; 1st Supplement, 1969; 2nd Supplement,
1973; 3rd Supplement, 1976.
____War Department, REVOLUTIONARY WAR PENSIONERS OF
1818, Genealogical Publishing Co., Baltimore, MD, 1959.
____War Department, PENSION ROLL OF 1835, Genealogical Publish-
ing Co., Baltimore, MD, 1968, 4 volumes.
____US Department of State, A CENSUS OF PENSIONERS FOR
REVOLUTIONARY OR MILITARY SERVICE TAKEN IN
1840, Genealogical Publishing Co., Baltimore, MD, 1974.
____National Society of the DAR, INDEX TO THE ROLLS OF
HONOR, (ANCESTOR'S INDEX) IN THE LINEAGE BOOKS,
Genealogical Publishing Co., Baltimore, MD, 1972, 2 volumes.
____J. Pierce, REGISTER OF CERTIFICATES TO US OFFICERS AND
SOLDIERS OF THE CONTINENTAL ARMY UNDER THE

___J. Pierce, REGISTER OF CERTIFICATES TO US OFFICERS AND
SOLDIERS OF THE CONTINENTAL ARMY UNDER THE
ACT OF 1783, Genealogical Publishing Co., Baltimore, MD,
1973.

___F. Rider, AMERICAN GENEALOGICAL INDEX, Godfrey Memorial Library, Middletown, CT, 1942-52, 43 volumes, and
AMERICAN GENEALOGICAL-BIOGRAPHICAL INDEX,
Godfrey Memorial Library, Middletown, CT, 1952-, in process,
over 190 volumes so far.

In addition, several printed OH sources for your search are in existence.
Among the better ones are:

___J. B. Clipson and K. B. Brinkdope, INDEX OF REVOLUTIONARY
WAR HEROES AND THEIR FAMILIES, Cincinnati Chapter,
DAR, Cincinnati, OH, 1983. Information from over 2000
applications.

___C. H. Hamlin, THE 1958 LINEAGE BOOK OF THE CINCINNATI
CHAPTER OF THE SONS OF THE AMERICAN REVOLU-
TION, The Chapter, Cincinnati, OH, 1958.

___W. T. Hutchinson, THE BOUNTY LANDS OF THE AMERICAN
REVOLUTION IN OH, Arno Press, New York, NY, 1979.

___OH Society, DAR, OFFICIAL ROSTER OF SOLDIERS OF THE
AMERICAN REVOLUTION BURIED IN THE STATE OF OH,
Heer Printing Co., Columbus, OH, 1929/38/59, 3 volumes.
Periodic additions to the listings are given in OH DAR NEWS,
The Society, Columbus, OH, 1960-.

___W. L. Phillips, ANNOTATED BIBLIOGRAPHY OF OH PATRI-
OTS, REVOLUTIONARY WAR AND WAR OF 1812, Heritage
Books, Bowie, MD, 1985.

___Sons of the American Revolution, OH Society, CENTENNIAL
REGISTER OF THE SAR, 1889-1989, The Sons, Columbus, OH,
1988.

___I. Waldenmaier, REVOLUTIONARY WAR PENSIONERS LIVING
IN OH BEFORE 1834, The Author, Tulsa, OK, 1983.

___S. M. Wilson, CATALOGUE OF REVOLUTIONARY SOLDIERS
AND SAILORS OF THE COMMONWEALTH OF VA TO
WHOM LAND BOUNTY WARRANTS WERE GRANTED,
Southern Book Co., Baltimore, MD, 1953.

Also do not fail to examine:

___OH VETERANS' GRAVE REGISTRATION FILE, OHS, Columbus,
OH.

Most of the reference works listed above are in OHS, SLO, WRHS, PLC,
OGS, ACPL, and FHL(FHC). Some of them are in RL and LGL.

Numerous other Revolutionary War records sources are listed in
the following work which goes into considerable detail and is recommended to all researchers who had Revolutionary War ancestors:

____Geo. K. Schweitzer, REVOLUTIONARY WAR GENEALOGY, The Author, 407 Ascot Court, Knoxville, TN 37923, 1988.

---

24. Military records: 1812-48

Over 26,000 soldiers from OH saw active service in the War of 1812, which was fought 1812-5. As was the case with the Revolutionary War, three types of records should be sought: military service, pension, and bounty land. The National Archives has original service records, pension records, and bounty land records, plus indexes of all three. These indexes are as follows:

____US Department of War, INDEX TO COMPILED SERVICE RECORDS OF VOLUNTEER SOLDIERS WHO SERVED DURING THE WAR OF 1812, National Archives, Washington, DC, Microfilm M602, 234 rolls.

____US Veterans Administration, INDEX TO WAR OF 1812 PENSION APPLICATION FILES, National Archives, Washington, DC, Microfilm M313, 102 rolls.

____US Bureau of Land Management, WAR OF 1812 MILITARY BOUNTY LAND WARRANTS, National Archives, Washington, DC, Microfilm M848, 14 rolls, with indexes on the first roll.

You can either have the National Archives look into the indexes, or if they are easily available, you can do it. They are located at NA, NARB, FHL(FHC), and some LGL. If you find your ancestor, or if you want the NA to look for him, write the following and request several copies of NATF Form 80:

____Military Service Records (NNCC), Washington, DC 20408.

Upon receiving them, fill three out, giving your ancestor's name and state, as much other pertinent data as you can, check the request box for military service on one, the pension box on another, and the bounty land record box on the third, attach a note asking for all records, then mail them back. There are also several nationally-applicable books which could be of assistance to you:

____F. I. Ordway, Jr., REGISTER OF THE GENERAL SOCIETY OF THE WAR OF 1812, The Society, Washington, DC, 1972.

____E. S. Galvin, 1812 ANCESTOR INDEX, National Society of US Daughters of 1812, Washington, DC, 1970.

____C. S. Peterson, KNOWN MILITARY DEAD DURING THE WAR OF 1812, The Author, Baltimore, MD, 1955.

In addition, there are materials relating specifically to OH. The following can be quite helpful:

____J. C. Diefenbach, INDEX TO THE GRAVE RECORDS OF SOLDIERS OF THE WAR OF 1812 BURIED IN OH, The Author, Columbus, OH, 1945.

_____OH Adjutant General's Office, ROSTER OF OH SOLDIERS IN THE WAR OF 1812, Genealogical Publishing Co., Baltimore, MD, 1968, with G. Garner, INDEX TO THE ROSTER OF OH SOLDIERS IN THE WAR OF 1812, Eastern WA Genealogical Society, Spokane, WA, 1974. Roster is not complete.

_____OH National Society of US Daughters of 1812, INDEX TO GRAVE RECORDS OF THE WAR OF 1812, The Society, Columbus, OH, 1969/74, 2 volumes. Supplements to Diefenbach.

_____OH National Society of US Daughters of 1812, ANCESTORS' ROSTER, The Society, Columbus, OH, 1943.

_____OH Historical Society, VETERANS' GRAVE REGISTRATION FILE, compiled by the WPA, The Society, Columbus, OH. Also on microfilm at FHL(FHC).

_____State Library of OH, GRAVE LOCATIONS, OH SOLDIERS OF THE WAR OF 1812, The Library, Columbus, OH, 18 volumes of forms.

_____OH Adjutant General's Office, SOLDIERS IN THE WAR OF 1812, various original records, including a card file of participants, The Office, Columbus, OH. Also on microfilm at FHL(FHC).

_____A. P. Stevens, THE MILITARY HISTORY OF OH, Hardesty, New York, NY, 1887.

OHS, SLO, WRHS, PLC, OGS, ACPL, and FHL(FHC) have many of the above books (both the national and OH), and those held by FHL can be borrowed through FHC. The nationally-oriented books are likely to be found in many LGL, and some of the national and OH volumes will be found in RL. Finally, do not overlook records that might be in the counties, most notably discharge and grave records.

Many other War of 1812 record sources are given in the following work which goes into considerable detail for tracing your ancestors who served in this war:

_____Geo. K. Schweitzer, WAR OF 1812 GENEALOGY, The Author, 407 Ascot Court, Knoxville, TN 37923, 1988.

During the Indian Wars period (1817-98), OH personnel were involved in several conflicts. National Archives again has military records, pension records, and bounty land records, plus indexes to all three. NATF Form 80 should be used in accordance with the above instructions to obtain records. Also some OH counties have records on the Wars. These are indicated under the counties in Chapter 4.

The Mexican War was fought 1846-8, with over 7000 OH soldiers and many navy personnel participating. Form 80 should be employed to obtain military service, pension, and bounty land records from the National Archives. The WPA indexed rosters of the OH soldiers in this war. Published sources include:

____OH Roster Commission, OFFICIAL ROSTER OF SOLDIERS IN THE STATE OF OH IN THE WAR OF THE REBELLION, 1861-6, AND IN THE MEXICAN WAR, 1846-8, Werner Co., Akron, OH, 1886-95, 12 volumes. Mexican War participants listed in Volume 12.

____W. H. Robarts, MEXICAN WAR VETERANS: A COMPLETE ROSTER, 1846-8, Washington, DC, 1887.

____C. S. Peterson, KNOWN MILITARY DEAD DURING THE MEXICAN WAR, The Author, Baltimore, MD, 1957.

These source materials should be sought in places such as OHS, SLO, OGS, WRHS, FHL, LGL, and may be borrowed through FHC.

---

25. Military records: Civil War

There are several major keys to the well-over 310,000 Civil War veterans of the state of OH:

____OH Roster Commission, OFFICIAL ROSTER OF SOLDIERS [AND SAILORS] IN THE STATE OF OH IN THE WAR OF THE REBELLION, 1861-6, AND IN THE MEXICAN WAR, 1846-8, Werner Co., Akron, OH, 1886-95, 12 volumes. Use with WPA, INDEX, typescript, The Administration, Columbus, OH, 1939, 4 volumes. INDEX at OHS, SLO, and FHL(FHC).

____INDEX TO COMPILED SERVICE RECORDS OF VOLUNTEER UNION SOLDIERS WHO SERVED IN ORGANIZATIONS FROM THE STATE OF OH, National Archives Microfilm, Washington, DC, M552, 122 rolls of microfilm.

The indexes should be looked into for your ancestor's name. Upon finding him, you will discover listed alongside his name his regiment, battalion, or ship, as well as his company. This information is what is needed to locate the detailed records. The above indexes should be sought at OHS, SLO, WRHS, PLC, OGS, ACPL, and FHL. They are available through FHC or the microfilms may be borrowed on interlibrary loan from:

____American Genealogical Lending Library, PO Box 244, Bountiful, UT 84010.

Once you know your ancestor's military unit, you can write the following address for several copies of NATF Form 80:

____Military Service Records (NNCC), Washington, DC 20408.

When your forms come, fill them out, giving as much data as you can, especially all the information from the above indexes. Then check the military service box on one form and the pension record box on another, ask for all records, and mail the forms back. In a few weeks you will receive a notice of military record data and/or pension data along with a bill.

In addition, there are several volumes and an index which will be useful to investigate:

____W. Reid, OH IN THE WAR, 1861-5, Moore, Wilsbach, and Baldwin, Cincinnati, OH, 1868, 2 volumes. Regimental histories.

____THE UNION ARMY, Volume 2, Madison, WI, 1908, pp. 353-483. Histories of OH Union regiments.

____F. H. Dyer, A COMPENDIUM OF THE WAR OF THE REBEL-LION, National Historical Society, Dayton, OH, 1979, pp. 1472-1556. Union regimental histories.

____A. P. Stevens, THE MILITARY HISTORY OF OH, Hardesty, New York, NY, 1887.

____OH Adjutant General's Office, OFFICIAL ROSTER OF COLORED TROOPS OF THE STATE OF OH IN THE WAR OF THE REBELLION, 1861-6, The Office, Columbus, OH.

____W. L. Phillips, INDEX TO PENSIONERS OF 1883, Heritage Books, Bowie, MD, 1987.

____Mrs. D. Seitz, OH VETERANS HOME DEATH RECORDS, 1889-1983, Erie County Chapter, OGS, Sandusky, OH, 1985.

____OH Historical Society, VETERANS' GRAVE REGISTRATION FILE, compiled by the WPA, The Society, Columbus, OH. Also on ymicrofilm at FHL(FHC).

The books listed above and several other similar books are available at OHS, SLO, OGS, WRHS, ACPL, and FHL(FHC).

If you care to go into considerable detail in researching your OH Civil War ancestor, this book will be of considerable help:

____Geo. K. Schweitzer, CIVIL WAR GENEALOGY, The Author, 407 Ascot Court, Knoxville, TN 37923, 1989.

This work treats local, state, and national records, service and pension records, regimental and naval histories, enlistment rosters, hospital records, court-martial reports, burial registers, national cemeteries, gravestone allotments, amnesties, pardons, state militias, discharge papers, officer biographies, prisons, prisoners, battle sites, maps, relics, weapons, museums, monuments, memorials, deserters, black soldiers, Indian soldiers, and many other topics.

There is in the National Archives an index to the service records of the Spanish-American War. This index is also available at RBNA. Again a properly filled out and submitted NATF Form 80 will bring you both military service and pension records. It is also possible that you will find the following volumes useful:

___OH Adjutant General's Office, THE OFFICIAL ROSTER OF OH
SOLDIERS IN THE WAR WITH SPAIN, 1898-9, The Office,
Columbus, OH, 1916. Index available in OHS, Columbus, OH.
___J. J. Erwin, THE NAVAL RESERVES OF OH IN THE WAR WITH
SPAIN, 1898-9, Ward and Shaw, Cleveland, OH, 1899.
Records for World War I and subsequent wars may be obtained from:
___National Personnel Records Center, GSA (Military Records), 9700
Page Blvd., St. Louis, MO 63132.
There is also a 23-volumed publication on OH World War I participants:
___OH Adjutant General's Office, OFFICIAL ROSTER OF THE SOL-
DIERS, SAILORS, AND MARINES IN THE WORLD WAR,
1917-8, The Office, Columbus, OH, 1920, 23 volumes.

26. Mortuary records

Very few OH mortuary records have been transcribed or micro-filmed. This means that you must write directly to the mortuaries which you know or suspect were involved in burying your ancestor. Sometimes the death certificate will name the mortuary; sometimes it is the only one nearby; sometimes you will have to write several in order to ascertain which one might have done the funeral arrangements. Mortuaries for OH with their addresses are listed in the following volume:
___C. O. Kates, editor, THE AMERICAN BLUE BOOK OF FUNERAL
DIRECTORS, Kates-Boylston Publications, New York, NY, latest
issue.
This reference book will usually be found in the offices of most mor-tuaries. In all correspondence with mortuaries be sure to enclose an SASE.

27. Naturalization records

Before OH became a state (1803), it was the Northwest Territory (1787-1803). During 1776-1789, the original states instituted naturalization regulations and/or procedures applying to their own areas. These requirements usually specified a period of residence, an oath of allegiance, and sometimes a confession of Protestant religion, all to be taken in a court of law. In 1790, the US Congress passed a naturalization act, followed in 1802 by a more com-prehensive act. Although there were many modifying laws, the basic citizenship requirement until 1906 was that an alien to become a citizen, must live in the US 5 years, must file a declaration of intent, must wait two years, must then petition for naturalization, and finally take an oath of loyalty before a circuit or district court of the US, a supreme or district court of a territory, or any court of record of a state. The declaration of intent and the petition and oath-taking could occur in different courts. Following June 1906, about the same procedure was employed, but records and court actions were centralized by the US government. For this post-1906 period, write to the following address for a Form G-641, which you can use to request records:

___Immigration and Naturalization Service, 425 I St., Washington, DC 20536.

Prior to June 1906, the naturalization process could have taken place in a US, state, or local court. This often makes locating the records a fairly difficult process. What it means is that all possible court records must be gone through in the quest. Unfortunately, few indexes have been made, so this is almost a page-by-page endeavor. The most likely OH courts for these naturalizations are the county Courts of Common Pleas before 1852, the county District Courts after 1852, and the US District and US Circuit Courts. Other courts, however, must not be overlooked. The records are generally filed under headings such as declaration of intent, first papers, second papers, petitions, naturalization records, court journal, and court minutes. From 1855 to 1922, it is well to recognize that wives and children were automatically naturalized along with the husband.

Naturalization records for over 60 OH counties are on microfilm at OHS and FHL(FHC). Most of these are noted under the pertinent counties in Chapter 4. Others need to be sought in the counties and in the ONAHRC. County naturalization records are also to be found in genealogical journals. These articles are indexed in the following publications:

___C. W. Bell, OH GENEALOGICAL PERIODICAL INDEX, A COUNTY GUIDE, The Author, Youngstown, OH, latest edition.

___For periodicals published 1847-1985, then annually 1986-present, consult Allen County Public Library Foundation, PERIODICAL SOURCE INDEX, The Foundation, Fort Wayne, In, 1986-.

Many of the records of the US Circuit and District Courts for OH are in the Chicago Regional Branch of the National Archives. US District courts have operated from 1789 to the present. US Circuit Courts operated from 1789 to 1911, at which time their records were transferred to the US District Courts. The available records consist of:

___US Circuit and District Courts, NATURALIZATION INDEXES, Record Group 21, Cincinnati 1852-1942, Cleveland 1855-1906, Toledo 1869-1940, Chicago Branch, National Archives, 7358 South Pulaski Road, Chicago, IL 60629.

___US Circuit and District Courts, NATURALIZATION RECORDS, Record Group 21, Cincinnati 1852-1956, Cleveland 1855-1925, Columbus 1916-30, Dayton 1906-30, Toledo 1869-1900 and 1907-29, Declarations of Intent and Final Naturalizations,

Chicago Branch, National Archives, 7358 South Pulaski Road, Chicago, IL 60629.

---

28. Newspaper records

A number of original and micro-filmed newspapers are available for towns, cities, and counties of OH. A few of them have been indexed. These records are likely to contain information on births, deaths, marriages, anniversaries, divorces, family reunions, land sales, legal notices, ads of professionals and businesses, and local news. The largest OH collections are to be found in OHS, WRHS, and the Cincinnati Historical Society, both originals and microfilms being included. Available OH newspapers and their locations will be found listed in:

___C. S. Brigham, HISTORY AND BIBLIOGRAPHY OF AMERICAN NEWSPAPERS, 1690–1820, American Antiquarian Society, Worcester, MA, 1947, 1961, 2 volumes.

___W. Gregory, AMERICAN NEWSPAPERS, 1821–1936, H. W. Wilson Co., New York, NY, 1937.

___Library of Congress, NEWSPAPERS IN MICROFILM, US Library of Congress, Washington, DC, 1973; Supplements, 1978, 1979, etc.

___S. Gutgesell, GUIDE TO OH NEWSPAPERS, 1793–1973, OHS, Columbus, OH, 1976. Locations of over 3000 OH newspapers.

___OH Historical Society, CATALOG OF NEWSPAPERS AVAILABLE AT THE OHS, microfilm, OHS, Columbus, OH, 1990. For newspapers acquired by the OHS since 1990, consult them.

___N. G. Leggett and D. E. Smith, A GUIDE TO LOCAL GOVERN-MENT RECORDS AND NEWSPAPERS PRESERVED AT THE DEPARTMENT OF ARCHIVES AND SPECIAL COLLEC-TIONS, WRIGHT STATE UNIVERSITY, The University, Dayton, OH, 1987.

___M. Levinson, GUIDE TO NEWSPAPER HOLDINGS AT THE CENTER FOR ARCHIVAL COLLECTIONS, Bowling Green State University, Bowling Green, OH, 1987.

FHL, FHC, and RL have some OH newspapers. A few OH newspapers have been indexed. Some of these are listed in:

___A. C. Milner, NEWSPAPER INDEXES, Scarecrow Press, Metuchen, NJ, 1977, 1980, 1981, 3 volumes.

A few LL have newspaper indexes which are not listed in the above works, so it is always important to inquire.

Newspaper publication began in the Northwest Territory with the appearance of the CENTINEL OF THE NORTH-WESTERN TERRI-TORY in Cincinnati in 1793. Others followed in fairly rapid succession.

Abstracts of genealogical information from many of the earliest OH newspapers have been issued as:

___K. M. Green, PIONEER OH NEWSPAPERS, 1793-1818, Frontier Press, Galveston, TX, 1986/8, 2 volumes.

___M. B. Clegg, OH NEWSPAPER OBITUARY ABSTRACT BOOKS, 1812-70, The Author, Fort Wayne, IN, 1984, 4 volumes. Mah, Ott, Por, San, Tru.

___J. G. Herbert, INDEX OF DEATH AND MARRIAGE NOTICES APPEARING IN THE CINCINNATI DAILY GAZETTE, 1827-81, Heritage, Bowie, MD, 1992, 2 volumes.

___J. G. Herbert, INDEX TO DEATH AND OTHER NOTICES APPEARING IN THE CINCINNATI FREIE PRESSE, 1874-1920, Heritage, Bowie, MD, 1993, 2 volumes. Over 38,000 names.

___ANNALS OF CLEVELAND, MICROFICHE OF ABSTRACTS FROM 19TH CENTURY NEWSPAPERS, Bloch and Company, Cleveland, OH, 1982, indexed. Greatest emphasis on northeastern OH.

Not to be overlooked are the news letters and denominational newspapers of the various religious groups in OH. Many were published over considerable periods of time. These may be located in OHS. Newspaper abstracts also appear in genealogical journals. The periodical indexes mentioned in the previous section should be used to locate these useful materials.

---

29. Published genealogies

There are a large number of index volumes and microfilm indexes which list published genealogies at the national level. Among the larger ones which you might examine are:

___FHL and FHC, FAMILY HISTORY LIBRARY CATALOG, Surname index.

___F. Rider, AMERICAN GENEALOGICAL INDEX, Godfrey Memorial Library, Middletown, CT, 1942-52, 48 volumes (millions of references).

___F. Rider, AMERICAN GENEALOGICAL AND BIOGRAPHICAL INDEX, Godfrey Memorial Library, Middletown, CT, 1952-, over 190 volumes (millions of references).

___The Newberry Library, THE GENEALOGICAL INDEX OF THE NEWBERRY LIBRARY, G. K. Hall, Boston, MA, 1960, 4 volumes (500,000 names).

___The New York Public Library, DICTIONARY CATALOG OF THE LOCAL HISTORY AND GENEALOGY DIVISION OF THE NEW YORK PUBLIC LIBRARY, G. K. Hall, Boston, MA, 1974, 20 volumes (318,000 entries).

___M. J. Kaminkow, GENEALOGIES IN THE LIBRARY OF CON-
GRESS, Magna Carta, Baltimore, MD, 1976–86. (25,000 refer-
ences). Also see GENEALOGIES CATALOGED BY THE
LIBRARY OF CONGRESS SINCE 1986, Library of Congress,
Washington, DC, 1991.
___M. J. Kaminkow, COMPLEMENT TO GENEALOGIES IN THE
LIBRARY OF CONGRESS, Magna Carta, Baltimore, MD, 1981.
___J. Munsell's Sons, INDEX TO AMERICAN GENEALOGIES,
1771–1908, reprint, Genealogical Publishing Co., Baltimore, MD,
1967 (60,000 references).

The first index is available at FHL and all FHC. At least some of the
rest are held by OHS, SLO, WRHS, PLC, OGS, ACPL, FHL, FHC, most
RL, and some LGL.

For the state of OH, these volumes are likely to be of help since
most of them (with the exception those by Kaminkow) are largely eastern
and northern oriented. The best sources of published genealogies of
Ohioans are the Card Catalog, the special indexes, and the special
alphabetical files in OHS, SLO, WRHS, PLC, and ACPL. Surname listings
in card catalogs, special surname indexes, and family record files in RL
and LL should not be overlooked.

---

30. Regional publications

In addition to national,
state, and local publi-
cations, there are also
numerous regional publications which should not be
overlooked by any OH researcher. For the most part, these are volumes
which are basically historical in character, but are likely to carry much
genealogical information, sometimes incidentally, sometimes as addenda.
They vary greatly in accuracy and coverage, so it is well the treat the data
cautiously. In general, they cover specific regions which are made up of
many or a few OH counties. In deciding which ones of these books to
search for your forebears, you will need to make good use of the
historical detail and the maps of Chapter 1.

The following works are ones which should prove useful to you if
one or more deal with geographical areas of concern to you:
___I. W. Andrews, WASHINGTON COUNTY AND THE EARLY
SETTLEMENTS OF OH, Thomson, Cincinnati, OH, 1877.
___BIOGRAPHICAL HISTORY OF NORTHEASTERN OH, Lewis
Publishing Co., Chicago, IL, 1893, 2 volumes. Ash, Gea, Lak,
Mah, Tru.
___HISTORY OF THE UPPER OH VALLEY, Brant and Fuller,
Madison, WI, 1890–1, 4 volumes. Bel, Col, Jef.

____G. E. Carlyle and D. D. Davis, HISTORY OF PIONEER MEN AND PLANTS IN SOUTHERN OH AND KY, Authors, Portsmounth, OH, 1947.

____R. C. Downes, HISTORY OF LAKE SHORE OH, Lewis Historical Publishing Co., New York, NY, 1952, 3 volumes.

____W. A. Duff, HISTORY OF NORTH CENTRAL OH, Historical Publishing Co., Topeka, KS, 1931, 3 volumes. Ashl, Hur, Kno, Lor, Med, Ric, Way.

____N. W. Evans, A HISTORY OF SCIOTO COUNTY AND A PIONEER RECORD OF SOUTHERN OH, Unigraphic, Evansville, IN, 1975, 2 volumes.

____H. H. Hardesty, HISTORICAL AND GEOGRAPHICAL ENCY-CLOPEDIA OF NORTHWEST OH, Hardesty and Co, New York, NY, 1883.

____HISTORY OF HOCKING VALLEY, OH, Interstate Publishing Co., Chicago, IL, 1883, 2 volumes. Ath, Hoc, Vin.

____HISTORY OF THE LOWER SCIOTO VALLEY, OH, Interstate Publishing Co., Chicago, IL, 1884.

____HISTORY OF THE UPPER OH VALLEY, Brant and Fuller, 1890, 2 volumes.

____HISTORY OF WESTERN OH AND AUGLAIZE COUNTY, Unigraphic, Evansville, OH, 1977.

____J. C. Hover and J. D. Barnes, MEMOIRS OF THE MIAMI VALLEY, Law, Chicago, IL, 1920, 3 volumes. Editions for several counties were printed.

____J. O. Jones, SOUTHERN OH AND ITS BUILDERS, Southern OH Biographical Association, Cincinnati, OH, 1927.

____H. S. Knapp, HISTORY OF THE MAUMEE VALLEY, Blade, Toledo, OH, 1872. All, Cra, Def, Luc, Mer, Pau, Put, San, Sen, Wya.

____T. W. Lewis, HISTORY OF SOUTHEASTERN OH AND MUSK-INGUM VALLEY, 1788-1928, Clarke and Co., Chicago, IL, 1928, 3 volumes.

____Mahoning Valley Historical Society, HISTORICAL COLLECTIONS OF THE MAHONING VALLEY, The Society, Youngstown, OH, 1876.

____C. H. Mitchener, THE TUSCARAWAS AND MUSKINGUM VALLEYS, Maxwell, Columbus, OH, 1975.

____NORTHEASTERN OH BIOGRAPHICAL HISTORY, Lewis Publishing Co., New York NY, 1893. Ash, Lak, Gea.

____OH Historical Society, MIAMI VALLEY OF OH, LOCAL HISTORY AND GENEALOGY, OHS, Columbus, OH, 1921-39, 2 rolls of microfilm.

____OH Historical Society, WESTERN BOATMEN AND STEAMBOAT DIRECTORY, 1848-9, OHS, Columbus, OH, 1849.

____F. Maxwell, INDEX TO VOLUME TWO, 1795-1803, RECORDS OF WASHINGTON COUNTY, NORTHWEST TERRITORY, OH Genealogical Center, Columbus, OH, 1984.

____P. E. Rieger, THE UPPER OH VALLEY, A BIBLIOGRAPHY, Gateway Press, Baltimore, MD, 1983.

____O. G. Rust, HISTORY OF WEST CENTRAL OH, Historical Publishing Co., Indianapolis, IN, 1934, 3 volumes.

____W. E. Smith, HISTORY OF SOUTHWESTERN OH, THE MIAMI VALLEY, Lewis Historical Publishing Co., West Palm Beach, FL, 1964, 3 volumes.

____SOUTHEASTERN OH LOCAL AND FAMILY HISTORY SOURCES IN PRINT, Heritage Research, Atlanta, GA, 1977. For 22 counties in southern and southeastern OH.

____J. S. Stewart, HISTORY OF NORTHEASTERN OH, Historical Publishing Co., Indianapolis, IN, 1935, 3 volumes.

____H. T. Upton, HISTORY OF THE WESTERN RESERVE, Lewis Publishing Co., Chicago, IL, 1910, 3 volumes.

____C. S. Van Tassel, STORY OF THE MAUMEE VALLEY, TOLEDO, AND THE SANDUSKY REGION, Van Tassel, Chicago, IL, 1929, 4 volumes.

____W. H. Venable, FOOTPRINTS OF THE PIONEERS IN THE OH VALLEY, Heritage Books, Bowie, MD, 1987.

____G. V. R. Wickham, MEMORIAL TO THE PIONEER WOMEN OF THE WESTERN RESERVE, Ashtabula County Genealogical Society, Jefferson, OH, 1981, 5 parts, 2 volumes, indexed.

____W. W. Williams, HISTORY OF THE FIRELANDS, HURON, AND ERIE COUNTIES, 1879, Unigraphic, Evansville, IN, 1973. Over 14,000 entries, indexed.

____N. O. Winter, A HISTORY OF NORTHWEST OH, Lewis Publishing Co., Chicago, IL, 1917, 3 volumes.

____Western Reserve Historical Society, WOMEN IN THE WESTERN RESERVE BEFORE 1840, The Society, Cleveland, OH, 1976. About 75,000 entries.

31. Tax lists

Practically every OH county from the year of its formation collected tax from its residents annually. Records of those from whom tax was collected were kept, and fortunately, many of these tax lists have survived. Sometimes the tax lists are very simple, giving only the names of the taxpayers; at other times the lists also give the amount of property, its value, and its location. At still other times there are also tax record of taxes on personal property. The original tax records are in the CH and/or ONAHRC, there are many duplicates in OHS, and the FHL(FHC) has have microfilmed copies of many. Copies or originals of the earliest tax records are at the OHS: Washington County for 1800, VA Military

District for 1801, all counties 1806–1814 and 1816–38. For the period 1826–34, there are also personal property tax lists. Many counties have numerous tax records for the period of time after 1838. The tax lists available for the 88 OH counties are listed in Chapter 4. These are extremely valuable records, because when the tax records exist for long periods of time (as they often do), you can have a year-by-year accounting of your ancestor. The tax records often give indirect indications of death of a landowner, death of his widow, and distribution of the land to sons and daughters.

In addition to the original and microfilmed tax records, there are a number of books which contain many tax records, especially the earlier ones.

___M. Adams, SOUTHERN OH TAXPAYERS IN THE 1820s, Heritage Research, Jackson, OH, 1981.

___R. D. Craig, RESIDENT PROPRIETORS OF THE CT WESTERN RESERVE, AN OH TAX LIST OF 1804, The Author, Cincinnati, OH, 1963.

___R. V. Jackson, INDEX TO OH TAX LISTS, 1800–10, Accelerated Indexing Systems, Bountiful, UT, 1977. About 45,000 entries.

___G. M. Petty, OH 1810 TAX DUPLICATES, The Author, Columbus, OH, 1977.

___G. M. Petty, OH TAX DUPLICATES FOR 1812, card file, OGS, Mansfield, OH. Also on microfilm at OHS.

___G. M. Petty, INDEX OF THE OH 1825 TAX DUPLICATES, The Author, Columbus, OH, 1981.

___G. M. Petty, INDEX OF THE OH 1835 TAX DUPLICATES, The Author, Columbus, OH, 1987.

___E. W. Powell, EARLY OH TAX RECORDS, The Author, Akron, OH, 1971; use with SURNAME INDEX, The Compiler, Akron, OH, 1974. 130 tax lists, every early county included, about 1800–25.

There are quite a number of tax lists which have been published in genealogical journals. They may be located by looking in the following genealogical periodical indexes:

___C. W. Bell, OH GENEALOGICAL PERIODICAL INDEX, A COUNTY GUIDE, The Author, Youngstown, OH, latest edition.

___For periodicals published 1847–1985, then annually 1986–present, consult Allen County Public Library Foundation, PERIODICAL SOURCE INDEX, The Foundation, Fort Wayne, In, 1986-.

During and shortly after the Civil War, there were federal tax assessments on OH people. Some of these records are in the Chicago Branch of the National Archives:

___Internal Revenue Service, TAX ASSESSMENT LISTS, 1867–73, Record Group 58, Chicago Branch, National Archives, Chicago, IL.

32. Wills and probate records

When a person died leaving any property (the estate), it was necessary for the authorities in the county of residence to see that this property was properly distributed. If a will had been written (testate), its wishes were carried out; if no will was left (intestate), the law indicated to whom distribution had to be made. Throughout the distribution process, many records had to be kept. Up to 1852, these matters were managed by the Court of Common Pleas, afterwards by the Probate Court. In early years, copies of the wills and brief records of the proceedings were put into the regular court records. Later, they were usually recorded in books which may have carried many titles, containing such words as: accounts, administrator, appraisal, court of common pleas, minutes, record, estate, executor, guardian, inventory, probate, sales, settlement, will, and perhaps others. In addition to the books, there were usually folders (or packets or envelopes or files) in which the numerous detailed loose records pertaining to the estates were filed. The books carry references to the folders so that they can be found in the boxes or cabinets where they are filed. All of these records are quite valuable genealogically, because they generally mention the wife or husband, the children, and the spouses of the children. They may also mention the exact date of death, but if not, they indicate the approximate date. The records thereby serve, as very few others do, to solidly connect the generations.

The original books and file folders (packets, envelopes) of loose records are in the CH and/or the ONAHRC. OHS and the FHL(FHC) have microfilm copies of many of the books, and SLO, WRHS, PLC, and ACPL have transcripts of some of the books. A few transcripts are also available in RL, LGL, and LL. Very few of the loose records have been microfilmed or transcribed. Listed in Chapter 4 are the will and probate records available in the OH counties. In seeking records of this type, you need to realize that all books with any of the key words (accounts, administrator, appraisal, court of common pleas, minutes, record, estate, executor, guardian, inventory, probate, sales, settlement, will) need to be examined. Remember that quite often, especially in earlier years, estate records are mixed in with the regular court of common pleas records. Further, the titles on books may not be precise. For example, a book labelled simply Wills may also contain settlements, inventories, and sales. Or a book labelled Settlements may contain wills, executors, administrators, and inventories. The other court records also should be investigated because disputes over inherited land appear there.

A very useful index to OH wills, estates, and guardianships before 1851 is:

___C. W. Bell, OH WILLS AND ESTATES, 1790 TO 1850, The Author,
Youngstown, OH, 1981. About 100,000 names.
It is well for you to recognize that the Probate Court handled other
matters also. Of importance, are these: adoptions, birth and death (1867-
1908), insanity, marriage, name changes.

33. WPA works

The Works Progress Administration (WPA)
of the federal government established the
OH Historical Records Survey in 1936. The
purpose of the OH Survey was to inventory
state, county, municipal, and church records
of historical importance. In 1939, supervision of the project was taken
over by the OHS, and in 1941, OH State University became the sponsor.
The Survey ended in 1942, and the unpublished inventories were
deposited in the OHS, WRHS, and OH State University. The data which
the WPA Historical Records Survey accumulated are often very useful to
genealogists because they indicate where many records were located in
the period 1936-42. They, therefore, can alert you to what was available,
and can give you clues as to where to start in your search for them.
Remember that many of the items to which these works refer remain
where they were in 1936-42, but some have been moved to depositories
such as the OHS, ONAHRC, and various church record archives and/or
historical societies.

Among the materials which could be of assistance to you are the
following. Many of them are incomplete.
___WPA OH Historical Records Survey, INVENTORIES OF COUNTY
ARCHIVES OF OH, The Survey, Columbus, OH, 1936-42, 29
volumes. Include the counties: Ada, All, Ashl, Ath, Bro, Col,
Cuy, Fay, Fra, Gea, Ham, Han, Jac, Kno, Lak, Lor, Luc, Mad,
Mont, Pik, Ros, Sci, Sen, Sta, Sum, Tru, and Was. Unpublished
material on these other counties in OHS, Columbus, OH: Asht,
Aug, Bel, But, Car, Cha, Cla, Cle, Cli, Cos, Cra, Dar, Def, Del
Eri, Fai, Fay, Ful, Gal, Gre, Gue, Hard, Harr, Hen, Hig, Hoc,
Hol, Hur, Jef, Law, Lic, Log, Mah, Mar, Med, Mei, Mer, Mia,
Monr, Morg, Morr, Mus, Nob, Ott, Pau, Per, Pic, Por, Pre, Put,
Ric, San, She, Tus, Uni, Van, Vin, War, Way, Wil, Woo, and Wya.
Unpublished material on these other counties in OH University,
Athens, OH: Ath, Bel, Car, Gal, Gue, Harr, Hoc, Hol, Jef, Law,
Mei, Mia, Monr, Mor, Mus, Nob, Per, Tus, and Vin.
___WPA OH Historical Records Survey, INVENTORIES OF STATE
RECORDS BY AGENCY, The Survey, Columbus, OH, 1936-42.
Materials deposited in OHS, Columbus, OH. Those of special
genealogical interest include the Records of Adjutant General,
Attorney General, Department of Education, Executive Depart-
ment, Department of Health, Judicial Department, Department of

Public Welfare, Secretary of State, Department of Taxation, and the Treasurer.

___WPA OH Historical Records Survey, INVENTORIES OF MUNICI-PAL RECORDS, incomplete, The Survey, Columbus, OH, 1936–42. Materials on municipal records inventoried in the following counties are deposited in OHS, Columbus, OH: Ada, All, Asht, Ath, Aug, Bel, Bro, But, Car, Cha, Cla, Cle, Cli, Col, Cos, Cra, Cuy, Dar, Def, Del, Fai, Fay, Fra, Ful, Gal, Gue, Ham, Han, Hard, Harr, Hen, Hig, Hoc, Hol, Hur, Jac, Jef, Kno, Lak, Law, Lic, Log, Lor, Luc, Mad, Mah, Mar, Mei, Mer, Mia, Monr, Mont, Morg, Morr, Mus, Nob, Ott, Pic, Pre, Ric, Ros, San, Sci, Sen, She, Sta, Sum, Tru, Tus, Uni, Van, Vin, War, Was, Way, Wil, Woo, and Wya. Materials on municipal records inventoried in the following towns is deposited in OH University, Athens, OH: Albany, Amesville, Athens, Bartnesville, Beallsville, Belle Valley, Belmont, Belpre, Bergholz, Bethesda, Beverly, Brookside, Buchtel, Cadiz, Caldwell, Clarington, Coal Grove, Coolville, Corning, Crooksville, Crown City, Dexter City, Flushing, Gallipolis, Glenmont, Glouster, Hopedale, Ironton, Jamesville, Jacksonville, Jerusalem, Jewett, Junction Cityd, Killbuck, Lewisville, Logan, Lowell, McArthur, McConnelsville, Macksburg, Malta, Marietta, Middleport, Miltonsburg, Morristown, Nashville, Nelsonville, New Athens, New Straitsville, New Matamoras, Pomeroy, Racine, Renville, Rio Grande, Roseville, St. Clairsville, Salem, Shadyside, Somerset, South Zanesville, Stafforrd, Syracuse, Thornville, Vinton, Woodsfield, and Zaleski.

___WPA OH Historical Records Survey, INVENTORIES OF CHURCH RECORDS BY COUNTY, incomplete, The Survey, Columbus, OH, 1936–42. Materials on church records inventoried in the following counties are deposited in OHS, Columbus, OH: Ath, Bel, Car, Cos, Gal, Gue, Harr, Hoc, Hol, Jac, Jef, Law, Mei, Mia, Monr, Morg, Mus, Nob, Per, Tus, Vin, and Was. Materials on church records inventoried in the following counties are deposited in OH University, Athens, OH: Ath, Bel, Car, Cos, Gal, Gue, Harr, Hoc, Hol, Jac, Jef, Law, Mei, Mia, Monr, Morg, Mus, Nob, Per, Tus, Vin, and Was.

Chapter 3

RECORD LOCATIONS

1. Introduction

The purpose of this chapter is to describe for you the major genealogical record repositories for OH records. These repositories are of two major types, libraries and archives. In general, libraries hold materials which have been published in printed, typescript, photocopied, and microfilm (microcard, microfiche) forms. Archives, on the other hand, are repositories for original records, largely in manuscript (hand-written) form, but also often as microfilm copies. Usually, libraries will have some original materials, and archives will have some published materials, but the predominant character of each is as indicated. When visiting and making use of the materials of repositories, there are several rules which almost all of them have. (1) You are required to check all overcoats, brief cases, and packages. (2) You are required to present some identification and to sign a register or fill out a form. (3) There is to be no smoking, no eating, no loud talk, and the use of pencils only. (4) All materials are to be handled with extreme care, with no injury to or defacing of any of them. (5) Materials are usually not to be returned to the stacks or drawers from which they came, but are to be returned to designated carts, tables, or shelves. (6) Upon leaving you should submit all materials for inspection and/or pass through security devices.

Libraries and archives have finding aids to facilitate locating the records which they hold. These aids are usually alphabetically arranged lists or indexes according to names or locations or subjects or authors or titles, or combinations of these, or they may be by dates. They consist of computer catalogs, card catalogs, microform catalogs, printed catalogs, typed catalogs and lists, various indexes, inventories, calendars, and tables of contents. In using these aids, especially computer, card, and microform catalogs, they must be searched in as many ways as possible to ensure that you extract everything from them. These ways are by name, by location, by subject, by author, by title, and sometimes by date. Sometimes certain catalogs are arranged by only one or two of these categories, but otherwise be sure and search them for all that are applicable. To help you to recall these categories, remember the word SLANT, with S standing for subject, L for location, A for author, N for name, and T for title. This is not, however, the order in which they should be searched for the maximum efficiency. They should be searched N-L-S-A-T. First, search the catalog for N(name), that is, for the surnames of all your OH forebears. Second, search the catalog for L(location), that is, look under all places where your ancestor lived (OH state, region, county, city, town, village), but especially the county, city, and town. Examine <u>every</u> entry in order to make sure you miss nothing. <u>Third</u>, look under appropriate S(subject) headings, such as the titles related to the sections in Chapter 2 [Bible, biography, birth, cemetery, census, church denomination, church name, court, Daughters of the American Revolution, death, divorce, emigration, ethnic group name (such as Germans, Huguenots, Irish), genealogy, historical records, immigration, marriage, US-history-Revolutionary War, US-history-War of 1812, US-history-Civil War, naturalization, newspaper, pensions, tax, will], but never neglecting these [biography, deeds, epitaphs, family records, genealogy, registers of births etc., wills].   Then <u>finally</u>, look under A(author) and/or T(title) for books mentioned in the sections of Chapter 2 which you need to examine.

When you locate references in finding aids to materials you need to examine, you will usually find that a numbered or alphabetized or combined code accompanies the listing. This is the access code which you should copy down, since it tells you where the material is located. For books it will usually be a code which refers to shelf positions. For microfilms, it usually refers to drawers and reel numbers. For manuscripts, it usually refers to folders, files, or boxes. In some repositories, the materials will be out on shelves or in cabinets to which you have access. In other repositories you will need to give the librarian or archivist a call slip on which you have written the title and code for the material so that it can be retrieved for you. In the microfilm areas of repositories you will find microform readers which attendants can help you with, if necessary.

Never leave a library or archives without discussing your research with a librarian or archivist. These people are trained specialists who know their collections and the ways for getting into them. And they can often suggest innovative approaches to locating data relating to your progenitors. They also can usually guide you to other finding aids. When you do discuss your work with librarians and archivists, please remember that they are busy people with considerable demands on their time. So be brief, get to the point, and don't bore them with irrelevant detail. They will appreciate this, and you and others will get more and better service from them.

In general, you cannot expect to do much of your genealogy by corresponding with libraries and archives. The reason is that the hardworking professionals who run these repositories have little time to give to answering mail. This is because of the heavy demands of serving the institutions which employ them, of maintaining the collection, and of taking care of patrons who visit them. Some simply cannot reply to mail requests. Others will answer one brief question which can be quickly looked up in a finding aid, but none of them can do even brief research for you. If you do write them, make your letter very brief, get right to the point, enclose an SASE, and be prepared to wait. Repositories will generally not recommend researchers you can hire, but they will sometimes provide you with a list of researchers. Such a list will bear no warranty from the repository, and they in no way have any responsibility toward either you or the researcher, because they are not in the business of certifying searchers.

As mentioned at the beginning of Chapter 2, there are numerous record repositories in OH which will be of immense value in your genealogical research. The best collections of OH materials are to be found in the following repositories:

___(OHS) Archives-Library Division, OH Historical Society, 1985 Velma Avenue, Columbus, OH 43211. Original, microfilmed, and published national, county, municipal, and private records.

___(SLO) Genealogy Division, State Library of OH, 65 South Front Street, Columbus, OH 43266-0334. Published national, county, municipal, and private records.

___(FHL) Family History Library, Genealogical Library of the Church of Jesus Christ of Latter-day Saints, 35 North West Temple, Salt Lake City, UT 84150. Microfilmed and published national, county, municipal, and private records.

___(FHC) Family History Center(s), over 1700 of them, located all over the world. They are local branch affiliates of the Family History Library (FHL). They can be found in most major US cities, including 10 in OH. Most of the microfilmed national, county, municipal, and private records held by the FHL can be borrowed through the FHC.

___(ONAHRC) OH Network of American History Research Centers, seven Centers located at University of Akron, Wright State University in Dayton, University of Cincinnati, Western Reserve Historical Society in Cleveland, OH Historical Society in Columbus, Bowling Green State University, and OH University. Original, microfilmed, and published regional, county, and private records.

___(WRHS) Western Reserve Historical Society Library, 10825 East Boulevard, Cleveland, OH 44106. Published and microfilmed national, county, municipal, and private records.

___(PLC) Public Library of Cincinnati and Hamilton County, 800 Vine Street, Cincinnati, OH 45202-2071. Published and microfilmed national, county, municipal, and private records.

___(OGS) OH Genealogical Society Library, 34 Sturges Avenue, Mansfield, OH 44906. Published and some microfilmed national, county, municipal, and private records.

____(ACPL) Allen County Public Library, Genealogical Department, 900 Webster Street, Fort Wayne, IN 46802. Published and micro-filmed national, county, municipal, and private records.

____(RL) Regional Libraries in OH which hold larger genealogical collections than are usually held by most local libraries. Published and some microfilmed regional, county, and local private records.

____(LL) Local Libraries in the cities and towns of the OH counties. These include county, city, town, and private libraries. Published county, city, and local private records.

____(LR) Local Repositories which have special types of records in counties, cities, and towns : historical societies, genealogical societies, record archives and institutes, museums, cemetery offices, organizations, mortuaries, and newspaper offices.

____(CH) County Court Houses in the county seats of the 88 OH counties. Original and microfilmed county records.

Records which are national (federal) and those which are state-wide in scope have been treated in detail in Chapter 2. The locations of the records have also been given. Records which are basically county-wide in scope were treated generally in Chapter 2, and detailed listings of those available will be given in Chapter 4.

Most of the original county records referred to in Chapter 2 and listed in detail under the counties in Chapter 4 are stored in the court houses and/or in the seven ONAHRC (OH Network of American History Research Centers). The locations of the ONAHRC are indicated above, and the court houses are located in the county seats which are listed along with their zip codes in Chapter 4. The original records usually consist of variously-labelled books (usually handwritten), files with file folders in them, and boxes with large envelopes or file folders in them. The records are generally stored in the offices of various county officials, or in the case of older records they may be found in special storage vaults. In many instances, they are readily accessible. In a few cases, they are put away so that they are very difficult to get out and use. The records which will most likely be found in the county court houses include the following, these categories being taken largely from the WPA inventories:

____Auditor: assessment, enumerations of the handicapped, justice of the peace records, military bounties, military exemptions, military personnel enumerations, militia rolls, relief, school enumerations, tax lists, veteran burials.

____Clerk of Courts: case files, chancery records, civil case records, court of common pleas records (see below), criminal case records, dockets, journals, jury lists, order books, partition records, probate records (before 1852), supreme court records.

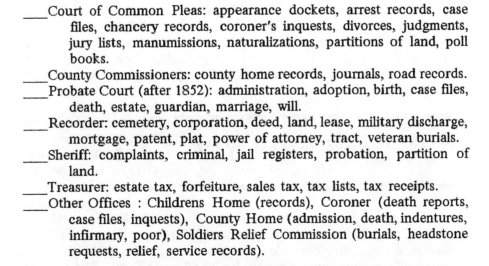

____Court of Common Pleas: appearance dockets, arrest records, case files, chancery records, coroner's inquests, divorces, judgments, jury lists, manumissions, naturalizations, partitions of land, poll books.

____County Commissioners: county home records, journals, road records.

____Probate Court (after 1852): administration, adoption, birth, case files, death, estate, guardian, marriage, will.

____Recorder: cemetery, corporation, deed, land, lease, military discharge, mortgage, patent, plat, power of attorney, tract, veteran burials.

____Sheriff: complaints, criminal, jail registers, probation, partition of land.

____Treasurer: estate tax, forfeiture, sales tax, tax lists, tax receipts.

____Other Offices : Childrens Home (records), Coroner (death reports, case files, inquests), County Home (admission, death, indentures, infirmary, poor), Soldiers Relief Commission (burials, headstone requests, relief, service records).

Once you have located the county in which your ancestor lived, it is usually not a good idea to go there first. It is best to explore the microfilmed, transcribed, and published copies of the records at some central repository such as OHS–SLO, WRHS, PLC, ACPL, and FHL(FHC). (OHS–SLO are hyphenated to remind you that both may be visited together since both are in Columbus.) This is because it is the business of these repositories to make the records available to you, but the primary task of the county officials and employees at the court houses is to conduct the record keeping task as an aid to regulating the society and keeping the law. Therefore, it is best not to encroach upon their time and their good graces until you have done as much work elsewhere as possible. Most of the major record books have been micro-filmed or transcribed so you can go through them nicely at OHS–SLO, WRHS, PLC, ACPL, and FHL(FHC). Or you can hire a researcher to do the investigating for you if a trip is not workable or would be too ex-pensive. Most of the contents of the case files, however, have not been copied. Hence, after doing work at OHS–SLO, WRHS, PLC, ACPL, and FHL(FHC) you then need to make a trip to the county (LL, LR, CH) and possibly to the ONAHRC, or hire a researcher to do so for you. In general, you will find the people there very helpful and cooperative, and often they will make photocopies for you or will give you access to a copying machine. It is usually best to visit the LL before going to the CH and the ONAHRC, and do not forget the many other possible LR in the counties.

Researchers who are near OHS–SLO, WRHS, PLC, ACPL, FHL, FHC, or the CH in the various counties will be listed in:

____G. B. Everton, Jr., editor, GENEALOGICAL HELPER, Everton Pub-lishers, Logan, UT, latest Jul–Aug issue.

In addition, staff members at OHS-SLO, WRHS, PLC, ACPL, FHL, and the LL in the various counties will often send you a list of researchers if you will dispatch a request and an SASE to them. Do not write the officials in the CH for researcher recommendations since they generally deem this a matter to be handled by the LL and therefore are ordinarily unable to help you.

2. The OH Historical Society (OHS)

The Archives-Library Division of the OH Historical Society (OHS) is composed of the OH State Archives (over 31,000 cubic feet of records) and a large associated library (about 130,000 books, 41,000 microfilms, and 20,000 volumes of newspapers) for OH historical and genealogical research. The OHS serves as one of the ONAHRC, and functions as the coordinating agency for all seven of them. The OHS is located at the intersection of Interstate 71 and 17th Avenue north of the downtown part of Columbus, OH. The mailing address is 1982 Velma Avenue, Columbus, OH 43211, and the telephone number is 1-(614)-297-2300. The hours of operation are 9am-5pm Tuesday-Saturday. Please note carefully that they are not open on Monday and Sunday. It is also important that you recognize that the opening times may change, so do not fail to call before you go. There is a motel very close to OHS, this being the Days Inn at the Fairgrounds, 1700 Clara Street, Columbus, OH 43211, [Phone 1-(614)-299-4300 or 1-(800)-325-2525]. The next nearest motel is two miles away, it being the Holiday Inn on the Lane, 328 West Lane Avenue, Columbus, OH 43201 [Phone 1-(614)-294-4848 Or 1-(800)-465-4329]. There is an ample free parking lot at the OHS.

Before going to OHS, you should make good use of two finding aids to the collections:
____S. Mettle, N. Weller, and C. W. Bell, GENEALOGICAL RESEARCHER'S MANUAL WITH SPECIAL REFERENCES FOR USING THE OHS LIBRARY, Franklin County Chapter, OGS, Columbus, OH, 1983. Can be purchased from Franklin County Chapter, OGS, PO Box 2503, Columbus, OH 43216.
____A. Lentz, GUIDE TO THE MANUSCRIPTS AT THE OHS, OHS, Columbus, OH, 1971. Holdings since 1971 are listed in a card catalog in OHS, but this 1971 book will show you many of the available materials.

When you enter the OHS, check in at the Visitor Desk and tell them that you want to work in the library. They will ask you to fill out a retgistration form and will then give you an identification card and a copy of the registration form. Take the elevator to the third floor, go in the library door, and present your identification card at the Reception Desk just inside the door. The attendant will ask you to put bags, briefcases, cameras, coats, purses, and umbrellas in a locker provided for you. You may take notes and pencils into the research area. Now begin to look around. You will find yourself in a large room with a Reference Desk situated to your left in the middle of the wall. Take a seat at one of the numerous study tables, and carefully read the Library Use Rules on the back of your copy of the registration form. After this, walk over to the center of the Reference Desk, then turn around facing out into the room. You will be looking north, with east on your right, west on your left, and south behind you. Notice that all four walls have book shelves filled with volumes. The shelves on the south (behind you) contain the following types of items:

____(S-1) current periodicals,

____(S-2) telephone books,

____(S-3) genealogical guidebooks,

____(S-4) city directories for Cincinnati and Columbus,

____(S-5) general reference works,

____(S-6) atlases,

____(S-7) military pensioner lists,

____(S-8) dictionaries, encyclopedias,

____(S-9) biographical works.

```
                        North

        [NW]      [NE] [NE]
                            [EC]
   W                        [EC]   E
   e                        [EC]   a
   s    [WC]                [EC]   s
   t                         [SE]  t
        [SW]                [SE]
              | Ref Dsk |

        South          Entry
```

On the west wall (to your left) will be found these types of materials:

____(W-1) biographical works,

____(W-2) Rider's AMERICAN GENEALOGICAL BIOGRAPHICAL INDEX,

____(W-3) DAR lineage books and DAR indexes,

____(W-4) ship passenger lists and indexes,

____(W-5) immigration records and indexes,

____(W-6) general historical works,

____(W-7) basic record volumes and periodicals for OH and for other states, and

____(W-8) the valuable periodical indexes PERIODICAL SOURCE INDEX (PERSI) and Bell's OH GENEALOGICAL PERIODI-CAL INDEX.

On the north wall (in front of you), these kinds of materials are shelved:

____(N-1) OH county histories,

____(N-2) OH regional histories,

____(N-3) OH county directories, and

____(N-4) OH city directories for cities other than Cincinnati and Columbus.

The shelves occupying the east wall (on your right) contain:

____(E-1) OH city directories,

____(E-2) general reference works, and

____(E-3) newspaper indexes.

Now, take a look at the numerous cabinets and book islands located just off the walls around the room. Beginning on your left in the southwest corner (SW) just out from the walls is a large island of cabinets. We will call them SW. The major items which these SW cabinets contain are:

___(SW-1) microfilms of OH censuses 1820–1920,

___(SW-2) microfilms of OH census Soundex/Miracode indexes 1880, 1900–20,

___(SW-3) microfilms of OH tax records 1800–38, only 1800–12, and 1825 indexed,

___(SW-4) microfilms of OH Civil War muster rolls,

___(SW-5) microfilms of the OH Graves Registration File,

___(SW-6) microfilms of OH local (OH counties and cities) governmental records,

___(SW-7) microfilms of OH state governmental records,

___(SW-8) microfiche of the FHL's INTERNATIONAL GENEALOGICAL INDEX, and

___(SW-9) microfiche of the Boston Transcript's Genealogical Columns.

Next, glance at the set of cabinets just out from the center of the west wall. This set we will call the west-central or WC cabinets. They contain the following:

___(WC-1) card catalog of OH local (OH counties and cities) governmental records,

___(WC-2) card catalog of OH state governmental records,

___(WC-3) card catalog of the small picture collection,

___(WC-4) card catalog of the audio-visual collection,

___(WC-5) card catalog of subjects in the manuscript collection,

___(WC-6) card catalog of titles in the manuscript collection,

___(WC-7) inventories of items in the audio-visual collection,

___(WC-8) inventories of manuscripts on microfilm, and

___(WC-9) inventories of manuscripts in the manuscript collection.

Further along the west wall, near the northwest corner, there is a high counter with book shelves beneath it. In accordance with its location, this counter will be called NW. The items on its shelves are:

___(NW-1) OH census indexes 1820–80,

___(NW-2) OH 1850 mortality census schedule index,

___(NW-3) census indexes for many other states,

___(NW-4) published indexes to OH tax lists, and

___(NW-5) indexed OH war rosters for the Revolution, War of 1812, Mexican War, Civil War, Spanish-American War, and World War I.

In the northeast corner, there are two cabinets which will be called NE. These have the following types of things in them:

___(NE-1) surname index to many OH county atlases,

___(NE-2) index to the periodical OLD NORTHWEST GENEAL-
OGICAL QUARTERLY,

___(NE-3) index to the periodical OH HISTORY, and

___(NE-4) surname index to many OH county histories.

Along the center of the east wall, you will see four cabinets which will be called EC (east-central). The contents of these cabinets are:

___(EC-1) a large card catalog to printed items in the library [books, periodicals, pamphlets, brochures, print-outs] <items marked R are on the shelves, others must be requested>,

___(EC-2) a card catalog labelled The Old Map Catalog [sections by area or locality, subject, title, author/publisher], and

___(EC-3) a card catalog labelled The New Map Catalog [sections by area or locality, subject, title, author/publisher].

In the southeast corner, which is where the entrance door is located, there are two important items, which we will designate SE. One is a sizable floor rack containing lists of newspapers held by the library, and the other is a cabinet with OH death certificate information.

___(SE-1) several listings of newspapers held by the library [one according to city, one according to county, one by title],

___(SE-2) an index to OH death certificates 1908-38, and

___(SE-3) OH death certificates 1908-36.

In order to use the abundant resources of the OHS to the fullest extent, you should _first_ examine those resources which provide large listings of _surnames_. Then, you should examine those finding aids which will lead you to other available records which might contain data on your ancestor. These will be chiefly finding aids which list records under your ancestor's locality (county, city, OH). So, your _first_ search is for your ancestor's _name_ in those of the following name indexes which you judge to be pertinent:

___(SW-8) International Genealogical Index,

___(EC-1) card catalog to the library,

___(NW-1) 1820-30-40-50-60-70 census indexes,

___(NW-2) 1850 mortality census schedule index,

___(SW-2) 1880, 1900-10-20 census indexes,

___(EC-1) Bell's book OH WILLS AND ESTATES 1790-1850

___(NE-4) surname index to some OH county histories,

___(NW-4) 1800-12, 1825 tax list indexes,

___(SW-5) veterans' grave index,

___(NW-5) OH war roster indexes,

___(W-8) periodical indexes, PERSI and Bell,

___(NE-1) surname index to some OH county atlases,

___(NE-2) index to Old Northwest Genealogical Quarterly

___(NE-3) index to OH History,

___(SE-2) index to deaths,

___(S-4), (N-4), and (E-1) city directories,
___(S-6) atlases,
___(W-2) Rider's AMERICAN GENEALOGICAL BIOGRAPHICAL INDEX, and
___(W-3) DAR lineage book and patriot indexes.

Your next or second step is to examine a number of finding aids to locate other records which might give data on your ancestor. This means searching the following finding aids for the localities in which your ancestor lived. Look at every card or item listed under your ancestor's county, town, and/or city. Then you should make your way carefully through all the many listings under the state of OH to see if any are pertinent.

___(WC-1) local governmental records held by the OHS,
___(WC-2) state governmental records held by the OHS,
___(EC-1) card catalog to the OHS library, look for records of the following sorts: atlas, Bible, biography, birth, cemetery, church, city directory, city history, county history, court, DAR, death, deed, divorce, ethnic, family history, gazetteer, genealogical periodical, genealogy, map, land, marriage, military, mortuary, naturalization, newspaper abstracts, probate, regional histories, registers of births, tax, and will,
___(WC-5) index to the manuscript collection,
___(EC-2) and (EC-3) map catalogs,
___(SE-1) newspaper holdings, and
___(W-8) periodical indexes, PERSI and Bell.

Now you are ready to take the third and the fourth steps to complete your coverage of the OHS resources. The third step is to check the appropriate items for any specialized subjects under which you think you might find information on your forebear. The headings of sections in Chapter 2 will suggest some of these subjects, and examples of others might be millwrights, Germans, Methodist Episcopal Church, epitaphs, War of 1812, underground railroad. The items that should be checked are EC-1, WC-5, and W-8. Fourth, look carefully at the large number of books and other items that are listed in the many sections of Chapter 2. As you find books and other items which you have not seen, locate them in the card catalog by author and/or title.

Do not fail to discuss your research with one of the competent staff of the OHS. Be brief, because their time is valuable. You will find that they will be able to save you much time and considerable effort. Remember, however, that they cannot do your work for you, they can only give you guidance.

3. The State Library of OH (SLO)

The State Library of OH (SLO) has a Genealogy Division which collects published historical and genealogical materials relating to the states of OH, WV, KY, and the colonial states. There are over 14,000 volumes and over 15,000 microforms. Included in the holdings are atlases, Bible records, cemetery records, censuses and their indexes, church records, DAR transcripts, county histories, family genealogies, family records, tax records, vital records (birth, marriage, death), and will records. The SLO is located in downtown Columbus, OH, near the Capitol, in the OH Departments Building, Room 308, at 65 South Front Street, Columbus, OH 43215. Its telephone number is 1-(614)-466-8050, and the hours of operation are 8am-5pm Monday-Thursday, and 9am-5pm Friday. Please note carefully that they are not open on Saturday and Sunday. It is also important that you recognize that the opening times may change, so do not fail to call before you go. Hotels near the SLO include the Quality Hotel City Centre, 4th and East Town Streets, Zip 43215 [Phone 1-(614)-221-3281], the Great Southern Hotel, Main and High Streets, Zip 43215 [Phone 1-(614)-228-3800], the Guest Quarters Suite Hotel, 50 South Front Street, Zip 43215 [1-(614)-228-4600], and the Hyatt on Capitol Square, 75 East State Street, Zip 43215 [Phone 1-(614)-228-1234].

Before going to SLO, it will save you time and energy if you have taken a careful look at a very comprehensive inventory of the OH holdings in the library. Pay particular attention to the listings under your progenitor's county and all the listings under the state of OH:

___P. Khouw and the SLO Staff, COUNTY BY COUNTY IN OH GENEALOGY, SLO, Columbus, OH, 1992 or latest edition. Can be purchased from the SLO at the address above.

You will enter the building on the first floor. Take the elevator to the third floor, walk down the hall to Room 308, and enter. Check in at the desk just to your left. At one corner of the desk is a Computer Catalog with a program called OHIOlink in it. As you stand at the desk, you will be viewing a long room running from far to your right to far to your left. The section to your left is filled with book shelves and stacks bearing the library's large collection. Directly in front of you is a Name Catalog. To your right you will see a few more book stacks, then an area with census indexes, then several microform readers and microform cabinets, and finally two computers. One computer has the International Genealogical Index of the FHL, and the other is a CDROM-equipped computer with numerous CDROM records, including OH marriages 1789-1863, and the Social Security Death Index.

The key to the large holdings of the SLO is the OHIOlink Computer Catalog. It should be searched first for all the OH names you are seeking. Also search these names in the International Genealogical Index, the Name Catalog, the census indexes, and periodical indexes (PERSI and Bell). Then seacrch the OHIOlink Computer Catalog for all the localities (county, city, state of OH) in which your ancestors lived. Take note of all pertinent records. Third, search the OHIOlink Computer Catalog for subjects which might lead you to information on your forebears. Suggestions for these subjects are the titles of the sections in Chapter 2, but also look under Registers of births, etc. Finally, search the OHIOlink Computer Catalog for the authors and/or titles of the many books mentioned in Chapter 2. These searches will lead you to the materials in the SLO which have the greatest possibility of adding to your ancestral data.

Do not fail to discuss your research with one of the competent staff of the SLO. Be brief, because their time is valuable. You will find that they will be able to save you much time and considerable effort. Because of the demands on them, the staff can only give you guidance, they cannot do your work for you.

4. The Western Reserve Historical Society (WRHS)

The Western Reserve Historical Society Library (WRHS) is one of the ten or twelve largest genealogical libraries in the US. It is located at 10825 East Boulevard, Cleveland, OH 44106. The library is open from 9am–5pm Tuesday–Saturday. Please note that the library is closed on Sunday and Monday. The telephone number is 1-(216)-721-5722. The resources of this repository are especially rich for the states northeast, east, and southeast of Cleveland. Do not forget to call before you go, in order to make sure that the opening times have not been changed. The library is located in the eastern part of Cleveland near the campus of Case Western Reserve University. There is a small daily fee for use of the facilities. The nearest accommodations are at the Omni International Hotel, Carnegie and East 96th Street, Cleveland, OH 44106, with the telephone number being 1-(216)-791-1900 or 1-(800)-THE-OMNI. Some useful guides to some of the collections in WRHS are:

___K. J. Pike, A GUIDE TO THE MANUSCRIPTS AND ARCHIVES OF THE WRHS, The Society, Cleveland, OH, 1972, with K. J. Pike, SUPPLEMENT FOR MANUSCRIPT COLLECTIONS ACCESSIONED 1970-1986, The Society, Cleveland, OH, 1987.

____The Staff, WRHS, A GUIDE TO THE SHAKER MANUSCRIPTS IN THE LIBRARY OF THE WRHS, The Society, Cleveland, OH, 1974.

____J. J. Grabowski and L. K. Arnold, A GUIDE TO JEWISH HISTORY SOURCES IN THE HISTORY LIBRARY OF THE WRHS, The Society, Cleveland, OH, 1983.

____B. Stith, A GUIDE TO LOCAL GOVERNMENTAL RECORDS IN THE LIBRARY OF THE WRHS, The Society, Cleveland, OH, 1981.

When you enter the main door of the WRHS building, you will find yourself in the Museum Foyer. Walk straight ahead down a long hall to double doors which lead to the library. Enter the library, register at the desk on your left, leave all purses, coats, umbrellas, briefcases, packages, bags, and cameras in the nearby lockers, then request copies of the Library Regulations and the Profile of Genealogy Collections. Find you a seat at the work tables in the center of the large room and read these two sheets thoroughly. Notice particularly that (1) you must not reshelve items, (2) all materials are to be handled carefully, (3) call slips must be used to request materials not on the open shelves, and (4) for manuscript users, a manuscript reader sheet must be filled out and its instructions must be strictly followed. The most important points regarding the usage of microforms are (1) you must sign up at the microforms desk in order to use a reader, (2) if there is a demand for readers, there is a one-hour time limit, (3) microforms are to be returned to the wooden truck, not to their drawers. For copying, please consult with the persons at the Main Desk.

Now, look around just a bit to get your bearings with regard to the layout of the library. The door where you entered is on the south, so when you are standing in the entrance, north is straight ahead, east is on your right, and west is on your left. Notice that the rest rooms are adjacent to the Main Desk and to the lockers in the southwest corner of the room. Next, look at the general layout of the long library room which runs from the door at the south end to the large semi-circular window at the north end. In the southeast corner of the room, there are more lockers and a small lunch room. You may use the lunch room from 10am–12noon and 1:30pm–3pm for conversation or snacking, however no food is available there, only a soft-drink machine. Now, look just in front of the Main Desk, and you will see 3 large card catalog cabinets, the 1st one housing the Manuscripts Card Catalog, and the 2nd and 3rd ones housing the Main Card Catalog to Published Materials. Over in the southeast corner from these 3 large catalog cabinets, you will observe 3 small card catalog cabinets. And then, you will notice a small table immediately north of the three large cabinets. These six cabinets (3 large, 3 small) and the small table hold the major finding aids at the

WRHS. They, and the microforms guide, will be your keys to WRHS's vast holdings.

Continue your survey of the library by noticing the large microform area over against the west wall. This area contains several microform storage cabinets and numerous microform readers. Along the far wall of this area (the north wall), there are shelves holding many published census indexes. On the opposite wall of this area (the south wall) there is the Microforms Room Guide. The entire far end (north end) of the large library room is occupied by book stacks and atlas shelves (northeast corner). Here you will find many of the published materials referenced in the Main Card Catalog. Those referenced in the Main Card Catalog but not in the open stacks can be obtained by submitting a call slip at the Main Desk. The rapid and efficient use of a library is dependent largely upon your facility with its finding aids. So it is these to which we now turn.

The major finding aids in the WRHS, which have been located for you above are as follows:

___(MainCC) The Main Card Catalog, 2 large cabinets in the southeast corner. This catalog should be searched by name, location (county, city, town, region, state), subject, record type (marriage, land, etc.), author, and title.

___(ManuCC) The Manuscript Card Catalog, 1 large cabinet in the southeast corner. To be searched by name, subject, organization, and locality. Be sure and use the guides sitting on top.

___(MRG) The Microforms Room Guide, sitting on the table at the south wall of the Microforms Room. Lists microforms available, cabinet number, and drawer number. Includes all available censuses 1790-1920 for all states, federal military records (for Revolutionary War, War of 1812, and Civil War), local newspapers, local records (chiefly for Cleveland and Cuyahoga County), OH county atlases, OH mortality schedules 1850-60-80, OHS surname index, OH Draper manuscripts, the FHL International Genealogical Index for OH, the FHL Ancestral File (careful!), the FHL Catalog, Revolutionary War Land Warrants for the OH Military District, and others. Do not fail to search the Microform Catalog in Small Cabinet Number 1, as indicated just below.

___(SC1) Small Cabinet Number 1, located in the southeast corner. Contains several card catalogs including the (SC1-C) Cleveland Index 1926-65 (search by name and topic), the (SC1-L) Local Records Index (search by county, city, town, and state), the (SC1-A) Atlas Catalog (search by county, city, town, state, and compiler), the (SC1-CD) City Directory Catalog (search by city), the (SC1-M) Microform Catalog (microfilms, microcards, and microfiche, search by county, city, town, manuscript title, and newspaper name), (SC1-CC) Cuyahoga County Archives Catalog, (SC1-CP), Cleveland Picture File Catalog, (SC1-F) Family Bible Catalog (search by surname), (SC1-MG) Manuscript Genealogies (search by surname), (SC1-MC) Map Catalog (search by county, city, town, state, and the US), (SC1-B) Baptist Associations Records (search by state), and the (SC1-AL) Almanac Catalog (search by state, city, and town).

___(SC2) Small Cabinet Number 2, located in the southeast corner. This is the Family History Catalog, which refers to names in books, manuscripts, Bible records, pamphlets, microfiche, town histories, and county histories. (Search by surname.)

___(SC3) Small Cabinet Number 3, located in the southeast corner. Contains several card catalogs including the (SC3-S) Surname Index (search by name), the (SC3-A) AAHGS Death Index (search by name), and the (SC3-J) Marriage and Death Index to the Jewish Review and Observer (search by names).

___(PCL) Periodical Checklist, Catalog, and Notebooks, located on a small table just north of the three large card catalog cabinets. (Search under county, city, town, and/or state and name of periodical).

___(NL) Newspaper Lists, these lists of the newspaper holding of WRHS are obtainable at the Main Desk.

A suggested procedure for your thorough use of the materials in the WRHS is as follows:

___1st NAME: Search for the names you are seeking in MainCC, ManuCC, the census indexes, Sc1-F, SC1-MG, SC2, SC3-S, the appropriate microforms as listed in MRG and SC1-M, and the appropriate periodical indexes as noted in PCL. Then find pertinent published name indexes and books containing indexes as listed in Chapter 2 by looking in the MainCC under the author and/or the title, and search for the name in them. Practically every section of Chapter 2 lists such published materials.

___2nd LOCALITY: Look up your ancestor's county in the following finding aids, then carefully examine the records to which you are referred: MainCC, ManuCC, MRG, SC1-L, SC1-A, SC1-M, SC1-MC, PCL, NL, and if applicable SC1-CP. Then repeat the procedure for the city or town: MainCC, ManuCC, MRG, SC1-L, SC1-A, SC1-M, SC1-MC, SC1-AL, PCL, NL, and if applicable SC1-F. Then repeat the procedure for the region. And finally, repeat the procedure for the state of OH: MainCC, ManuCC, MRG, SC1-L, SC1-A, SC1-M, SC1-MC, SC1-B, SC1-AL, and PCL.

___3rd SUBJECT, TITLE, AND AUTHOR: Look in MainCC, ManuCC, and MRG for pertinent subjects (such as the titles to the sections in Chapter 2), for authors of books you are interested in (see listings in Chapter 2), and for titles of books, periodicals, and manuscripts which you have not as yet seen (see listings in Chapter 2).

5. The Allen County Public Library (ACPL)

The Allen County Public Library (ACPL) has the second largest genealogical collection in the US. The holdings include genealogies, histories, indexes (births, marrriages, deaths, cemetery inscriptions, periodicals, probates, wills), federal and local record microfilms, city directories, and periodicals. Their OH collection is quite strong. Many of the materials mentioned in Chapter 2 will be found there. The facility is located at 900 Webster Street, Ft. Wayne, IN 46802, and the telephone number is 1-(219)-424-7241, Ext. 2242. The hours are 9am–9pm Monday–Thursday, 9am–6pm Friday–Saturday, and 1pm–6pm Sunday. Hours vary in the summer and they are subject to change, so if you are planning to go, telephone and inquire about the times.

6. The Public Library of Cincinnati (PLC)

The Public Library of Cincinnati (PLC) is a well-stocked genealogical library which has excellent OH material. The library is located at Library Square, 800 Vine Street, Cincinnati, OH 45202, and its telephone number is 1-(513)-369-6900. The hours are 9am–9pm Monday–Friday, and 9am–6pm Saturday. The library is closed on Sundays. Hours may change, so call about them before you pay the PLC a visit. Nearby hotels include the Cincinnati Terrace Hilton, 15 West Sixth Street, Zip 45202 [Phone 1-(513)-381-4000], the Clarion Hotel, 141 West Sixth Street, Zip 45202 [Phone 1-(513)-352-2100], the Hyatt Regency, 151 West Fifth Street, Zip 45202 [Phone 1-(513)-579-1234], and the Omni Netherland Plaza, 35 West Fifth Street, Zip 45202 [Phone 1-(513)-421-9100].

Most of the genealogically–pertinent materials in the PLC are to be found in the History Department, which is located on the 1st Floor South of the library. Among its abundant holdings are atlases, biographical works, census indexes and microfilms, Cincinnati city directories, gazetteers, genealogical periodicals and indexes, genealogies, guide books, histories, the International Genealogical Index, maps, military records, passenger lists, newspapers, and many books of compiled records. The major finding aids in the library are:

____Main Card Catalog (search by name, locality, subject, author, title),

___CINCH Computer Catalog (search by name, locality, subject, author, title),
___Local History Index (search by name and subject),
___Local Newspaper Indexes (search by name and subject),
___Genealogy Index (search by name),
___Newspaper Holdings List (search by town, city, and county).
These should all be searched according to the search technique described in Paragraph 2 of Section 1 of this chapter. You will remember that this involves SLANT: N = name, L = location, S = subject, A = author, and T = title. When you find items of interest to your search, they may be requested at the History Desk by submitting a carefully filled-out call slip.

If you are concerned with ancestors in Cincinnati or Hamilton County or the surrounding counties, there is another repository in Cincinnati that it might be well worth visiting. This is the Cincinnati Historical Society, Cincinnati Museum Center, 1301 Western Avenue, Cincinnati, OH 45203. The telephone number is 1-(513)-287-7097, and the hours are 9am – 5pm, Monday through Saturday. Their collection includes records, manuscripts, maps, vital statistics, histories, church records, directories, and censuses, mainly for Hamilton County and the surrounding southwestern OH area.

---

7. The Family History Library and its Branch Family History Centers (FHL/FHC)

The largest genealogical library in the world is the Family History Library of the Genealogical Society of UT (FHL). This library, which holds almost two million rolls of microfilm, almost 400,000 microfiche, plus a vast number of books, is located at 50 East North Temple St., Salt Lake City, UT 84150. The basic keys to the library are composed of six indexes. (1) The International Genealogical Index, (2) The Surname Index in the FHL Catalog, (3) Listings of the Indexes to the Family Group Records Collection, (4) The Ancestral File, (5) The Social Security Death Index, and (6) The Locality Index in the FHL Catalog. In addition to the main library, the Society maintains a large number of Branches called Family History Centers (FHC) all over the US. Each of these branches has microfiche and computer copies of the International Genealogical Index, the Surname Index, the Index to the Family Group Records Collection, the Ancestral File, the Social Security Death Index, and the Locality Index. In addition each FHC has a supply of forms for borrowing microfilm copies of the records from the main library. This means that the astonishingly large holdings of the FHL are available through each of its numerous FHC branches.

The FHC in or near OH are as follows:
___Akron FHC, 735 N. Revere Rd., Akron, OH.
___Cincinnati FHC, 5505 Bosworth Place, Cincinnati, OH.
___Cleveland FHC, 25000 Westwood Rd., Westlake, OH.
___Columbus FHC, 3648 Leib St., Dublin, OH.
___Dayton FHC, 1500 Shiloh Springs Rd., Dayton, OH.
___Fairborn FHC, 3080 Bell Drive, Fairborn, OH.
___Kirtland FHC, Chillicothe Rd., Kirtland, OH.
___Mansfield FHC, 1951 Middle, Bellville, OH.
___Reynoldsburg FHC, 2135 Baldwin Rd., Reynoldsburg, OH.
___Sandusky FHC, Galloway Rd., Sandusky, OH.
___Toledo FHC, 1545 East Gate, Toledo, OH.

Other FHC are to be found in the cities listed below. They may be located by looking in the local telephone directory under the listing CHURCH OF JESUS CHRIST OF LATTER-DAY SAINTS-GENE-ALOGY LIBRARY or in the Yellow Pages under CHURCHES-LATTER-DAY SAINTS.
___In AL: Bessemer, Birmingham, Dothan, Huntsville, Mobile, Montgomery, Tuscaloosa, in AK: Anchorage, Fairbanks, Juneau, Ketchikan, Kotzebue, Sitka, Sodotna, Wasilla, in AZ: Benson, Buckeye, Camp Verde, Casa Grande, Cottonwood, Eagar, Flagstaff, Glendale, Globe, Holbrook, Kingman, Mesa, Nogales, Page, Payson, Peoria, Phoenix, Prescott, Safford, Scottsdale, Show Low, Sierra Vista, Snowflake, St. David, St. Johns, Tucson, Winslow, Yuma, in AR: Fort Smith, Jacksonville, Little Rock, Rogers,
___In CA (Bay Area): Antioch, Concord, Fairfield, Los Altos, Menlo Park, Napa, Oakland, San Bruno, San Jose, Santa Clara, Santa Cruz, Santa Rosa, In CA (Central): Auburn, Clovis, Davis (Woodland), El Dorado (Placerville), Fresno, Hanford, Merced, Modesto, Monterey (Seaside), Placerville, Sacramento, Seaside, Stockton, Turlock, Visalia, Woodland, In CA (Los Angeles County): Burbank, Canoga Park, Carson, Cerritos, Chatsworth (North Ridge), Covina, Glendale, Granada Hills, Hacienda Heights, Huntington Park, La Crescenta, Lancaster, Long Beach (Los Alamitos), Los Angeles, Monterey Park, Northridge, Norwalk, Palmdale, Palos Verdes (Rancho Palos Verdes), Pasadena, Torrance (Carson), Valencia, Van Nuys, Whittier, In CA (Northern): Anderson, Chico, Eureka, Grass Valley, Gridley, Mt. Shasta, Quincy, Redding, Susanville, Ukiah, Yuba City, In CA (Southern, except Los Angeles): Alpine, Anaheim, Bakersfield, Barstow, Blythe, Buena Park, Camarillo, Carlsbad, Corona, Cypress (Buena Park), El Cajon (Alpine), Escondido, Fontana, Garden Grove (Westminster), Hemet, Huntington Beach, Jurupa (Riverside), Los Alamitos, Mission Viejo, Moorpark, Moreno Valley, Needles, Newbury Park, Orange, Palm Desert, Palm

Springs (Palm Desert), Poway (San Diego), Redlands, Ridgecrest, Riverside, San Bernardino, San Diego, San Luis Obispo, Santa Barbara, Santa Maria, Simi Valley, Thousand Oaks (Moorpark), Upland, Ventura, Victorville, Vista, Westminster,

___In CO: Alamosa, Arvada, Aurora, Boulder, Colorado Springs, Columbine, Cortez, Craig, Denver, Durango, Fort Collins, Frisco, Grand Junction, Greeley, La Jara, Littleton, Louisville, Manassa, Meeker, Montrose, Longmont, Northglenn, Paonia, Pueblo, in CT: Bloomfield, Hartford, Madison, New Canaan, New Haven, Waterford, Woodbridge, in DC: Kensington, MD, in DE: Newark, Wilmington, in FL: Boca Raton, Cocoa, Ft. Lauderdale, Ft. Myers, Gainesville, Hialeah, Homestead, Jacksonville, Lake City, Lake Mary, Lakeland, Miami, Orange Park, Orlando, Palm City, Panama City, Pensacola, Plantation, Rockledge, St. Petersburg, Tallahassee, Tampa, West Palm Beach, Winterhaven, in GA: Atlanta, Augusta, Brunswick, Columbus, Douglas, Gainesville, Jonesboro, Macon, Marietta, Powder Springs, Roswell, Savannah, Tucker, in HI: Hilo, Honolulu, Kaneohe, Kauai, Kona, Laie, Lihue, Miliani, Waipahu,

___In ID: Basalt, Blackfoot, Boise, Burley, Caldwell, Carey, Coeur D'Alene, Driggs, Emmett, Firth, Hailey, Idaho Falls, Iona, Lewiston, McCammon, Malad, Meridian, Montpelier, Moore, Mountain Home, Nampa, Pocatello, Paris, Preston, Rexburg, Rigby, Salmon, Sandpoint, Shelley, Soda Springs, Twin Falls, Weiser, in IL: Champaign, Chicago Heights, Fairview Heights, Nauvoo, Peoria, Rockford, Schaumburg, Wilmette, in IN: Bloomington, Evansville, Fort Wayne, Indianapolis, New Albany, Noblesville, South Bend, Terre Haute, West Lafayette, in IA: Ames, Cedar Rapids, Davenport, Sioux City, West Des Moines, in KS: Dodge City, Olathe, Salina, Topeka, Wichita, in KY: Hopkinsville, Lexington, Louisville, Martin, Paducah, in LA: Alexandria, Baton Rouge, Denham Springs, Monroe, Metairie, New Orleans, Shreveport, Slidell,

___In ME: Augusta, Bangor, Cape Elizabeth, Caribou, Farmingdale, Portland, in MD: Annapolis, Baltimore, Ellicott City, Frederick, Kensington, Lutherville, in MA: Boston, Foxboro, Tyngsboro, Weston, Worcester, in MI: Ann Arbor, Bloomfield Hills, East Lansing, Escanaba, Grand Blanc, Grand Rapids, Hastings, Kalamazoo, Lansing, Ludington, Marquette, Midland, Muskegon, Traverse City, Westland, in MN: Anoka, Duluth, Minneapolis, Rochester, St. Paul, in MS: Clinton, Columbus, Gulfport, Hattiesburg, in MO: Cape Girardeau, Columbia, Farmington, Frontenac, Hazelwood, Independence, Joplin, Kansas City, Liberty, Springfield, St. Joseph, St. Louis, in MT: Billings, Bozeman, Butte, Glasgow, Glendive, Great Falls, Havre, Helena,

Kalispell, Missoula, Stevensville, in NE: Grand Island, Lincoln, Omaha, Papillion,

____In NV: Elko, Ely, Henderson, LaHonton Valley, Las Vegas, Logandale, Mesquite, Reno, Tonapah, Winnemucca, in NH: Concord, Exeter, Nashua, Portsmouth, in NJ: Caldwell, Dherry Hill, East Brunswick, Morristown, North Caldwell, in NM: Albuquerque, Carlsbad, Farmington, Gallup, Grants, Las Cruces, Santa Fe, Silver City, in NY: Albany, Buffalo, Ithaca, Jamestown, Lake Placid, Liverpool, Loudonville, New York City, Pittsford, Plainview, Queens, Rochester, Scarsdale, Syracuse, Vestal, Williamsville, Yorktown, in NC: Asheville, Charlotte, Durham, Fayetteville, Goldsboro, Greensboro, Hickory, Kinston, Raleigh, Skyland, Wilmington, Winston-Salem, in ND: Bismarck, Fargo, Minot, in OH: Akron, Cincinnati, Cleveland, Columbus, Dayton, Dublin, Fairborn, Kirtland, Perrysburg, Reynoldsburg, Tallmadge, Toledo, Westlake, Winterville,

____In OK: Lawton, Muskogee, Norman, Oklahoma City, Stillwater, Tulsa, in OR: Beaverton, Bend, Brookings, Central Point, Coos Bay, Corvallis, Eugene, Grants Pass, Gresham, Hermiston, Hillsboro, Keizer, Klamath Falls, LaGrande, Lake Oswego, Lebanon, Minnville, Medford, Newport, Nyssa, Ontario, Oregon City, Portland, Prineville, Roseburg, Salem, Sandy, The Dallas, in PA: Altoona, Broomall, Clarks Summit, Erie, Kane, Philadelphia(Broomall), Pittsburgh, Reading, Scranton(Clarks Summit), State College(Altoona), York, in RI: Providence, Warwick, in SC: Charleston, Columbia, Florence, Greenville, North Augusts, in SD: Gettysburg, Rapid City, Rosebud, Sioux Falls, in TN: Chattanooga, Franklin, Kingsport, Knoxville, Madison, Memphis, Nashville, in TX: Abilene, Amarillo, Austin, Bay City, Beaumont, Bryan, Conroe, Corpus Christi, Dallas, Denton, Duncanville, El Paso, Ft. Worth, Friendswood, Harlingen, Houston, Hurst, Katy, Kileen, Kingwood, Longview, Lubbock, McAllen, Odessa, Orange, Pasadena, Plano, Port Arthur, Richland Hills, San Antonio, Sugarland,

____In UT: American Fork, Altamont, Beaver, Blanding, Bloomington, Bluffdale, Bountiful, Brigham City, Canyon Rim, Castle Dale, Cedar City, Delta, Duchesne, Escalante, Farmington, Ferron, Fillmore, Granger, Heber, Helper, Highland, Holladay, Hunter, Huntington, Hurricane, Hyrum, Kanab, Kaysville, Kearns, Laketown, Layton, Lehi, Loa, Logan, Magna, Manti, Mapleton, Midway, Moab, Monticello, Moroni, Mt. Pleasant, Murray, Nephi, Ogden, Orem, Panguitch, Parowan, Pleasant Grove, Price, Provo, Richfield, Riverton, Roosevelt, Rose Park, Salt Lake City, Sandy, Santaquin, South Jordan, Springville, St. George, Syracuse, Tooele, Trementon, Tropic, Vernal, Wellington, Wendover, West Jordan, West Valley City, in VA: Annandale, Bassett, Charlottesville, Chesapeake, Dale City, Falls Church, Fredericksburg, Hamilton, Martinsville, McLean, Newport News, Norfolk, Oakton, Pembroke, Richmond, Roanoke, Salem, Virginia Beach, Waynesboro, Winchester, in VT: Berlin, Montpelier,

___In WA: Auburn, Bellevue, Bellingham, Bremerton, Centralia, Colville, Edmonds, Ellensburg, Elma, Ephrata, Everett, Federal Way, Ferndale, Lake Stevens, Longview, Lynnwood, Marysville, Moses Lake, Mt. Vernon, North Bend, Olympia, Othello, Port Angeles, Pullman, Puyallup, Quincy, Renton, Richland, Seattle, Silverdale, Spokane, Sumner, Tacoma, Vancouver, Walla Walla, Wenatchee, Yakima, in WV: Charleston, Fairmont, Huntington, in WI: Appleton, Eau Clair, Hales Corner, Madison, Milwaukee, Shawano, Wausau, in WY: Afton, Casper, Cheyenne, Cody, Gillette, Green River, Jackson Hole, Kemmerer, Laramie, Lovell, Lyman, Rawlins, Riverton, Rock Springs, Sheridan, Urie, Worland. The FHL is constantly adding new branches so this list will probably be out-of-date by the time you read it. An SASE and a $2 fee to the FHL (address in first paragraph above) will bring you an up-to-date listing of FHC.

When you go to FHL or FHC, first ask for the OH International Genealogical Index and examine it for the name of your ancestor, then if you are at FHL, request the record. If you are at FHC, ask them to borrow the microfilm containing the record from FHL. The cost is only a few dollars, and when your microfilm arrives (usually 4 to 6 weeks), you will be notified so that you can return and examine it. Second, ask for the Surname Catalog. Examine it for the surname of your ancestor. If you think any of the references relate to your ancestral line, and if you are at FHL, request the record. If you are at FHC, ask them to borrow the record for you. Third, ask for the Listings of Indexes to the Family Group Records Collection which will be found in the Author/Title Section of the FHL Catalog. There are several listings, so be sure you see them all. Locate the microfilm number which applies to the index of the surname you are seeking. If you are at FHL, request the microfilm. If you are at FHC, ask them to borrow the microfilm for you. When it comes, examine the microfilm to see if any records of your surname are indicated. If so, obtain them and see if they are pertinent.

Fourth, ask for the Ancestral File and look up the name you are seeking. If it is there, you will be led to sources of information, either people who are working on the line, or records pertaining to the line. Be careful with the material in this file, because in some of the cases, there appears to be no documentation. Fifth, if you are seeking a person who died after 1937, request the Social Security Death Index and look her/him up in it. Sixth, ask for the OH Locality Catalog. Examine all listings under the main heading of OHIO. Then examine all listings under the subheading of the county you are interested in. These county listings will follow the listings for the state of OH. Toward the end of the county listings, there are listed materials relating to cities and towns in the county. Be sure not to overlook them. If you are at FHL, you can request the materials which are of interest to you. If you are at FHC, you may have the librarian borrow them for you. A large number of the records referred to in Chapter 2 and those listed under the counties in Chapter 4 will be found in the OH locality catalog.

The FHL and each FHC also have a set of Combined Census Indexes. These indexes are overall collections of censuses and other records for various time periods. Set 1 covers all colonies and states 1607–1819, Set 2 covers all states 1820–9, Set 3 covers all states 1830–9, Set 4 covers all states 1840–9, Set 5 covers the southern states 1850–9, Set 6 covers the northern states 1850–9, Set 7 covers the midwestern and western states 1850–9, Set 7A covers all the states 1850–9, and further sets cover various groups of states 1860 and after. Additional details concerning the records in FHL and FHC along with instructions for finding and using them will be found in:

____J. Cerny and W. Elliott, THE LIBRARY, A GUIDE TO THE LDS FAMILY HISTORY LIBRARY, Ancestry Publishing, Salt Lake City, UT, 1988.

8. The National Archives (NA)

The National Archives and Records Service (NA), located at Pennsylvania Avenue and 8th Street, Washington, DC 20408, is the central national repository for federal records, many being of importance to OH genealogical research. The NA does not concern itself with colonial records (pre-1776), state, county, city, or town records. Among the most important NA records which pertain to OH are the following:

____Census records: Federal census records for OH, 1800–1920 (1800 and 1810 for one county, 1820 two counties missing)

____Non–population census schedules: farm, manufacture, and mortality records for OH, 1850–80 (incomplete)

____Military records: Service, bounty land, pension, claims records, and indexes for the Revolution, War of 1812, Mexican War, Civil War, Spanish–American War

____Land records: Land warrant applications, land warrant redemptions, land sales, surveys, land grants for OH, 1787–, records are in both NA and Chicago Branch of the NA

____Naturalization records: For US District and Circuit Courts in OH, 1852–1956, records are in the Chicago Branch of the NA

___Federal District and Circuit Court records: For OH   1803–1962, records are in the Chicago Branch of the NA
___Bounty land warrants: Revolutionary warrants used in the US Military District of OH

Details on all of these have been given in the pertinent sections of Chapter 2. Further detail on them may be obtained in:

___NA Staff, GENEALOGICAL RESEARCH IN THE NATIONAL ARCHIVES, NA, Washington, DC, 1982.

The numerous records of the NA may be examined in Washington in person or by a hired researcher. Microfilm copies of many of the major records and/or their indexes may also be seen in Regional Branches of the National Archives (NARB) which are located in or near Atlanta (1557 St. Joseph Ave., East Point, GA 30344), Boston (380 Trapelo Rd., Waltham, MA 02154), Chicago (7358 S. Pulaski Rd., Chicago, IL 60629), Denver (Bldg. 48, Federal Center, Denver, CO 80225), Fort Worth (501 West Felix St., Ft. Worth, TX 76115), Kansas City (2312 E. Bannister Rd., Kansas City, MO 64131), Los Angeles (24000 Avila Rd., Laguna Niguel, CA 92677), New York (201 Varick St., New York, NY 10014), Philadelphia (9th and Market Sts., Philadelphia, PA 19107), San Francisco (1000 Commodore Dr., San Bruno, CA 94066), and Seattle (6125 Sand Point Way, NE, Seattle, WA 98115). Take special note of the Chicago Branch in Chicago, IL. It holds many OH census records, Revolutionary War service, pension, and bounty land records, US Courts of OH, naturalizations in US Circuit and District Courts, Internal Revenue tax records 1862–66, OH Union service records 1861–65, and the OH non-population census schedules.

Many of the NA records pertaining to OH, as was noted in detail in Chapters 2 and 3, are also available at OHS, SLO, WRHS, PLC, ACPL, and the FHL (FHC), and some are available at LGL and RL. In addition, practically any local library in the US can borrow NA microfilms for you from AGLL (American Genealogical Lending Library, PO Box 244, Bountiful, UT 84010). Or you may borrow from them directly. Included are NA census records and military records (Revolutionary War, War of 1812, Mexican War, Civil War).

9. The OH Network of American History Research Centers (ONAHRC)

In 1970, the State of OH evidenced a concern for the preservation of local government records by establishing the OH Network of American History Research Centers (ONAHRC). The network is presently made up of seven repositories to which local governments may send records for preservation and safekeeping. Numerous records have been transferred to these regional centers. In some cases, microfilm copies of the removed records have been left with the county or city from which they have come.

Each center keeps an inventory of its records arranged by county. The seven centers, along with the counties they serve, are:

____ONAHRCenter, Bierce Library, University of Akron, Akron, OH 44325. Counties: Ashl, Car, Col, Cos, Har, Hol, Jef, Mah, Por, Ric, Sta, Sum, Tus, Way. See L. Folck, LOCAL GOVERNMENT RECORDS AT THE UNIVERSITY OF AKRON, University of Akron, Akron, OH, 1982. Also see their more recent in-house inventory.

____ONAHRCenter, Archives and Special Collections, Wright State University, Dayton, OH 45435. Counties: Aug, Cha, Cla, Dar, Gre, Log, Mer, Mia, Mont, Pre, She. See N. G. Leggett and D. E. Smith, A GUIDE TO LOCAL GOVERNMENT RECORDS AND NEWSPAPERS, Wright State University, Dayton, OH, 1993. Also see their more recent in-house inventory.

____ONAHRCenter, University of Cincinnati, 462 Central Library, Cincinnati, OH 45221. Counties: Ada, Bro, But, Cle, Cli, Ham, Hig, War. See INVENTORY OF GOVERNMENT DOCU-MENTS FOR EIGHT COUNTIES OF SOUTHWEST OH, Bleden Library, University of Cincinnati, Cincinnati, OH, 1993. See their in-house inventory.

____ONAHRCenter, Western Reserve Historical Society, 10825 East Boulevard, Cleveland, OH 44106. Counties: Asht, Cuy, Gea, Lak, Lor, Med, Tru. See B. Stith, A GUIDE TO LOCAL GOVERN-MENTAL RECORDS IN THE LIBRARY OF THE WRHS, The Society, Cleveland, OH, 1981. Also see section on WRHS above.

____ONAHRCenter, OH Historical Society, Interstate 71 at 17th Avenue, Columbus, OH 43211. Counties: Del, Fai, Fay, Fra, Kno, Lic, Mad, Mar, Mor, Pic, Uni. See K. Matusoff, CENTRAL OH LOCAL GOVERNMENT RECORDS AT THE OHS, The Society, Columbus, OH, 1978. Also see section on OHS above, as well as their more recent in-house inventory.

____ONAHRCenter, Center for Archival Collections, Bowling Green State University, Bowling Green, OH 43403. Counties: All, Cra, Def, Eri, Ful, Han, Har, Hen, Hur, Luc, Ott, Pau, Put, San, Sen, Van, Wil, Woo, Wya. See S. M. Charter, GUIDE TO LOCAL GOVERNMENT RECORDS AT THE CENTER FOR ARCHI-VAL COLLECTIONS, Bowling Green State University, Bowling Green, OH, 1993, and D. K. Christian, GUIDE TO NEWS-PAPER HOLDINGS AT THE CENTER FOR ARCHIVAL COLLECTIONS, Bowling Green State University, Bowling Green, OH, 1980. Also see their more recent in-house inventory.

___ONAHRCenter, Special Collections, OH University, Athens, OH 45701. Counties: Ath, Bel, Gal, Gue, Hoc, Jac, Law, Mei, Monr, Mor, Mus, Nob, Per, Pik, Ros, Sci, Vin, Was. See OH University Library, GUIDE TO LOCAL GOVERNMENT RECORDS AT OH UNIVERSITY, The Library, Athens, OH, 1992, and E. Smith and others, GUIDE TO GENEALOGICAL RESOURCES OF THE OH UNIVERSITY LIBRARY, Athens County Historical Society, Athens, OH, 1983. Also see their more recent in-house inventory.

---

10. The OH Genealogical Society (OGS)

The OH Genealogical Society (OGS) maintains an extensive genealogical research library (over 16,000 volumes and microfilms) at its headquarters. The location is 34 Sturges Avenue, Mansfield, OH 44906. The hours are 9am to 5pm, Tuesday-Saturday, the library being closed on Sunday and Monday. But check because times change; the telephone number is 1-(419)-522-9077. Their collection focuses on OH family history research, with Bible records, censuses, cemetery lists, manuscripts, newspapers, and numerous genealogies which their members and others have submitted. They also have most of the important OH publications mentioned in Chapter 2. Their county record collection contains birth records for 16 counties, 1870 census indexes for 14 counties, death records for 15 counties, land records for 17 counties, marriage records for 51 counties, pre-1816 tax records for most existing counties, post-1815 tax records for 14 counties, and will records for 25 counties.

Among the hotel facilities near the library are the Holiday Inn Conference Center, 116 Park Avenue West, Zip 44902 [Phone 1-(419)-525-6000], and the 191 Park Place Hotel, 191 Park Avenue West, Zip 44902 [Phone 1-(419)-522-7275]. Out in the county are numerous motels and some bed-and-breakfasts. For a list, call the Visitor's Bureau at 1-800-642-8282.

---

11. Regional libraries (RL)

Regional libraries (RL) in OH are defined as those libraries which have sizable genealogical collections for the region, rather than just for the immediate locality. Included among them are the seven ONAHRCenters discussed in the second section back. In addition, the following are to be noted:

___Akron Public Library, 55 South Main Street, Akron, OH 44309, Phone 1-(216)-762-7621.

___Stark County District Library, 715 Market Avenue, North, Canton, OH 44702, Phone 1-(216)-452-0665, Ext. 225.

___Dayton and Montgomery County Public Library, 215 East Third Street, Dayton, OH 45402, Phone 1-(513)-227-9500, Ext. 211.

___Lorain Public Library, 351 Sixth Street, Lorain, OH 44052, Phone 1-(216)-244-1192.

___Toledo-Lucas County Public Library, 325 Michigan Street, Toledo, OH 43624, Phone 1-(419)-255-7055, Ext. 233.

___Greene County District Library, 76 East Market Street, Xenia, OH 45385, Phone 1-(513)-376-4952.

___Public Library of Youngstown and Mahoning County, 305 Wick Avenue, Youngstown, OH 44503, Phone 1-(216)-744-8636, Ext. 51.

When a visit is made to any of these libraries, your _first_ endeavor is to search the card and/or computer catalog. You can remember what to look for with the acronymn SLANT. A detailed treatment of its use was given back in Section 1 of this chapter. This procedure should give you very good coverage of the library holdings which are indexed in the catalog. The _second_ endeavor at any of these libraries is to ask about any special indexes, catalogs, collections, finding aids, or materials which might be pertinent to your search. You should make it your aim particularly to inquire about Bible, cemetery, church, map, manuscript, military, mortuary, and newspaper materials. In some cases, microform (microfilm, microfiche, microcard) records are not included in the regular catalog but are separately indexed. It is important that you be alert to this possibility.

12. Local repositories

Local libraries, court houses, and other repositories (LL, CH, LR) are located in every county seat, and sometimes libraries and other repositories will be found in other towns in the county. The most significant libraries are listed under the counties in Chapter 4. At the libraries, it is important for you to inquire about other record repositories in the county: cemeteries, churches, mortuaries, newspaper offices, organization offices, schools, society offices. Please look back at the last third of Section 1 for information about Court Houses, and remember that they should be visited only after going to the library.

13. Large genealogical libraries (LGL)

Spread around the US there are a number of large genealogical libraries

(LGL) which have at least some OH genealogical source materials. In general, those libraries nearest OH are the ones that have the larger OH collections, but there are exceptions. Among these libraries are the following:

____In AL: Birmingham Public Library, Library at Samford University in Birmingham, AL Archives and History Department in Montgomery, in AZ: Southern AZ Genealogical Society in Tucson, in AR: AR Genealogical Society in Little Rock, AR History Commission in Little Rock, Little Rock Public Library, in CA: CA Genealogical Society in San Francisco, Los Angeles Public Library, San Diego Public Library, San Francisco Public Library, Sutro Library in San Francisco,

____In CO: Denver Public Library, in CT: CT State Library in Hartford, Godfrey Memorial Library in Middletown, in DC: Library of Congress, DAR Library, National Genealogical Society Library in Washington, in FL: FL State Library in Tallahassee, Miami-Dade Public Library, Orlando Public Library, Tampa Public Library, in GA: Atlanta Public Library, in ID: ID Genealogical Society, in IL: Newberry Library in Chicago, in IN: IN State Library in Indianapolis, Public Library of Fort Wayne, in IA: IA State Department of History and Archives in Des Moines, in KY: KY Historical Society in Frankfurt, Filson Club in Louisville,

____In LA: LA State Library in Baton Rouge, in ME: ME State Library in Augusta, in MD: MD State Library in Annapolis, MD Historical Society in Baltimore, in MA: Boston Public Library, New England Historic Genealogical Society Library in Boston, in MI: Detroit Public Library, in MN: MN Public Library, in MS: MS Department of Archives and History in Jackson, in MO: Kansas City Public Library, Mid-Continent Public Library in Independence, St. Louis Public Library, In NE: NE State Historical Society in Lincoln, Omaha Public Library, in NV: Washoe County Library in Reno, in NY: NY Public Library, NY Genealogical and Biographical Society in NY City, in NC: NC State Library in Raleigh, in OK: OK State Historical Society in Oklahoma City, in OR: Genealogical Forum of Portland, Portland Library Association, in PA: Historical Society of PA in Philadelphia, PA State Library in Harrisburg,

____In SC: The South Caroliniana Library in Columbia, in SD: State Historical Society in Pierre, in TN: TN State Library and Archives in Nashville, in TX: Dallas Public Library, Fort Worth Public Library, TX State Library in Austin, Houston Public Library, Clayton Library in Houston, in UT: Brigham Young University Library in Provo, in VA: VA Historical Society Library and VA State Library in Richmond, in WA: Seattle Public Library, in WV: WV Department of Archives and History in Charleston, in WI: Milwaukee Public Library, State Historical Society in Madison.

When you visit a LGL, the general procedure described earlier in this chapter should be followed: First, search the card catalog. Look under the headings summarized by SLANT: subject, location, author, name, title. Then, second, inquire about special indexes, catalogs, collections, materials, and microforms.

The above list of LGL is not inclusive. There may be other medium-sized and large libraries near you. Just because they do not appear in the above list, do not fail to check out their OH genealogical holdings.

Abbreviations

ACPL	Allen County Public Library
C	1890 Union pension census
CH	County court houses
D	Death or mortality censuses
DAR	Daughters of the American Revolution
F	Farm and ranch censuses
FHC	Family History Center
FHL	Family History Library
LGL	Large genealogical libraries
LL	Local libraries
LR	Local repositories
M	Manufactures censuses
NA	National Archives
NARB	National Archives Regional Branches
OGS	Ohio Genealogical Society
OHS	Ohio Historical Society
ONAHRC	Ohio Network of American History Research Centers
P	1840 Revolutionary War veteran census
PLC	Public Library of Cincinnati
R	Regular censuses
RL	Regional libraries
SLO	State Library of Ohio
T	Tax substitutes for censuses
WPA	Works Progress Administration
WRHS	Western Reserve Historical Society

Chapter 4

RESEARCH PROCEDURE AND COUNTY LISTINGS

━━━━━━━━━━━━━━━━━━━━━━━

1. Introduction

━━━━━━━━━━━━━━━━━━━━━━━

Now you should have a good idea of OH history, its genealogical records, and the locations and availabilities of these records. The emphasis in the first three chapters was on records at levels higher than the county. Detailed information on national, state-wide, and regional records was given, but county records were normally treated only in general. We now will turn our focus upon the county records, treating them in detail. We will also emphasize non-governmental records available at the county level (such as Bible, biography, cemetery, directories, DAR, ethnic, genealogies, histories, manuscripts, maps, mortuary, newspaper, and periodicals). The reason for all this attention to county records is that these records are more likely to contain more information on your ancestors than any other type. Such records were generally recorded by people who knew your forebears, and they often relate to the personal details of her/his life.

In the state of OH, many of the original governmental records of the counties and cities remain within the counties, but some have been transferred to the ONAHRCenters. Many of these original county/city governmental records and some non-governmental records have been microfilmed by the FHL, and the microfilms are available at FHL, and by interlibrary loan through the many FHC branches throughout the US. Microfilms of some of these original records are also available at the OHS. Some of the original county/city governmental records and numerous non-governmental records have been published either in printed volumes or as typescripts. Most of these publications are available at SLO, WRHS, PLC, OGS, and ACPL. Some are available at OHS, LGL, RL, and LL.

This chapter, Chapter 4, will deal with county and city records in detail. We will first discuss procedures for finding the county in which your OH progenitor(s) lived. This is important because knowing that your ancestors were simply from OH is not enough to permit genealogical research. You need to know the county or city since many genealogically-applicable records were kept on a local basis, and since you will often find more than one person in OH bearing the name of your ancestor. In such a case, the county/city location will often let you tell them apart. After discussing ways to find the county, we will second suggest approaches for doing OH genealogy, recommending the order in which the various repositories should be used.

2. Finding the county

As you will recall from Chapter 1, official OH record keeping began with the territorial period (1787), even though there had been some records pertaining to the area which were kept by the states which initially claimed the territory, especially VA. Counties were established in the Northwest Territory beginning in 1788, and they kept records from the start. As time went on, the population increased, more counties were established, and more and more of the keeping of records was shifted to them. It is, therefore, of considerable importance for you to know your OH predecessor's county in order to direct yourself efficiently to many of the pertinent records. It is also important because the local county officials probably knew your ancestor personally, and further, kept more detailed records on him, his family, his property, and his activities than did the territory or state. If you happen to know your ancestor's county, you may skip the remainder of this section. If not, your first priority must be a successful search for the county. The most efficient method for discovering the county depends on the time period during which your forebear lived in OH. We will discuss county-finding techniques for three periods of time in OH history: (a) 1787–1820, (b) 1820–1908, and (c) 1908–present.

If your forebear's time period was 1787–1820, you should look in the following major sources for your progenitor's name. Items more generally available (indexes in FHC, published and microfilm indexes in LGL) will be listed before those available chiefly in OH repositories (OHS, SLO, WRHS, PLC, OGS) or available by ordering from FHL through FHC.

____(1a) INTERNATIONAL GENEALOGICAL INDEX (IGI), OH SECTION; FAMILY SEARCH; ANCESTRAL FILE; FAMILY GROUP RECORDS COLLECTION; all available at FHL and at FHC.

____(2a) F. Rider, AMERICAN GENEALOGICAL[-BIOGRAPHICAL] INDEX, Godfrey Memorial Library, Middletown, CT, 1942-, 2 series, 1st containing 48 volumes, 2nd containing over 190 volumes.

____(3a) M. Kaminkow, GENEALOGIES IN THE LIBRARY OF CONGRESS, Magna Carta, Baltimore, MD, 1972-7, 3 volumes, plus SUPPLEMENTS; also A COMPLEMENT TO GENEALO-GIES IN THE LIBRARY OF CONGRESS [GENEALOGIES IN OTHER LIBRARIES], Magna Carta, Baltimore, MD, 1981.

____(4a) Published early OH land records by these authors: Bell, Berry, Clark, Dyer, Maxwell, McMullin, Page, and Riegel. See Section 20, Chapter 2, for full references.

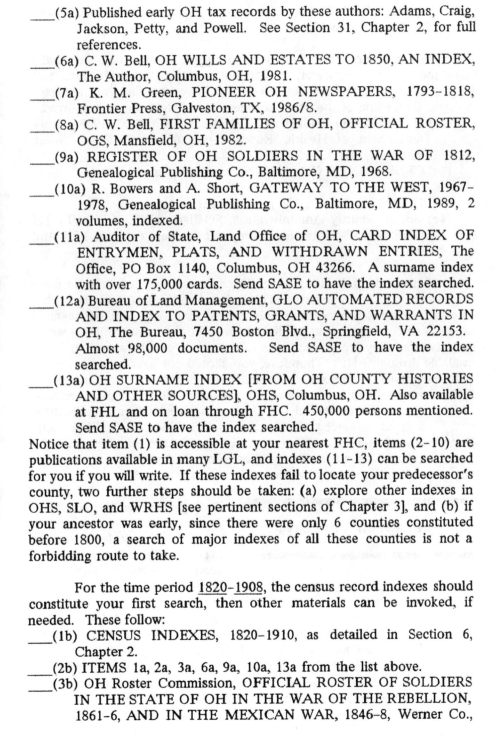

____(5a) Published early OH tax records by these authors: Adams, Craig, Jackson, Petty, and Powell. See Section 31, Chapter 2, for full references.

____(6a) C. W. Bell, OH WILLS AND ESTATES TO 1850, AN INDEX, The Author, Columbus, OH, 1981.

____(7a) K. M. Green, PIONEER OH NEWSPAPERS, 1793-1818, Frontier Press, Galveston, TX, 1986/8.

____(8a) C. W. Bell, FIRST FAMILIES OF OH, OFFICIAL ROSTER, OGS, Mansfield, OH, 1982.

____(9a) REGISTER OF OH SOLDIERS IN THE WAR OF 1812, Genealogical Publishing Co., Baltimore, MD, 1968.

____(10a) R. Bowers and A. Short, GATEWAY TO THE WEST, 1967–1978, Genealogical Publishing Co., Baltimore, MD, 1989, 2 volumes, indexed.

____(11a) Auditor of State, Land Office of OH, CARD INDEX OF ENTRYMEN, PLATS, AND WITHDRAWN ENTRIES, The Office, PO Box 1140, Columbus, OH 43266. A surname index with over 175,000 cards. Send SASE to have the index searched.

____(12a) Bureau of Land Management, GLO AUTOMATED RECORDS AND INDEX TO PATENTS, GRANTS, AND WARRANTS IN OH, The Bureau, 7450 Boston Blvd., Springfield, VA 22153. Almost 98,000 documents. Send SASE to have the index searched.

____(13a) OH SURNAME INDEX [FROM OH COUNTY HISTORIES AND OTHER SOURCES], OHS, Columbus, OH. Also available at FHL and on loan through FHC. 450,000 persons mentioned. Send SASE to have the index searched.

Notice that item (1) is accessible at your nearest FHC, items (2-10) are publications available in many LGL, and indexes (11-13) can be searched for you if you will write. If these indexes fail to locate your predecessor's county, two further steps should be taken: (a) explore other indexes in OHS, SLO, and WRHS [see pertinent sections of Chapter 3], and (b) if your ancestor was early, since there were only 6 counties constituted before 1800, a search of major indexes of all these counties is not a forbidding route to take.

For the time period 1820-1908, the census record indexes should constitute your first search, then other materials can be invoked, if needed. These follow:

____(1b) CENSUS INDEXES, 1820-1910, as detailed in Section 6, Chapter 2.

____(2b) ITEMS 1a, 2a, 3a, 6a, 9a, 10a, 13a from the list above.

____(3b) OH Roster Commission, OFFICIAL ROSTER OF SOLDIERS IN THE STATE OF OH IN THE WAR OF THE REBELLION, 1861-6, AND IN THE MEXICAN WAR, 1846-8, Werner Co.,

Akron, OH, 1886-95, 12 volumes.   Mexican War participants
listed in Volume 12.

For the time period from <u>1908-</u> forward, family members usually
know the county.   However, if they do not, the state-wide birth and
death records provide the best source. Should you not find your ancestor
in them, then some of the other sources listed below can be employed.

___(1c) INDEXES TO BIRTH AND DEATH RECORDS, 1908-, State
       Department of Health, Room G-20, 65 South Front Street,
       Columbus, OH 43215.

___(2c) CENSUS INDEXES, 1910-20, as detailed in Section 6, Chapter
       2.

___(3c) ITEMS 1a, 3a, and 13a from the list above.

___(4c) Social Security Administration, SOCIAL SECURITY DEATH
       INDEX, 1937-88, on four computer compact discs, at FHL and
       FHC.

The work of locating your OH ancestor can generally be done
from where you live or nearby. This is because the key items are either
indexes or indexed records which means that they can be scanned
rapidly. Also, many are in published form (books or microfilms), which
indicates that they are in numerous LGL outside of OH, as well as being
available through FHC. Therefore, you should not have to travel too far
to find many of the indexes you need. Some of the important indexes in
OH repositories can be searched for you upon written request (enclose
SASE).   Or, if you prefer, all the above resources can be examined for
you by a hired researcher in Columbus, OH (OHS, SLO, FHC, State
Department of Health). This ought not to cost too much because the
searches can all be made in very short time, and your hired researcher
can stop when the county has been identified.

3. Research approaches

Having identified the county of
your forebear's residence, you
are in position to ferret out the
details.   This means that you
need to identify what non-
governmental, federal, state, and county records are available, then to
locate them, and finally to examine them in detail. The most useful non-
governmental records have been discussed in Chapter 2 (atlas, Bible,
biography, cemetery, church, city directory, county/city history, court,
DAR, ethnic, gazetteer, genealogical compilation, genealogical index,
genealogical periodical, land, manuscript, map, mortuary, newspaper,
regional publication). The federal governmental records which are most
important for consideration have also been treated in Chapter 2 (census,
court, military, naturalization). State governmental records which are of
the greatest utility for genealogical research are examined in Chapter 2

(birth, court, death, divorce, land, marriage, military, tax). And the types of records which were generated by OH's counties are listed in Chapter 3 (Section 1), and they were discussed in general in Chapter 2. To remind you of the various types of county governmental records, the list from Chapter 3 is repeated here:

___Auditor: assessment, enumerations of the handicapped, justice of the peace records, military bounties, military exemptions, military personnel enumerations, militia rolls, relief, school enumerations, tax lists, veteran burials.

___Clerk of Courts: case files, chancery records, civil case records, court of common pleas records (see below), criminal case records, dockets, journals, jury lists, order books, partition records, probate records (before 1852), supreme court records.

___Court of Common Pleas: appearance dockets, arrest records, case files, chancery records, coroner's inquests, divorces, judgments, jury lists, manumissions, naturalizations, partitions of land, poll books.

___County Commissioners: county home records, journals, road records.

___Probate Court (after 1852): administration, adoption, birth, case files, death, estate, guardian, marriage, will.

___Recorder: cemetery, corporation, deed, land, lease, military discharge, mortgage, patent, plat, power of attorney, tract, veteran burials.

___Sheriff: complaints, criminal, jail registers, probation, partition of land.

___Treasurer: estate tax, forfeiture, sales tax, tax lists, tax receipts.

___Other Offices : Childrens Home (records), Coroner (death reports, case files, inquests), County Home (admission, death, indentures, infirmary, poor), Soldiers Relief Commission (burials, headstone requests, relief, service records).

County and city governmental record originals are found in the counties, usually at the CH or in a special repository, and at the relevant ONAHRC. Many microfilm copies of county and city governmental records are located at FHL (available through FHC), and some are at OHS. Most published (printed and typescript) county and city governmental records are at SLO, WRHS, PLC, and ACPL. Some will be found at OHS, OGS, LGL, RL, and LL. Both the major microfilmed records and the major types of published records (both governmental and non-governmental) for the 88 OH counties will be listed in detail in later sections of this chapter. These listings have been obtained from the catalogs at FHL, OHS, WRHS, SLO, and then compared to similar listings in works by Bell, Khouw, Clark, and Harter.

The general approach for doing an utterly thorough job of researching an OH ancestor is to follow this pattern:

____1st, check all family sources (oral, records, mementos, Bible), making a continuing effort to contact more and more of the many descendants of the ancestor

____2nd, locate your forebear's county (Section 2, this Chapter)

____3rd, use the nearest LGL (catalogs, indexes, publications, microfilms)

____4th, use the nearest FHC or the FHL (IGI, Ancestral File, family Group Records Archives, FHL Catalog surname and locality indexes, integrated census indexes), if at FHC, order the pertinent microfilms

____5th, borrow any major federal records you have not seen from AGLL (census, military)

____6th, either go to Columbus, OH (OHS, SLO), or hire a researcher in Columbus to look at microfilms and publications you have not seen

____7th, write a letter to the ONAHRCenter which serves your ancestor's county, and ask for a list of their record holdings for that county; if they have anything you have not seen, either go there or hire a researcher to look at them for you

____8th, either visit the county, or hire a researcher in the county to look in the LL (catalogs, indexes, manuscripts, local records), and to visit offices of cemeteries, churches, mortuaries, newspapers, and organizations to obtain records you have not seen

____9th, then you or your researcher should go to the CH, and the offices of the county and city record keepers, and/or the county and city record repositories, to examine records you have not seen

____10th, use the NARB and NA (for further federal census, court, military, and naturalization materials)

____11th, address inquiries to pertinent Church Archives, if church records have still not been found

The precise way in which you use this scheme will be determined chiefly by how far you are from Salt Lake City, UT (FHL) and Columbus, OH (OHS, SLO), and the relevant OH county. The major idea that you need to recognize is that eventually you will have to go to OH, or you will need to hire a researcher there, perhaps two, one for Columbus, and one for the county.

In using the above steps to set forth your own research plan, you ought to think about three items. The _first_ is expense. You need to balance the cost of a hired researcher over against the cost of personal visits (to Columbus, to the ONAHRC, and to the county): travel, meals, lodging. You need also to compare the costs of borrowing microfilms from your nearest FHC (a few dollars per roll) to a trip to Salt Lake City, where the films can be read off-the-shelf at no charge. Of course, your desire to visit your ancestor's area, and your desire to look at the records yourself may be an important consideration.

The second item is a reminder about interlibrary loans. With the exception of the microfilms FHL (available through FHC) and those of AGLL (available personally or through your local library), very few libraries and practically no archives will lend out genealogical materials. The third item is also a reminder. Correspondence with librarians, governmental officials, and archivists is ordinarily of very limited use. The reason is that these helpful and hard-working federal, state, local, and private employees do not have time to do any detailed work for you because of the demanding duties of their offices. In some cases, these people will have time to look up one specific item for you (a land grant, a catalog entry, a deed record, a will, a military record) if an overall index is available. Please do not ask them for detailed data, and please do not write them a long letter. If you do write, enclose a long SASE, a check for $5 with the payee line left blank, and a brief request (no more than one-third page) for one specific item in an index or catalog. Ask them to use the check if there is a charge for their services or for copying, and if they do not have time to look themselves, that they hand the check and your letter to a researcher who can do the work.

---

4. Format of county listings

In the following sections of this chapter, you will find listings of many of the major records of the OH counties. The records are mostly county based, many of them being governmental records, and many non-governmental or private records. In addition, libraries and genealogical societies in the counties will be shown because they are valuable sources of ancestral information.

Please take a look at the next section (Section 5) which will serve as an example of the format of the county listings. This section deals with Adams County. First, the name of the county is given, then the dates on which the county was established and organized, along with the parent county or counties. This is followed by the name of the county seat and the zip code of the CH. After this, you will find notes regarding losses of county records, if such has occurred. Then the regional ONAHRCenter is given. This is followed by the available census records. Remember what the abbreviations refer to: R = regular census records, I = index to regular census records, M = manufactures census records, F = farm census records, P = 1840 census of military pensioners, D = mortality census records, and C = 1890 census of Civil War Union veterans.

Second, microfilmed records which are available at the FHL are shown. These microfilms may be borrowed through any of the numerous FHC. Third, microfilmed records and other records which are available at the OHS are listed. <u>Fourth</u>, types of volumes which the DAR has produced for this county are specified. These should be looked for in SLO, WRHS, PLC, ACPL, in the DAR Library in Washington, DC, and sometimes in RL and LL. The <u>fifth</u> list is one which sets out the types of published volumes which are available for this county. These can be sought in SLO, WRHS, PLC, ACPL, LGL, and in pertinent RL and LL. <u>Sixth</u>, you will find notations as to where manuscripts, newspapers, and genealogical periodical articles relating to the county may be sought.

And finally, <u>seventh</u>, there will be listed the library or libraries in the county which will be essential for your genealogical quest. Following the library listing, the genealogical society or societies in the area will be named. Since these societies sometimes undergo address changes when they elect new officers, you will be advised to contact the library for the most recent address. For this purpose, the library's telephone number is given along with its listing.

Now, a few remarks about the listings of county records need to be made. The listings are not complete, but are meant to give you a good general idea of the materials which are available. The emphasis in the listings has been in the pre-1900 period, since this is the time domain of major concern to most researchers. Further, when a set of inclusive dates is given, such as (1817-1903), it does not necessarily mean that every year is included; there may be a few gaps.

Do not forget that the listings of records under the names of the counties in this chapter represent only a fraction of what is available in the counties. A visit to the OH county (or a hired searcher) and a search of its records is an absolute must if you want to do a thorough investigation. Even though the microfilmed and published records are often those of greatest genealogical utility, the records which have not been put into microfilm or published form are very valuable, particularly the court records, and among them, especially the probate packets or files. These records are usually only in the county, although some may have gotten into the ONAHRCenters.

---

5. ADAMS COUNTY

Adams County, established/organized 1797/1797 from Hamilton County. County seat West Union (45693), court house fire in 1910, many records lost.

ONAHRC: University of Cincinnati. Censuses: 1820RIM, 1830RI, 1840RIP, 1850RIMF, 1860RIFD, 1870RFM, 1880RID, 1890C, 1900RI, 1910RI, 1820RI.

FHL(FHC) microfilms: administrat/or/ion (1910-67), birth (1888-93), cemetery, death (1888-93), deed (1797-1900), guardian (1910-67), marriage (1910-67), Presbyterian (1829-), tax (1801, 1806-38), will (1910-67).

OHS microfilms and records: administrat/or/ion, Bible, inventory (1816-26), marriage (1803-1902), school (1866-86), tax (1801, 1806-38). DAR volumes: Bible, cemetery, church, marriage, school.

Published volumes: atlas, Bible, birth, Black, cemetery, census, church, death, estate, family, gazetteer, genealogy, history, inventory of court records, land, marriage, newspaper abstracts, plat, probate, school, survey, will.

Manuscripts in OHS, WRHS, FHL. For newspapers, see repositories and reference volumes given in Chapter 2, section 30. For genealogical periodical articles, see indexes referred to in Chapter 2, section 19. Library: OH Valley District Free Library, Fourth and Pike Sts., Manchester, OH 45144. Phone 1-(513)-549-3359. Society: Adams County Genealogical Society (contact library for current address). Publishes OUR HERITAGE.

6. ALLEN COUNTY

Allen County, authorized/established 1820/31 from Shelby County. County seat Lima (45801). ONAHRC: Bowling Green State University. Censuses: 1830RI, 1840RIP, 1850RIMF, 1860RIFD, 1870-RFM, 1880RIF, 1890C, 1900RI, 1920RI.

FHL(FHC) microfilms: accounts (1837-85), administrator (1831-99), birth (1867-1940), cemetery, chancery (1833-57), civil court cases (1832-57), clerk of courts (1832-57), common pleas court (1859-1947), coroner (1886-92, 1911-17), death (1867-1909), deed (1831-1902), district court (1852-64), estate (1835-1926), guardian (1859-1913), inventory (1853-86), jail (1870-1923), marriage (1831-1919), Mennonite (1840-), military (1865-1923), naturalization (1851-1929), probate (1837-87), quadrennial enumeration (1883-87), school (1865-77), supreme court (1837-51), Swiss Reformed (1870-), tax (1831-50), voters (1904-60), will (1836-1905), witness (1859-1907).

OHS microfilms and records: administrator (1882-87), Bible, cemetery, chancery (1833-57), clerk of courts (1832-57), district court (1852-64), marriage (1831-64), military (1865-1923), naturalization (1906-12, 1921-29), supreme court (1837-51), will (1904-10).

DAR volumes: Bible, cemetery, marriage. Published volumes: atlas, biography, Black, cemetery, church, city/county directories, family, history, inventory of county records, land marriage, military, plat, newspaper abstracts.

For newspapers, see repositories and reference volumes given in Chapter 2, section 30. For genealogical periodical articles, see indexes referred to in Chapter 2, section 19. Library: Lima Public Library, 650 W. Market St., Lima, OH 45801. Phone 1-(419)-228-5113. Society:

154

Allen County Chapter, OGS (contact library for current address).
Publishes NEWSLETTER.

---

7. ASHLAND COUNTY

Ashland County, authorized/established
1846/1846 from Huron, Lorain, Richland, and Wayne Counties. County
seat Ashland (44805). ONAHRC:
University of Akron. Censuses: 1850-
RIMF, 1860RIFD, 1870RFM, 1880RID, 1890C, 1900RI, 1910RI, 1920RI.

FHL(FHC) microfilms: cemetery, chancery (1847–52), civil court
cases (1846–52), common pleas court (1847–52), deed (1846–1901),
Presbyterian (1841–), supreme court (1847–52).

OHS microfilms and records: cemetery, chancery (1846–53),
common pleas court (1846–67), CT Land Company (1795–1809),
marriage (1846–65), supreme court (1847–52).

DAR volumes: cemetery, marriage. Published volumes: biography,
Black, cemetery, census, church, city/county directories, gazetteer,
genealogy, history, inventory of county records, land, marriage, military.

Manuscripts in WRHS. For newspapers, see repositories and
reference volumes given in Chapter 2, section 30. For genealogical
periodical articles, see indexes referred to in Chapter 2, section 19.
Library: Ashland County Public Library, 224 Claremont Ave., Ashland,
OH 44805. Phone 1-(419)-289-8188. Society: Ashland County Chapter,
OGS (contact library for current address). Publishes PASTFINDER.

---

8. ASHTABULA COUNTY

Ashtabula County, author-
ized/established 1808/1811 from
Geauga and Trumbull Counties.
County seat Jefferson (44047).
ONAHRC: WRHS in Cleveland.
Censuses: 1820RIM, 1830RI, 1840RIP, 1850RIMF, 1860RIFD,
1870RFM, 1880RID, 1890C, 1900RI, 1910RI, 1920RI.

FHL(FHC) microfilms: Baptist, birth (1867–1908), census (1811–
35, 1843), church incorporation (1818–73), death (1867–1908), deed
(1798–1947), marriage (1812–1915), naturalization (1858–1906),
Presbyterian (1814–), probate (1811–1955), tax (1812–38), will (1853–88).

OHS microfilms and records: CT Land Company (1795–1809),
deed (1798–1947), marriage (1811–68), naturalization (1875–1906),
religious organizations (1818–34), tax (1812–38). Death (1869–1937) in
SLO, also birth and estate.

DAR volumes: cemetery, census, church, marriage. Published
volumes: atlas, Bible, biography, birth, Black, cemetery, census, church,
death, city/county directories, genealogy, history, naturalization, plat.

Manuscripts in OHS, SLO, WRHS. For newspapers, see
repositories and reference volumes given in Chapter 2, section 30. For
genealogical periodical articles, see indexes referred to in Chapter 2,

section 19. Library: Henderson Memorial Library, 54 E. Jefferson St., Jefferson, OH 44047. Phone 1-(216)-576-3761. Society: Ashtabula County Chapter, OGS (contact library for current address). Publishes ANCESTOR HUNT.

9. ATHENS COUNTY

Athens County, authorized/established 1805/1805 from Washington County. County seat Athens (45701). ONAHRC: OH University in Athens. Censuses: 1820RIM, 1830RI, 1840RIP, 1850RIM, 1860RIFD, 1870RFM, 1880RIFD, 1890C, 1900RI, 1910RI, 1920RI.

FHL(FHC) microfilms: administrator (1842-76), birth (1867-1960), chancery (1837-55), childrens home (1882-1911), common pleas court (1807-60), county home (1857-1928), death (1867-1908), deed (1792-1876), district court (1852-60), estate (1800-1945), executor (1857-97), guardian (1875-92), marriage (1817-1911), military (1861-1916), naturalization (1858-78), probate (1852-88), supreme court (1809-60), tax (1806-38), will (1814-79).

OHS microfilms and records: chancery (1837-5), childrens home (1882-1911), common pleas court (1807-54), county home (1857-1928), district court (1852-60), jail (1881-1900), marriage (1805-65), military (1861-1902), naturalization (1880-1906), supreme court (1809-60), tax (1806-38), will (1795-1845).

DAR volumes: marriage, will. Published volumes: atlas, biography, Black, cemetery, census, church, death, city/county directories, genealogy, history, land, marriage, plat.

For newspapers, see repositories and reference volumes given in Chapter 2, section 30. For genealogical periodical articles, see indexes referred to in Chapter 2, section 19. Library: Charles & Rita Levering Genealogical Library, Athens County Historical Society and Museum, 65 North Court St., Athens, OH 45701. Phone 1-(614)-592-2280. Society: Athens County Chapter, OGS (contact library for current address). Publishes BULLETIN.

10. AUGLAIZE COUNTY

Auglaize County, authorized/established 1848/1848 from Allen and Mercer Counties. County seat Wapakoneta (45895). ONAHRC: Wright State University in Dayton. Censuses: 1850RIMF, 1860RIFD, 1870RFM, 1880RIFD, 1890C, 1900RI, 1910RI, 1920RI.

FHL(FHC) microfilms: administrator (1861-99), birth (1867-1908), chancery (1848-58), civil court cases (1848-58), clerk of courts (1850-8), county home (1889-1935), death (1867-1938), deed (1835-1967), district court (1852-84), guardian (1861-1925), inventory (1857-72), marriage (1848-1926), military (1861-1927), naturalization (1854-

1905), probate (1848-1902), settlements (1852-83), supreme court (1850-84), will (1864-1903).

OHS microfilms and records: cemetery, chancery (1848-58), civil court cases (1848-58), county home (1889-1935), district court (1852-84), military (1861-1927), supreme court (1850-84).

DAR volumes: cemetery, history. Published volumes: atlas, biography, Black, cemetery, church, city/county directories, family, genealogy, history, plat, newspaper abstracts.

For newspapers, see repositories and reference volumes given in Chapter 2, section 30. For genealogical periodical articles, see indexes referred to in Chapter 2, section 19. Library: Auglaize County Public District Library, 203 Perry S. St., Wapakoneta, OH 45895. Phone 1-(419)-738-2921. Society: Auglaize County Chapter, OGS (contact library for current address). Publishes FALLEN TIMBERS ANCES-TREE.

11. BELMONT COUNTY

Belmont County, author-ized/established 1801/1801 from Jefferson and Washington Counties. County seat St. Clairsville (43950), court house fire in 1980, some records lost. ONAHRC: OH University in Athens. Censuses: 1820RIM, 1830RI, 1840RIP, 1850RIMF, 1860RIFD, 1870RFM, 1880RIFD, 1890C, 1900RI, 1910RI, 1920RI.

FHL(FHC) microfilms: administrator (1804-89), birth (1867-1940), chancery (1824-58), childrens home (1880-1947), clerk of courts (1808-55), common pleas court (1808-53), county home (1883-1930), death (1867-1908), deed (1800-1942), district court (1852-4), estate (1801-1935), executor (1849-67), inventory (1832-87), law (1808-55), marriage (1803-1917), military (1865-1919), naturalization (1860-1906), Presbyterian (1821-), probate (1852-87), supreme court (1804-54), tax (1806-38), will (1804-87).

OHS microfilms and records: Black (1809-54), chancery (1824-58), childrens home (1880-1947), commissioners (1804-1902), common pleas court (1805-58), county home (1877/1930), district court (1852), jail (1866-1922), law (1808-55), military (1865-1919), supreme court (1804-51), tax (1806-38).

DAR volumes: deed, land, will. Published volumes: atlas, Black, cemetery, church, city/county directories, gazetteer, genealogy, history, land, marriage, newspaper abstracts, plat.

For newspapers, see repositories and reference volumes given in Chapter 2, section 30. For genealogical periodical articles, see indexes referred to in Chapter 2, section 19. Libraries: Belmont County Public Library, 108 West Main St., St. Clairsville, OH 43950. Phone 1-(614)-695-2062. Barnesville-Hutton Memorial Library, 308 E. Main St., Barnesville, OH 43713. Phone 1-(614)-425-1651. Society: Belmont

County Chapter, OGS (contact library for current address). Publishes BELMONT COUNTY GENEALOGY NEWS.

12. BROWN COUNTY

Brown County, authorized/established 1818/ 1818 from Adams and Clermont Counties. County seat Georgetown (45121). ONAHRC: University of Cincinnati. Censuses: 1820RIM, 1830RI, 1840RIP, 1850RIMF, 1860RIFD, 1870RF, 1880RIFD, 1890C, 1900RI, 1910RI, 1920RI.

FHL(FHC) microfilms: administrator (1852-87), Baptist, birth (1867-1909, 1909-), bonds (1852-71), cemetery, chancery (1820-54), childrens home (1886-1921), civil court cases (1818-88), clerk of courts (1821-54), death (1867-1909), deed (1818-1916), guardian (1882-96), law (1818-26), marriage (1818-1939), military (1864-99), naturalization (1822-34, 1856-1906), probate (1820-52), supreme court (1821-56), tax (1819-38).

OHS microfilms and records: cemetery, chancery (1820-54), childrens home (1885-1935), civil court cases (1818-50), commissioners (1843-1904), common pleas court (1821-54), district court (1852-56), jail (1909-27), law (1818-54), marriage (1818-65), military (1864-99), naturalization (1833-34), quadrennial enumeration (1887-91, 1903), school (1829-87), supreme court (1819-56), tax (1819-38).

DAR volumes: cemetery, genealogy, history, marriage. Published volumes: atlas, Black, cemetery, city/county directories, family, genealogy, history, marriage, naturalization, plat, will.

For newspapers, see repositories and reference volumes given in Chapter 2, section 30. For genealogical periodical articles, see indexes referred to in Chapter 2, section 19. Library: Mary P. Shelton Library, 700 West Grant Ave., Georgetown, OH 45121. Phone 1-(513)-378-3197. Society: Brown County Chapter, OGS (contact library for current address). Publishes ON THE TRAIL.

13. BUTLER COUNTY

Butler County, authorized/established 1803/1803 from Hamilton County. County seat Hamilton (45011). ONAHRC: University of Cincinnati. Censuses: 1820RIM, 1830RI, 1840RIP, 1850RIFM, 1860RIFMD, 1870RF, 1880RIFM, 1890C, 1900RI, 1920RI.

FHL(FHC): birth (1856-57, 1867-1908), cemetery, common pleas court (1803-1939), court (1852-1916), criminal (1824-35), death (1856-57, 1867-1908), deed (1803-76), estate (1851-1929), Friends (1807-), guardian (1867-1960), marriage (1803-1937), Presbyterian (1850-), probate (1852-1939), tax (1806-38), will (1851-1912).

OHS microfilms and records: commissioners (1804-1901), county home (1880-1913), deed (1803-76), marriage (1835-47), surveyor (1803-55), tax (1806-38).

DAR volumes: cemetery, church, marriage. Published volumes: atlas, Bible, biography, Black, cemetery, census, church, city/county directories, family, genealogy, history, land, marriage, will.

Manuscripts in WRHS. For newspapers, see repositories and reference volumes given in Chapter 2, section 30. For genealogical periodical articles, see indexes referred to in Chapter 2, section 19. Libraries: Lane Public Library, N. Third & Buckeye Sts., Hamilton, OH 45011. Phone 1-(513)-894-7156. Middletown Public Library, 125 South Broad St., Middletown, OH 45044. Phone 1-(513)-424-1251. Society: Butler County Chapter, OGS (contact library for current address). Publishes PATHWAYS.

14. CARROLL COUNTY

Carroll County, authorized/established 1833/1833 from Columbiana, Harrison, Jefferson, Stark, and Tuscarawas Counties. County seat Carrollton (44615). ONAHRC: University of Akron. Censuses: 1840RIP, 1850 RIM, 1860RID, 1870RMF, 1880RIFD, 1890C, 1900RI, 1910RI, 1920RI.

FHL(FHC) microfilms: birth (1867-1909), chancery (1834-54), common pleas court (1833-71), death (1867-1908), deed (1826-93), guardian (1900-26), land (1833-50), naturalization (1860-1903), Presbyterian (1828-), probate (1822-1910), supreme court (1833-51), tax (1833-38), will (1833-79).

OHS microfilms and records: chancery (1834-54), supreme court (1833-51), tax (1833-38).

DAR volumes: Bible, cemetery, church, family. Published volumes: atlas, biography, birth, cemetery, census, church, death, city/county directories, genealogy, history, land, marriage, newspaper abstracts, plat, tax, will.

Manuscripts in OHS, WRHS. For newspapers, see repositories and reference volumes given in Chapter 2, section 30. For genealogical periodical articles, see indexes referred to in Chapter 2, section 19. Library: Carroll County District Library, 70 North Lisbon St., Carrollton, OH 44615. Phone 1-(216)-627-2613. Society: Carroll County Chapter, OGS (contact library for current address). Publishes CARROLL COUSINS.

15. CHAMPAIGN COUNTY

Champaign County, authorized/established 1805/1805 from Franklin and Greene Counties. County seat Urbana (43078), court house fire in 1948, some

records lost. ONAHRC: Wright State University in Dayton. Censuses:
1820RIM, 1830RI, 1840RIP, 1850RIM, 1860RID, 1870RFM, 1880RIFD,
1890C, 1900RI, 1910RI.

FHL(FHC) microfilms: administrator (1861-1967), Baptist, birth
(1867-1908), cemetery, chancery (1833-54), childrens home (1892-1910),
common pleas court (1805-55), county home (1838-1963), death (1867-
1909), deed (1805-1968), guardian (1808-1967), land (1852-91), marriage
(1805-1967), military (1865-1968), naturalization (1860-98), Presbyterian
(1844-), probate (1852-1967), settlements (1804-1968), supreme court
(1805-51), tax (1806-38), will (1808-1967).

OHS microfilms: cemetery, chancery (1833-54), childrens home
(1892-1910), clerk of courts (1805-78), common pleas court (1805-55),
county home (1838-1963), death, marriage (1805-64), supreme court
(1805-51), tax (1806-38).

DAR volumes: Bible, cemetery, church, family, marriage,
mortuary. Published volumes: atlas, Bible, biography, Black, death, deed,
city/county directories, family, genealogy, history, land, marriage,
newspaper abstracts, plat, will.

Manuscripts in WRHS. For newspapers, see repositories and
reference volumes given in Chapter 2, section 30. For genealogical
periodical articles, see indexes referred to in Chapter 2, section 19.
Libraries: Champaign County Library, 160 W. Market, Urbana, OH
43078. Phone 1-(513)-635-6557. St. Paris Public Library, 127 E. Main
St., St. Paris, OH 43072. Phone 1-(513)-663-4399. Society: Champaign
County Chapter, OGS (contact library for current address). Publishes,
MAD RIVER CURRENT.

16. CLARK COUNTY

Clark County, authorized/established
1818/1818 from Champaign, Greene, and
Madison Counties. County seat Springfield (45502). ONAHRC: Wright State
University in Dayton. Censuses: 1820-
RIM, 1830RI, 1840RIP, 1850RIM, 1860RID, 1870RM, 1880RIFD,
1890C, 1900RI, 1910RI, 1920RI.

FHL(FHC) microfilms: administrator (1860-1904), birth (1867-
1968), cemetery, chancery (1820-55), childrens home (1878-1920), civil
court cases (1821-52), clerk of courts (1818-1906), common pleas courts
(1820-55), county home (1836-1922), death (1867-1908), deed (1818-
1968), executor (1860-1904), Friends (1815-), law (1819-50), marriage
(1818-1968), military (1864-1964), mortgage (1818-1968), naturalization
(1861-1906), Presbyterian (1810-), probate bonds (1824-1904), school
(1822-33), settlement (1827-1903), supreme court (1819-50), tax (1818-
38).

OHS microfilms and records: chancery (1820-55), childrens home
(1878-1920), civil court cases (1821-52), clerk of courts (1818-1906),
common pleas court (1820-54), county home (1836-1922), law (1819-50),

military (1865-1900), naturalization (1856-77), school (1822-33), Springfield (1827-1926), supreme court (1821-51), tax (1818-38).

DAR volumes: cemetery, church, marriage, tax, will. Published volumes: atlas, Bible, biography, Black, cemetery, church, city/county directories, family, genealogy, history, land, marriage, military, naturalization, newspaper abstracts, plat, probate, tax, will.

Manuscripts in OHS. For newspapers, see repositories and reference volumes given in Chapter 2, section 30. For genealogical periodical articles, see indexes referred to in Chapter 2, section 19. Library: Clark County Public Library, 201 S. Fountain Ave., Springfield, OH 45501. Phone 1(513)-323-9751. Society: Clark County Chapter, OGS (contact library for current address). Publishes CLARK COUNTY KIN.

---

17. CLERMONT COUNTY

Clermont County, authorized/established 1800/1800 from Hamilton County. County seat Batavia (45103). ONAHRC: University of Cincinnati. Censuses: 1820RIM, 1830RI, 1840RIP, 1850RIM, 1860RID, 1870RM, 1880RIFD, 1890C, 1900RI, 1910RI, 1920RI.

FHL(FHC) microfilms: birth (1856-7, 1867-1908), bonds (1860-1916), cemetery, chancery (1824-58), civil court cases (1817-53, 1873-89), death (1856-7, 1867-1908), deed (1800-79), guardian (1849-1910), marriage (1801-1910), military (1863-93), naturalization (1880-1905), petition (1896-1974), probate (1852-89), settlement (1865-1912), supreme court (1801-51),

OHS microfilms and records: Bible, cemetery, chancery (1824-58), civil court cases (1817-53), marriage (1800-54), military (1863-93), supreme court (1801-51), tax (1806-38).

DAR volumes: Bible, cemetery, marriage. Published volumes: atlas, Bible, biography, Black, cemetery, census, church, death, city/county city/county directories, estate, gazetteer, genealogy, guardian, history, land, marriage, mortuary, plat, will.

For newspapers, see repositories and reference volumes given in Chapter 2, section 30. For genealogical periodical articles, see indexes referred to in Chapter 2, section 19. Library: Clermont County Public Library, 180 South Third St., Batavia, OH 45103. Phone 1-(513)-732-2736. Society: Clermont County Chapter, OGS (contact library for current address). Publishes NEWSLETTER.

---

18. CLINTON COUNTY

Clinton County, authorized/established 1810/1810 from Highland and Warren Counties. County seat Wilmington (45177). ONAHRC: University of Cincinnati.

Censuses: 1820RIM, 1830RI, 1840RIP, 1850RIM, 1860RID, 1870RM, 1880RIFD, 1890C, 1900RI, 1810 RI, 1920RI.

FHL(FHC) microfilms: administrator (1853-1901), birth (1868-1908), Black (1838-61), cemetery, chancery (1812-55), childrens home (1884-1926), civil court cases (1810-57), clerk of courts (1812-1906), county home (1836-1909), death (1867-1900), deed (1806-1963), estate (1825-1902), Friends (1754-), guardian (1858-1904), indenture (1824-31), jail (1917-27), marriage (1817-1904), military (1865-1919), mortgage (1836-1913), naturalization (1872-95), probate (1852-1901), quadrennial enumeration (1907), settlement (1874-97), tax (1810-38), votes (1880-90), will (1810-1931).

OHS microfilms and records: Black (1838-61), chancery (1812-55), childrens home (1884-1926), civil court cases (1810-57), clerk of courts (1812-1906), commissioners (1875-1907), county home (1836-1909), indenture (1824-31), jail (1912-27), marriage (1810-93), military (1865-1919), quadrennial enumeration (1907), supreme court (1810-50), tax (1810-38), votes (1880-90).

DAR volumes: cemetery, church, genealogy, marriage, tax. Published volumes: atlas, Black, cemetery, census, church, death, city/county directories, family, genealogy, history, land, newspaper abstracts.

For newspapers, see repositories and reference volumes given in Chapter 2, section 30. For genealogical periodical articles, see indexes referred to in Chapter 2, section 19. Library: Wilmington Public Library of Clinton County, 268 North South St., Wilmington, OH 45177. Phone 1-(513)-382-2417. Society: Clinton County Chapter, OGS (contact library for current address). Publishes THE CLINTON CHRONICAL.

19. COLUMBIANA COUNTY

Columbiana County, authorized/established 1803/1803 from Jefferson and Washington Counties. County seat Lisbon (44432), court house fire in 1976, some records lost. ONAHRC: University of Akron. Censuses: 1820RIM, 1830RI, 1840RIP, 1850RIM, 1860RID, 1870RM, 1880RIFD, 1890C, 1900RI, 1920RI.

FHL(FHC) microfilms: administrator (1861-88), Baptist (1820-), birth (1867-1908), church incorporation (1845-79), commissioners (1803-29, 1859-1905), common pleas court (1831-36), county home (1834-1911), death (1867-1908), deed (1803-1969), executor (1857-88), Friends (1762-), guardian (1852-90), inventory (1834-36, 1856-87), land (1837-48), marriage (1803-1957), Methodist (1864-), mortgage (1846-80), Presbyterian (1832-), probate (1803-1940), quadrennial enumeration (1899-1903), tax (1806-38), will (1853-87).

OHS microfilms and records: Civil War, commissioners (1803-29, 1859-1905), county home (1834-1911), marriage (1804-35), quadrennial enumeration (1899-1903), tax (1806-38), will (1803-50).

DAR volumes: atlas, biography, Black, cemetery, census, church, death, deed, city/county directories, genealogy, history, land, marriage, newspaper abstracts, pensioners, plat, will.

Manuscripts in OHS, WRHS. For newspapers, see repositories and reference volumes given in Chapter 2, section 30. For genealogical periodical articles, see indexes referred to in Chapter 2, section 19. Libraries: Lepper Public Library, 303 East Lincoln Way, Lisbon, OH 44432. Phone 1-(216)-424-3117. Salem Public Library, 821 East State St., Salem, OH 44460. Phone 1-(216)-332-0042. Society: Columbiana County Chapter, OGS (contact library for current address). Publishes THE COLUMBIANA COUNTY CONNECTIONS.

---

20. COSHOCTON COUNTY

Coshocton County, authorized/established 1810/1811 from Muskingum and Tuscarawas Counties. County seat Coshocton (43812). ONAHRC: University of Akron. Censuses: 1820RIM, 1830RI, 1840RIP, 1850RIM, 1860RID, 1870RM, 1880RIFD, 1890C, 1900RI, 1910RI, 1920RI.

FHL(FHC) microfilms: administrator (1811-1921), birth (1867-1908), chancery (1814-57), clerk of courts (1811-52), commissioners (1812-1902), common pleas court (1811-52), death (1867-1908), deed (1800-1907), district court (1849-63), estate (1853-1944), executor (1839-1923), guardian (1837-1925), inventory (1837-1918), jail (1870-1927), Lutheran (1876-), marriage (1811-1917), militia (1857-8), naturalization (1839-1906), Presbyterian (1827-), probate (1811-95), quadrennial enumeration (1883, 1891), supreme court (1814-63), tax (1812-38), will (1811-1912).

OHS microfilms and records: administrator (1839-1921), chancery (1814-57), clerk of courts (1811-52), commissioners (1812-1902), common pleas court (1811-52), executor (1839-1923), guardian (1839-1925), inventory (1837-55, 1887-1918), militia (1857-58), naturalization (1866, 1880-1932), probate (1811-85), quadrennial enumeration (1883, 1891), supreme court (1814-63), tax (1812-38), will (1888-1912).

DAR volumes: birth, cemetery, church, death, marriage, will. Published volumes: atlas, birth, Black, cemetery, census, church, city/county directories, death, history, land, marriage, school, will.

Manuscripts in WRHS. For newspapers, see repositories and reference volumes given in Chapter 2, section 30. For genealogical periodical articles, see indexes referred to in Chapter 2, section 19. Library: Coshocton Public Library, 655 Main St., Coshocton, OH 43812. Phone 1-(614)-622-0956. Society: Coshocton County Chapter, OGS (contact library for current address). Publishes KINSMAN COURIER.

---

21. CRAWFORD COUNTY

Crawford County, authorized/established 1800/1826 from Delaware County. County seat Bucyrus (44820), court house fire in 1831, some records lost. ONAHRC: Bowling Green State University. Censuses: 1830RI, 1840RIP, 1850RIM, 1860RID, 1870RM, 1880RIFMD, 1890C, 1900RI, 1910RI, 1820RI.

FHL(FHC) microfilms: administrator (1826–88), birth (1866–1908), cemetery, chancery (1851–54), church incorporation (1875–1933), commissioners (1831–1910), common pleas court (1839–73), death (1868–1909), deed (1816–1967), district court (1832–84), estate (1834–1969), Evangelical-Reformed (1859–), executor (1883–99), guardian (1826–1940), Lutheran (1829–), marriage (1831–1929), Methodist (1850–), military (1861–1965), naturalization (1847–1905), newspapers (1850–), Presbyterian (1853–), probate (1852–1913), supreme court (1832–84), tax (1826–38), United Brethren (1850–), will (1831–1901).

OHS microfilms and records: cemetery, chancery (1851–54), common pleas (1839–73), district court (1832–84), supreme court (1832–84), tax (1826–38).

DAR volumes: Bible, cemetery, family, marriage. Published volumes: atlas, Bible, biography, cemetery, church, city/county directories, family, history, newspaper abstracts, probate.

Manuscripts in OHS, WRHS. For newspapers, see repositories and reference volumes given in Chapter 2, section 30. For genealogical periodical articles, see indexes referred to in Chapter 2, section 19. Library: Bucyrus Public Library, 200 E. Mansfield St., Bucyrus, OH 44820. Phone 1-(419)-562-7327. Society: Crawford County Chapter, OGS (contact library for current address). Publishes TRACKING IN CRAWFORD COUNTY.

---

22. CUYAHOGA COUNTY

Cuyahoga County, authorized/established 1808/1810 from Geauga County. County seat Cleveland (44113). ONAHRC: WRHS in Cleveland. Censuses: 1820RIM, 1830RI, 1840RIP, 1850RIM, 1860RID, 1870RM, 1880-RIFMD, 1890C, 1900RI, 1910RI, 1920RI.

FHL(FHC) microfilms: administrator (1811–96), alien (1818–56), Baptist (1820–), birth (1867–1908), cemetery, common pleas court (1823–52), Congregational (1816–), death (1868–1908), deed (1810–1900), Episcopal (1835–), marriage (1810–1929), Methodist (1874–), mortgage (1810–1900), naturalization (1858–1906), Presbyterian (1807–), probate (1811–86), supreme court (1831–51), tax (1810–38), will (1852–93).

OHS microfilms and records: Bible, cemetery, church, common pleas court (1823–52), land (1795–1809), naturalization (1888–89, 1902–06), supreme court (1831–42), tax (1810–38).

DAR volumes: Bible, cemetery, church, family, land, marriage, tax. Published volumes: atlas, baptisms, Bible, biography, Black, cemetery, church, city/county directories, family, genealogy, history, inventory of county records, land, marriage, mortuary, newspaper abstracts.

Manuscripts in WRHS. For newspapers, see repositories and reference volumes given in Chapter 2, section 30. For genealogical periodical articles, see indexes referred to in Chapter 2, section 19. Libraries: Cuyahoga County Public Library, 4510 Memphis Ave., Cleveland, OH 44144. Phone 1-(216)-398-1880. Cleveland Public Library, 325 Superior Ave., Cleveland, OH 44114. Phone 1-(216)-623-2800. Western Reserve Historical Society (WRHS), 10825 East Blvd., Cleveland, OH 44106. Phone 1-(216)-721-5722. Societies: Brecksville Chapter, OGS (contact library for current address). Publishes FOOT-STEPS TO THE PAST. East Cuyahoga Chapter, OGS (contact library for current address). Publishes SPEAKING RELATIVELY. Greater Cleveland Chapter, OGS (contact library for current address). Publishes CERTIFIED COPY. Parma Chapter, OGS (contact library for current address). Southwest Cuyahoga Chapter, OGS (contact library for current address). Publishes NEWSLETTER. West Cuyahoga Chapter, OGS (contact library for current address). Publishes TRACER.

23. DARKE COUNTY

Darke County, authorized/established 1809/1817 from Miami County. County seat Greenville (45331). ONAHRC: Wright State University of Dayton. Censuses: 1820RIM, 1830RI, 1840RIP, 1850RIMF, 1860RIFD, 1870RM, 1880RIFMD, 1890C, 1900RI, 1810RI, 1920RI.

FHL(FHC) microfilms: Bible, birth (1867-1908), cemetery, chancery (1818-53), childrens home (1889-1915), civil court cases (1817-87), county home (1856-1951), death (1867-1905), deed (1820-38), estate (1818-1925), marriage (1817-1911), naturalization (1856-1906), probate (1818-53), supreme court (1817-51), tax (1818-38). will (1818-1910).

OHS microfilms and records: biography (1867-1908), cemetery, chancery (1818-53), childrens home (1889-1915), civil court cases (1817-87), county home (1856-1951), death (1867-1905), estate (1818-1925), Greenville (1857-1976), marriage (1817-1911), naturalization (1856-1906), probate (1818-53), supreme court (1817-51), tax (1818-38), will (1818-1910).

DAR volumes: Bible, birth, cemetery, church, death. Published volumes: atlas, Bible, biography, cemetery, census, church, city/county directories, death, family, genealogy, history, inventory of county records, land, marriage, naturalization, newspaper abstracts, will.

Manuscripts in OHS. For newspapers, see repositories and reference volumes given in Chapter 2, section 30. For genealogical periodical articles, see indexes referred to in Chapter 2, section 19. Library: Greenville Public Library, 520 Sycamore St., Greenville, OH 45331. Phone 1-(513)-548-3915. Society: Darke County Chapter, OGS (contact library for current address). Publishes DARKE COUNTY KINDLING.

---

24. DEFIANCE COUNTY

Defiance County, authorized/established 1845/1845 from Henry, Paulding, and Williams Counties. County seat Defiance (43512). ONAHRC: Bowling Green State University. Censuses: 1850RIMF, 1860RIFD, 1870RM, 1880 RIFMD, 1890C, 1900RI, 1910RI, 1920RI.

FHL(FHC) microfilms: administrator (1845-1905), birth (1867-1908), chancery (1845-65), civil court cases (1853-1908), clerk of courts (1845-84), county home (1880-1980), death (1867-1908), deed (1823-1969), guardian (1860-1905), inventory (1853-86), marriage (1845-1918), military (1869-1972), naturalization (1848-1906), Presbyterian (1836-), probate (1845-1972), supreme court (1846-84), veteran (1869-1972), will (1845-1910).

OHS microfilms and records: administrator (1845-53), birth (1867-1908), chancery (1845-65), childrens home (1884-1925), clerk of courts (1845-84), county home (1880-1980), deed (1880-86), marriage (1840-64), naturalization (1884-94), probate (1845-89), supreme court (1846-84), will (1902-10).

DAR volumes: Bible, marriage, will. Published volumes: atlas, Bible, biography, Black, church, city/county directories, death, family, history, newspaper abstracts, plat, will.

For newspapers, see repositories and reference volumes given in Chapter 2, section 30. For genealogical periodical articles, see indexes referred to in Chapter 2, section 19. Library: Defiance Public Library, 320 Fort St., Defiance, OH 43512. Phone 1-(419)-782-1456. Society: Defiance County Chapter, OGS (contact library for current address). Publishes YESTERYEARS TRAIL.

---

25. DELAWARE COUNTY

Delaware County, authorized/established 1808/1808 from Franklin County. County seat Delaware (43015), court house fire in 1835, many records lost. ONAHRC: OHS in Columbus. Censuses: 1820 RIM, 1830RI, 1840RIP, 1850RIMF, 1860RIFD, 1870RM, 1880RIFMD, 1890C, 1900RI, 1910RI, 1920RI.

FHL(FHC) microfilms: administrator (1860-84), birth (1867-1909), cemetery, chancery (1825-54), clerk of courts (1821-55), common pleas court (1818-27, 1835-38), death (1867-99), estate (1835-49), executor (1853-79), guardian (1858-79), marriage (1835-1927), Presbyterian (1814-), probate (1852-1908), supreme court (1833-51), tax (1808-38), veteran (1884-98), will (1812-1952).

OHS microfilms and records: cemetery, chancery (1825-54), clerk of courts (1821-55), common pleas court (1919-27, 1835-38), estate (1835-49), marriage (1832-65), military, supreme court (1833-51), tax (1808-38), veteran (1884-98).

DAR volumes: cemetery, marriage, will. Published volumes: atlas, Black, cemetery, church, city/county directories, family, genealogy, history, land, marriage, mortuary, probate, tax, will.

Manuscripts in OHS, WRHS. For newspapers, see repositories and reference volumes given in Chapter 2, section 30. For genealogical periodical articles, see indexes referred to in Chapter 2, section 19. Library: Delaware County District Library, 84 E. Winter St., Delaware, OH 43015. Phone 1-(614)-362-3861. Society: Delaware County Chapter, OGS (contact library for current address). Publishes DELAWARE GENEALOGIST.

26. ERIE COUNTY

Erie County, authorized/established 1838/1838 from Huron and Sandusky Counties. County seat Sandusky (44870). ONAHRC: Bowling Green State University. Censuses: 1840RIP, 1850RIMF, 1860RIFD, 1870RM, 1880 RIFMD, 1890C, 1900RI, 1910RI, 1920RI.

FHL(FHC) microfilms: administrator (1838-1907), birth (1856-1913), cemetery, clerk of courts (1838-), commissioners (1860-1904), common pleas court (1838-54), death (1856-65, 1870-1913), deed (1837-1905), district court (1852-57), executor (1866-1907), guardian (1866-1907), inventory (1855-1902), marriage (1838-1920), military (1865-1930, 1944-45), naturalization (1838-44, 1852-1929), oaths (1838-1919), probate (1838-1961), supreme court (1839-52), tax (1838-51), will (1853-1911).

OHS microfilms and records: administrator (1838-88), common pleas court (1838-54), deed (1881-86), district court (1852-57), military (1865-1919, 1944-45), supreme court (1839-52), will (1901-11).

DAR volumes: cemetery, marriage, will. Published volumes: atlas, biography, birth, cemetery, city/county directories, death, family, genealogy, history, marriage, newspaper abstracts, will.

Manuscripts in OHS, WRHS. For newspapers, see repositories and reference volumes given in Chapter 2, section 30. For genealogical periodical articles, see indexes referred to in Chapter 2, section 19. Library: Sandusky Library, 114 West Adams St., Sandusky, OH 44870. Phone 1-(419)-625-3834. Society: Erie County Chapter, OGS (contact library for current address). Publishes ERIE COUNTY CONNECTION.

27. FAIRFIELD COUNTY

Fairfield County, author-zed/established 1800/1800 from Ross and Washington Counties. County seat Lancaster (43130). ONAHRC: OHS in Columbus.

Censuses: 1820RIM, 1830RI, 1840RIP, 1850RIMF, 1860RIFMD, 1870RF, 1880RIMD, 1890C, 1900RI, 1910RI, 1920RI.

FHL(FHC) microfilms: administrator (1835-59), Bible, birth (1867-1909), cemetery, commissioners (1812-1962), common pleas court (1838-54), death (1867-1909), deed (1801-99), guardian (1835-1913), LDS (1931-), marriage (1803-80), naturalization (1820-1904), Presbyterian (1806-), probate (1802-1969), quadrennial enumeration (1831, 1839, 1847-51, 1859), quarter sessions (1801-38), supreme court (1803-22, 1833-79), tax (1806-38), will (1803-77).

OHS microfilms and records: Bible, cemetery, commissioners (1812-1962), common pleas court (1838-54), marriage (1803-65), naturalization (1820-1904), quadrennial enumeration (1831, 1839, 1847-51, 1859), supreme court (1803-22, 1833-79), tax (1806-38).

DAR volumes: Bible, cemetery, family, marriage. Published volumes: atlas, Bible, Black, cemetery, census, church, city/county directories, family, genealogy, history, inventory of county records, land, marriage, naturalization, will.

For newspapers, see repositories and reference volumes given in Chapter 2, section 30. For genealogical periodical articles, see indexes referred to in Chapter 2, section 19. Library: Fairfield County District Library, 219 North Broad St., Lancaster, OH 43130. Phone 1-(614)-653-2745. Society: Fairfield County Chapter, OGS (contact library for current address). Publishes FAIRFIELD TRACE.

28. FAYETTE COUNTY

Fayette County, author-ized/established 1810/1810 from Highland and Ross Counties. County seat Washington Court House (43160), court house fire in 1828, some records lost. ONAHRC: OHS in Columbus. Censuses: 1820RIM, 1830RI, 1840RIP, 1850RIMF, 1860RIFD, 1870RFM, 1880RIFMD, 1890C, 1900RI, 1910RI.

FHL(FHC) microfilms: administrator (1828-78), Bible, birth (1867-1908, cemetery, commissioners (1828-1902), county home (1885-1913), death (1868-1907), deed (1810-1913), executor (1828-59), Friends (1827-), guardian (1828-90), marriage (1810-1937), militia (1865), naturalization (1880-1900), Presbyterian (1834-), probate (1852-1900), quadrennial enumeration (1887-1891, 1899), tax (1810-38), will (1810-1957).

OHS microfilms and records: Bible, cemetery, commissioners (1828-1902), common pleas court (1870-1905), county home (1885-

1913), deed (1810–15), marriage (1843–55), militia (1865), tax (1810–38), will (1825–1900).

DAR volumes: Bible, cemetery, church, court, death, deed, family, guardian, marriage, will. Published volumes: atlas, Bible, biography, birth, Black, cemetery, census, church, city/county directories, court, deed, family, genealogy, history, land, marriage, will.

Manuscripts in OHS, WRHS. For newspapers, see repositories and reference volumes given in Chapter 2, section 30. For genealogical periodical articles, see indexes referred to in Chapter 2, section 19. Library: Carnegie Public Library, 127 South North St., Washington Court House, OH 43160. Phone 1-(614)-335-3540. Society: Fayette County Chapter, OGS (contact library for current address). Publishes FAYETTE CONNECTION.

29. FRANKLIN COUNTY

Franklin County, authorized/established 1803/1803 from Ross and Wayne (MI) Counties. County seat Columbus (43215), court house fire in 1879, some records lost. ONAHRC: OHS in Columbus. Censuses: 1830RI, 1840RIP, 1850RIMF, 1860RIFD, 1870RFM, 1880RIFMD, 1890C, 1900RI, 1910RI, 1920RI.

FHL(FHC) microfilms: administrator (1831–86), appraisal (1803–18), Bible, birth (1867–1907), cemetery, chancery (1823–52), clerk of courts (1803–72), common pleas court (1809–53), death (1811–32, 1867–1908), deed (1804–77), estate (1801–1919), executor (1855–86), guardian (1806–1919), incorporation (1821–22), Jewish (1906–), LDS (1931–), marriage (1803–1918), naturalization (1846–1906), Presbyterian (1831–), probate (1852–86), supreme court (1810–51), tax (1806–38), will (1805–1932.

OHS microfilms and records: administrator (1831–1951), Bible, birth (1867–1907), cemetery, chancery (1823–52), city directories (1843–62), clerk of courts (1803–72), commissioners (1908–56), common pleas court (1809–53), coroner (1904–20), county home (1859–99), death (1867–1908), estate (1801–1970), executor (1849–1900), guardian (1806–1919), incorporation 1821–22), Jewish (1868–), marriage (1803–1976), naturalization (1846–1906), probate (1852–1932), supreme court (1810–51), tax (1806–38), will (1803–1932).

DAR volumes: Bible, cemetery, church, death, family, genealogy, marriage, will. Published volumes: atlas, biography, cemetery, census, church, city/county directories, death, divorces, family, genealogy, guardian, history, inventory of county records, land, marriage, naturalization, newspaper abstracts, probate, tax, will.

For newspapers, see repositories and reference volumes given in Chapter 2, section 30. For genealogical periodical articles, see indexes referred to in Chapter 2, section 19. Libraries: Ohio Historical Society,

1985 Velma Ave., Columbus, OH 43211. Phone 1-(614)-297-2510. State Library of OH, 65 South Front St., Columbus, OH 43266. Phone 1-(614)-644-7061; Columbus Metropolitan Library, 28 South Hamilton Rd., Columbus, OH 43213. Phone 1-(614)-645-2800. Society: Franklin County Chapter, OGS (contact library for current address). Publishes THE FRANKLINTONIAN.

---

30. FULTON COUNTY

Fulton County, authorized/established 1850/1850 from Henry, Lucas, and Williams Counties. County seat Wauseon (43567), court house fire in the 1860s, a few records lost. ONAHRC: Bowling Green State University. Censuses: 1850RIMF, 1860RIFD, 1870RFM, 1880RIFMD, 1890C, 1900RI, 1910RI, 1920RI.

FHL(FHC) microfilms: administrator (1868-93), birth (1867-1951), cemetery, commissioners (1874-1926), coroner (1888-1948), death (1867-1951), deed (1835-93), executor (1868-93), guardian (1864-89), jail (1869-1922), marriage (1864-1930), militia (1864), military 1865-1952), naturalization (1872-1906), Presbyterian (1848-), probate (1864-1972), school (1861-79, 1892-1902), will (1853-1972).

OHS microfilms and records: cemetery, church, deed (1881-87), marriage (1863-66), military (1865-1952).

DAR volumes: Bible, cemetery, church, court, marriage, will. Published volumes: atlas, Bible, biography, Black, cemetery, census, church, death, family, history, inventory of court records, land, newspaper abstracts, plat.

For newspapers, see repositories and reference volumes given in Chapter 2, section 30. For genealogical periodical articles, see indexes referred to in Chapter 2, section 19. Libraries: Wauseon Public Library, 117 East Elm St., Wauseon, OH 43567. Phone 1-(419)-335-6626. Swanton Public Library, 305 Chestnut St., Swanton, OH 43558. Phone 1-(419)-826-2760. Society: Fulton County Chapter, OGS (contact library for current address). Publishes FULTON FOOTPRINTS.

---

31. GALLIA COUNTY

Gallia County, authorized/established 1803/1803 from Adams and Washington Counties. County seat Gallipolis (45631), court house fire in 1981, some records lost. ONAHRC: OH University of Athens. Censuses: 1820RIM, 1830RI, 1840RIP, 1850RIMF, 1860RIFD, 1870RFM, 1880RIMD, 1890C, 19100RI, 1910RI, 1920RI.

FHL(FHC) microfilms: birth (1864-1921), chancery (1835-52), childrens home (1885-1942), clerk of courts (1849-52), commissioners (1860-1904), common pleas court (1811-53), county home (1877-1974), death (1867-1916), deed (1789-1892), jail (1869-1928), marriage (1803-1941), military (1862-1903, 1918), naturalization (1880-1906), Presbyterian (1829–), probate (1852–81), quadrennial enumeration (1899), school (1867–99), supreme court (1829–51), tax (1806–38), will (1803–1963).

OHS microfilms and records: chancery (1835–52), childrens home (1885–1942), clerk of courts (1849–52), commissioners (1860–1904), common pleas court (1811–53), county home (1877–1974), jail (1869–1928), marriage (1805–65), military (1862–1903, 1918), quadrennial enumeration (1899), school (1867–99), supreme court (1829–51), tax (1806–38).

DAR volumes: marriage, tax. Published volumes: atlas, biography, cemetery, census, court, city/county directories, death, gazetteer, history, inventory of county records, land, marriage, newspaper abstracts, plat, tax, will.

Manuscripts in OHS, WRHS. For newspapers, see repositories and reference volumes given in Chapter 2, section 30. For genealogical periodical articles, see indexes referred to in Chapter 2, section 19. Library: Dr. Samuel L. Bossard Memorial Library, 641 Second Ave., Gallipolis, OH 45631. Phone 1-(614)-446-7323. Society: Gallia County Chapter, OGS (contact library for current address). Publishes GALLIA COUNTY HISTORICAL SOCIETY NEWSLETTER.

32. GEAUGA COUNTY

Geauga County, authorized/established 1806/1806 from Trumbull County. County seat Chardon (44024). ONAHRC: WRHS in Cleveland. Censuses: 1820RIM, 1830RI, 1840RIP, 1850RIMF, 1860RIFD, 1870RFM, 1880RIMD, 1890C, 1900RI, 1920RI.

FHL(FHC) microfilms: administrator (1870–98), Baptist (1817–), birth (1867–1908), chancery (1839–52), clerk of courts (1806–52), common pleas court (1807–90), death (1867–1908), deed (1795–86), district court (1853–57), executor (1870–97), guardian (1867–1910), incorporation (1845–1906), indenture (1825–58), inventory (1853–86), land (1806–08), lease (1830–1921), marriage (1806–1919), military, mortgage (1795–1880), naturalization (1860–1906), Presbyterian (1814–), probate (1806–87), road (1806–84), school (1839–66), settlement (1806–89), supreme court (1806–84), surveyor (1834–74), tax (1807–50), treasurer (1819–72), will (1853–1910).

OHS microfilms and records: administrator (1871–98), chancery (1839–52), common pleas court (1807–95), CT Land Company (1795–1809), deed (1835–86), marriage (1805–65), supreme court (1806–62), tax (1807–38), will (1891–1910).

DAR volumes: Bible, cemetery, family, marriage, will. Published volumes: atlas, biography, Black, cemetery, church, city/county directories, gazetteer, genealogy, history, inventory of county records, land, marriage, newspaper abstracts.

Manuscripts in WRHS. For newspapers, see repositories and

reference volumes given in Chapter 2, section 30. For genealogical
periodical articles, see indexes referred to in Chapter 2, section 19.
Library: Geauga County Public Library, 121 South St., Chardon, OH
44024. Phone 1-(216)-286-6811. Society: Geauga County Chapter, OGS
(contact library for current address). Publishes RACONTEUR.

33. GREENE COUNTY

Greene County, authorized/established
1803/1803 from Hamilton and Ross
Counties. County seat Xenia (45385).
ONAHRC: Wright State University of
Dayton. Censuses: 1820RIM, 1830RI,
1840RIP, 1850RIMF, 1860RIFD, 1870RFM, 1880RIM, 1890C, 1900RI,
1910RI, 1920RI.

FHL(FHC) microfilms: administrator (1814-1967), birth (1869-
1909), Black (1805-44), cemetery, chancery (1821-54), childrens home
(1896-1926), circuit court (1885-1913), civil court cases (1804-1909),
clerk of courts (1802-1910), commissioners (1804-1902), common pleas
court (1853-1902), county home (1829-1908), death (1870-1903), deed
(1798-1965), district court (1852-85), executor (1814-1967), final
settlement (1852-1960), Friends (1925-), guardian (1868-1962), indenture
(1896-1919), marriage (1803-1968), military (1863-1965), mortgage
(1839-1967), naturalization (1880-1906), Presbyterian (1829-), probate
(1852-1967), school (1831-33), superior court (1870-82), supreme court
(1810-60), tax (1806-50), will (1803-1959).

OHS microfilms and records: Black (1805-44), chancery (1821-
54), childrens home (1896-1926), circuit court (1885-1913), civil court
cases (1804-1909), clerk of courts (1802-1910), commissioners. (1804-
1902), common pleas court (1853-1902), county home (1829-1908),
district court (1852-85), indenture (1896-1919), marriage (1803-70),
military (1862-1949), naturalization (1880-1906), school (1831-33),
superior court (1871-82), supreme court (1803-60), tax (1806-50), Xenia
(1834-1977), Yellow Springs (1861-1977).

DAR volumes: cemetery, history, marriage. Published volumes:
atlas, Bible, biography, cemetery, census, church, city/county directories,
death, gazetteer, genealogy, history, inventory of county records, land,
marriage, naturalization, newspaper abstracts, plat, school.

Manuscripts in OHS, WRHS. For newspapers, see repositories
and reference volumes given in Chapter 2, section 30. For genealogical
periodical articles, see indexes referred to in Chapter 2, section 19.
Library: Greene County District Library, 76 East Market St., Xenia, OH
45385. Phone 1-(513)-376-2996. Society: Greene County Chapter, OGS
(contact library for current address). Publishes LEAVES OF GREENE.

34. GUERNSEY COUNTY

Guernsey County, author-ized/established 1810/1810 from Belmont and Muskingum Counties. County seat Cambridge (43725). ONAHRC: OH University in Athens. Censuses: 1820RIM, 1830RI, 1840RIP, 1850RIMF, 1860RIFD, 1870RFM, 1880RIM, 1890C, 1900RI, 1910RI, 1920RI.

FHL(FHC) microfilms: administrator (1829-86), birth (1867-1909), cemetery, chancery (1836-62), childrens home (1884-1929), commissioners (1810-1901), common pleas court (1810-53), county home (1868-1945), death (1867-1908), deed (1802-1968), district court (1852-56), inventory (1826-87), jail (1893-1902), law (1838-61), marriage (1810-1930), military (1861-65), naturalization (1864-1906), Presbyterian (1840-), probate (1812-1942), supreme court (1811-52), tax (1810-34), will (1812-1972).

OHS microfilms and records: cemetery, chancery (1836-62), childrens home (1884-1929), commissioners (1810-1901), common pleas court (1810-53), county home (1868-1945), district court (1852-56), jail (1893-1902), military (1861-65), supreme court (1811-52), tax (1810-34).

DAR volume: cemetery. Published volumes: atlas, biography, cemetery, census, church, city/county directories, death, deed, estate, family, gazetteer, history, Indians, inventory of county records, land, marriage, will.

Manuscripts in WRHS. For newspapers, see repositories and reference volumes given in Chapter 2, section 30. For genealogical periodical articles, see indexes referred to in Chapter 2, section 19. Library: Guernsey County District Public Library, 800 Steubenville Ave., Cambridge, OH 43728. Phone 1-(614)-432-5946. Society: Guernsey County Chapter, OGS (contact library for current address). Publishes GUERNSEY ROOTS AND BRANCHES.

35. HAMILTON COUNTY

Hamilton County, author-ized/established 1790/1790 as an original county. County seat Cincinnati (45702), court house fires in 1814, 1849, and 1884, numerous records lost. ONAHRC: University of Cincinnati. Censuses: 1820RIM, 1830RI, 1840RIP, 1850RIMFD, 1860RIFD, 1870RFM, 1880RIOM, 1890C, 1900RI, 1910RI, 1920RI.

FHL(FHC) microfilms: administrator (1852-87), alien (1880-90), birth (1863-1908), cemetery, circuit court (1844-47), city directories (1819-1910), death (1881-1908), deed (1787-1877), Friends (1762-), guardian (1852-1901), incorporation (1847-1919), Jewish (1850-), LDS (1856-), marriage (1808-1928), naturalization (1830-1902), Presbyterian (1795-), probate (1790-1891), tax (1801-38), will (1792-1901).

OHS microfilms and records: alien (1880-90), cemetery, marriage (1817-46), Methodist (1861-), naturalization (1830-1902), tax (1801-38). DAR volumes: Bible, cemetery, church, family. Published volumes: atlas, Bible, biography, Black, cemetery, census, church, city/county directories, court, death, deed, family, gazetteer, history, inventory of county records, land, marriage, mortuary, newspaper abstracts, school.

Manuscripts in WRHS, Cincinnati Historical Society. For newspapers, see repositories and reference volumes given in Chapter 2, section 30. For genealogical periodical articles, see indexes referred to in Chapter 2, section 19. Library: Public Library of Cincinnati & Hamilton County, 800 Vine St., Cincinnati, OH 45202. Phone 1-(513)-369-6000. Society: Hamilton County Chapter, OGS (contact library for current address). Publishes THE TRACER.

36. HANCOCK COUNTY

Hancock County, authorized/established 1820/1828 from Logan County. County seat Findlay (45840). ONAHRC: Bowling Green State University. Censuses: 1830RI, 1840RIP, 1850RIMFD, 1860RIFD, 1870RFM, 1880RIF, 1890C, 1900RI, 1910RI, 1820RI.

FHL(FHC) microfilms: administrator (1845-1916), birth (1867-1909), cemetery, chancery (1847-56), clerk of courts (1833-74), common pleas court (1828-57), county home (1868-1947), death (1867-80), deed (1820-1936), district court (1852-67), final settlement (1857-89), marriage (1828-1918), military (1865-1946), Presbyterian (1830-), probate (1828-1970), supreme court (1833-51), tax (1828-38), will (1829-1903).

OHS microfilms and records: administrator (1845-50), cemetery, chancery (1847-56), clerk of courts (1833-74), common pleas court (1828-57), county home (1868-1947), deed (1881-87), district court (1852-67), marriage (1828-1918), military (1865-1946), supreme court (1833-51), tax (1828-38).

DAR volumes: Bible, cemetery, marriage. Published volumes: atlas, Bible, biography, cemetery, census, church, city/county directories, gazetteer, history, inventory of county records, land, marriage, naturalization, newspaper abstracts, plat, will.

For newspapers, see repositories and reference volumes given in Chapter 2, section 30. For genealogical periodical articles, see indexes referred to in Chapter 2, section 19. Library: Findlay-Hancock County Public Library, 206 Broadway, Findlay, OH 45840. Phone 1-(419)-422-1712. Society: Hancock County Chapter, OGS (contact library for current address). Publishes HANCOCK COUNTY HERITAGE.

174

37. HARDIN COUNTY

Hardin County, authorized/established 1820/1833 from Logan County. County seat Kenton (43326), court house fire in 1853, many records lost.

ONAHRC: Bowling Green State University. Censuses: 1820RI, 1830RI, 1840RIF, 1850RIMFD, 1860RIFD, 1870RFM, 1880RIF, 1890C, 1900RI, 1910RI, 1920RI.

FHL(FHC) microfilms: administrator (1866-95), birth (1867-1908), chancery (1842-46), clerk of courts (1833-67), commissioners (1853-1903), common pleas court (1833-50), coroner (1885-1921), death (1867-1908), deed (1831-1968), district court (1852-57), estate (1850-1960), executor (1871-95), final settlement (1834-98), guardian (1865-93), infirmary (1871-1957), inventory (1849-87), jail (1868-85, 1897-1938), jury (1885-90), marriage (1833-1960), military (1861-65), naturalization (1875-1900), Presbyterian (1869-), probate (1834-85), quadrennial enumeration (1887-1907), supreme court (1836-52), surveyor (1820-57), tax (1821-50).

OHS microfilms and records: administrator (1873-82), chancery (1842-46), clerk of courts (1833-67), commissioners (1853-1903), common pleas court (1833-50), deed (1881-86), district court (1852-57), executor (1873-82), final settlement (1834-98), guardian (1865-89), marriage (1833-65), supreme court (1836-52), tax (1833-38), will (1901-12).

DAR volumes: Bible, family, marriage. Published volumes: atlas, biography, cemetery, city/county directories, family, history, land, newspaper abstracts.

For newspapers, see repositories and reference volumes given in Chapter 2, section 30. For genealogical periodical articles, see indexes referred to in Chapter 2, section 19. Library: Mary Lou Johnson-Hardin County District Library, 325 East Columbus St., Kenton, OH 43326. Phone 1-(419)-673-2278. Society: Hardin County Chapter, OGS (contact library for current address). Publishes TRACE AND TRACE.

38. HARRISON COUNTY

Harrison County, authorized/established 1813/1813 from Jefferson and Tuscarawas Counties. County seat Cadiz (43907).

ONAHRC: University of Akron. Censuses: 1820RIM, 1830RI, 1840RIP, 1850RIMFD, 1860RIFD, 1870RFM, 1880RIF, 1890C, 1900RI, 1910RI, 1820RI.

FHL(FHC) microfilms: administrator (1813-55), birth (1867-1971), commissioners (1824-1909), death (1867-1941), deed (1812-1911), executor (1826-51), final settlement (1853-87), Friends (1820-), guardian (1826-51, 1882-1913), inventory (1813-87), jail (1913-36), marriage (1813-1820), Presbyterian (1813-), probate (1852-87), tax (1814-35), will (1813-92).

OHS microfilms and records: commissioners (1824-1909), jail (1913-36), tax (1814-35).

DAR volume: marriage. Published volumes: biography, birth, cemetery, census, church, city/county directories, court, death, deed, family, gazetteer, genealogy, history, infirmary, land, marriage.

For newspapers, see repositories and reference volumes given in Chapter 2, section 30. For genealogical periodical articles, see indexes referred to in Chapter 2, section 19. Library: Puskarich Public Library, 200 Market St., Cadiz, OH 43907. Phone 1-(614)-942-2623. Society: Harrison County Chapter, OGS (contact library for current address). Publishes OUR HARRISON HERITAGE.

39. HENRY COUNTY

Henry County, authorized/established 1820/1834 from Shelby County. County seat Napoleon (43545), court house fire in 1847, some records lost. ONAHRC: Bowling Green State University. Censuses: 1830RI, 1840RIP, 1850RIMFD, 1860RIFD, 1870RFM, 1880RIF, 1890C, 1900RI, 1910RI, 1920RI.

FHL(FHC) microfilms: administrator (1847-89), birth (1867-1921), cemetery deeds (1872-1976), clerk of courts (1847-73), county home (1870-1979), death (1867-1908), deed (1846-), district court (1852-85), guardian (1874-82), incorporation (1874-1903), marriage (1847-1930), military (1865-1945), mortgage (1847-1902), naturalization (1852-1906), probate (1847-1917), supreme court (1847-53), tax (1835-38), veterans' graves (1835-1976), will (1852-1910).

OHS microfilms and records: administrator (1847-89), county home (1870-1979), guardian (1874-82), naturalization (1852-1906), probate (1847-1917), tax (1835-38), will (1899-1910).

DAR volume: marriage. Published volumes: Bible, biography, cemetery, church, city/county directories, family, history, newspaper abstracts, school.

For newspapers, see repositories and reference volumes given in Chapter 2, section 30. For genealogical periodical articles, see indexes referred to in Chapter 2, section 19. Libraries: Patrick Henry School District Public Library, 208 North East Ave., Deshler, OH 43516. Phone 1-(419)-278-3616. Napoleon Public Library, 310 W. Clinton St., Napoleon, OH. Phone 1-(419)-592-2531. Society: Henry County Chapter, OGS (contact library for current address). Publishes Henry County Genealogical Society NEWSLETTER.

40. HIGHLAND COUNTY

Highland County, authorized/established 1805/1805 from Adams, Clermont, and Ross Counties. County seat Hillsboro (45133). ONAHRC: University of Cincinnati.

Censuses: 1820RIM, 1830RI, 1840RIP, 1850RIMFD, 1860RIFD, 1870RFM, 1880RIFM, 1890C, 1900RI, 1910RI, 1920RI.

FHL(FHC) microfilms: accounts (1853-99), administrator (1852-1913), birth (1867-1909), Black (1828-43), bonds, cemetery, chancery (1849-53), commissioners (1811-1903), common pleas court (1805-76), county home (1909-12), death (1868-1909), deed (1804-1964), executor (1852-71), Friends (1806-1948), guardian (1852-1906), indenture (1852-59), marriage (1805-1946), military (1864-65), mortgage (1859-1909), naturalization (1879-91), poll (1806-91), Presbyterian (1810-36), probate (1852-1901), supreme court (1806-51), tax (1806-35), veteran (1850-1908), will (1809-1968).

OHS microfilms and records: Black (1828-43), cemetery, chancery (1849-53), commissioners (1811-1903), common pleas court (1805-76), county home (1909-12), indenture (1852-59), marriage (1805-20), poll (1806-91), supreme court (1806-51), tax (1806-35).

DAR volumes: cemetery, church, court, marriage. Published volumes: adoptions, atlas, biography, birth, Black, cemetery, census, church, city/county directories, court, death, family, gazetteer, genealogy, guardian, history, inventory of county records, land, marriage, newspaper abstracts, tax, will.

For newspapers, see repositories and reference volumes given in Chapter 2, section 30. For genealogical periodical articles, see indexes referred to in Chapter 2, section 19. Library: Highland County District Library, 10 Willettsville Pike, Hillsboro, OH 45133. Phone 1-(513)-393-3114. Society: Southern OH Genealogical Society (contact library for current address). Publishes ROOTS AND SHOOTS.

41. HOCKING COUNTY

Hocking County, authorized/established 1818/1818 from Athens, Fairfield, and Ross. County seat Logan (43138). ONAHRC: OH University in Athens. Censuses: 1820RIM, 1830RI, 1840RIP, 1850RIMFD, 1860RIFD, 1870RFM, 1880RIF, 1890C, 1900RI, 1910RI, 1920RI.

FHL(FHC) microfilms: administrator (1852-97), birth (1867-1908), civil court cases (1821-51), clerk of courts (1818-60), commissioners (1818-1903), death (1867-1908), deed (1818-1905), district court (1852-59), estray (1818-39), executor (1848-97), guardian (1874-96), jail (1881-1927), marriage (1818-1938), militia (1818-1903), military (1861-65), naturalization (1906-28), partition (1821-33), poll (1821-70), Presbyterian (1829-87), probate (1840-60), sales (1831-62), supreme court (1837-79), tax (1819-38), votes (1828-30, 1844), will (1819-94).

OHS microfilms and records: cemetery, civil court cases (1821-51), commissioners (1818-1903), district court (1852-59), jail (1881-1927), marriage (1818-65), militia (1818-1903), military (1861-65), partition (1821-33), probate (1840-60), supreme court (1837-79), tax (1819-38), votes (1828-30, 1844).

DAR volumes: cemetery, marriage, will. Published volumes: atlas, cemetery, church, city/county directories, death, gazetteer, history, inventory of county records, land, tax, will.

For newspapers, see repositories and reference volumes given in Chapter 2, section 30. For genealogical periodical articles, see indexes referred to in Chapter 2, section 19. Library: Logan-Hocking County District Library, 10 N. Walnut St., Logan, OH 43138. Phone 1-(614)-385-2348. Society: Hocking County Chapter, OGS (contact library for current address). Publishes THE HOCKING SENTINEL.

42. HOLMES COUNTY

Holmes County, authorized/established 1824/1825 from Coshocton, Tuscarawas, and Wayne Counties. County seat Millersburg (44654). ONAHRC: University of Akron. Censuses: 1830RI, 1840RIP, 1850RIMFD, 1860RIFD, 1870RFM, 1880RIF, 1890C, 1900RI, 1910RI, 1920RI.

FHL(FHC) microfilms: administrator (1841-86), birth (1867-1966), chancery (1827-52), common pleas court (1825-52), death (1867-1908), deed (1808-1941), delinquent tax (1826-55), executor (1841-97), guardian (1849-88), marriage (1821-1954), military (1865-1959), naturalization (1840-1961), Presbyterian (1830-89), probate (1825-98), supreme court (1826-52), tax (1825-38), will (1825-1965).

OHS microfilms and records: chancery (1827-52), common pleas court (1825-52), delinquent tax (1826-55), naturalization (1840-1940), probate (1825-52), supreme court (1826-52), tax (1825-38).

DAR volume: court. Published volumes: atlas, biography, cemetery, census, church, city/county directories, court, genealogy, history, land, marriage, newspaper abstracts, will.

For newspapers, see repositories and reference volumes given in Chapter 2, section 30. For genealogical periodical articles, see indexes referred to in Chapter 2, section 19. Library: Holmes County District Public Library, 10 W. Jackson St., Millersburg, OH 44654. Phone 1-(216)-674-5972. Society: Holmes County Chapter, OGS (contact library for current address). Publishes HOLMES COUNTY HEIRS.

43. HURON COUNTY

Huron County, authorized/established 1809/1815 from Cuyahoga and Portage Counties. County seat Norwalk (44857). ONAHRC: Bowling Green State University. Censuses: 1820RIM, 1830RI, 1840RIP, 1850RIMFD, 1860RIFD, 1870RFM, 1880RIF, 1890C, 1900RI, 1910RI, 1920RI.

FHL(FHC) microfilms: administrator (1815-1900), birth (1867-1908), cemetery, civil court cases (1852-1903), clerk of courts (1818-53), commissioners (1848-1945), common pleas court (1818-53), Congregational (1787-1969), county home (1848-1945), death (1867-1908), deed (1809-1901), estate (1815-52), executor (1852-1900), guardian (1815-1900), licenses (1815-28), marriage (1818-1919), Methodist (1852-86), military (1865-1931), naturalization (1859-1905), Presbyterian (1838-41, 1871), probate (1851-95), settlement (1851-89), tax (1816-38), tax (1816-38), United Church of Christ (1861-1983), will (1828-1911).

OHS microfilms and records: administrator (1815-32, 1849-1900), common pleas court (1818-53), deed (1809-1900), estate (1815-52), executor (1815-22), 1849-1900), guardian (1815-55), military (1865-1931), tax (1816-38), will (1903-11).

DAR volumes: Bible, cemetery, census, church, family, marriage, will. Published volumes: atlas, biography, cemetery, census, church, city/county directories, court, genealogy, history, marriage, newspaper abstracts, plat, school, will.

Manuscripts in OHS, WRHS. For newspapers, see repositories and reference volumes given in Chapter 2, section 30. For genealogical periodical articles, see indexes referred to in Chapter 2, section 19. Library: Norwalk Public Library, 46 West Main St., Norwalk, OH 44857. Phone 1-(419)-668-6063. Society: Huron County Chapter, OGS (contact library for current address). Publishes HURON COUNTY KINOLOGIST.

---

44. JACKSON COUNTY

Jackson County, authorized/established 1816/1816 from Athens, Gallia, Ross, and Scioto Counties. County seat Jackson (45640). ONAHRC: OH University in Athens. Censuses: 1820RIM, 1830RI, 1840RIP, 1850RIMFD, 1860-RIFD, 1870RFM, 1880RIF, 1890C, 1900RI, 1910RI, 1920RI.

FHL(FHC) microfilms: alien (1865-1906), birth (1867-1908), common pleas court (1816-1904), death (1867-1908), deed (1816-77), district court (1852-58), estate (1819-83), marriage (1816-1913), naturalization (1880-1906), supreme court (1817-51), tax (1819-38), will (1819-85).

OHS microfilms and records: Black (1816-54), common pleas court (1816-1904), district court (1852-58), marriage (1816-68), supreme court (1817-51), tax (1819-38).

DAR volume: marriage. Published volumes: atlas, biography, birth, cemetery, census, church, death, history, inventory of county records, land, naturalization, tax.

For newspapers, see repositories and reference volumes given in Chapter 2, section 30. For genealogical periodical articles, see indexes referred to in Chapter 2, section 19. Library: Jackson City Library, 21

Broadway St., Jackson, OH 45640. Phone 1-(614)-286-4111. Society: Jackson County Chapter, OGS (contact library for current address). Publishes POPLAR ROW.

45. JEFFERSON COUNTY

Jefferson County, authorized/established 1797/ 1797 from Washington County. County seat Steubenville (43952). ONAHRC: University of Akron. Censuses: 1820RIM, 1830RI, 1840RIP, 1850RIMFD, 1860RIFD, 1870RF, 1880RIF, 1890C, 1900RI, 1910RI, 1920RI.

FHL(FHC) microfilms: administrator (1838-95), birth (1867-1908), civil court cases (1804-54, 1879-), commissioners (1802-1908), common pleas court (1803-51), criminal (1896-1906), death (1867-1908), deed (1795-1939), estate (1803-89), executor (1849-85), guardian (1838-1905), manuscripts (1788-1877), marriage (1803-1916), naturalization (1823-28, 1854-1904), Presbyterian (1818-1933), probate (1852-87), quadrennial enumeration (1883-1907), tax (1806-38), will (1798-1884).

OHS microfilms and records: civil court cases (1804-54, 1879-), commissioners (1808-1908), common pleas court (1803-51), criminal (1896-1906), deed (1795-1941), Friends, marriage (1789-1839), quadrennial enumeration (1883-1907), tax (1806-38).

DAR volumes: church, marriage. Published volumes: atlas, cemetery, census, church, city/county directories, death, deed, estate, family, gazetteer, genealogy, guardian, history, inventory of county records, land, marriage, naturalization, newspaper abstracts, will.

Manuscripts in OHS, WRHS. For newspapers, see repositories and reference volumes given in Chapter 2, section 30. For genealogical periodical articles, see indexes referred to in Chapter 2, section 19. Libraries: Jefferson County Historical Society Genealogical Library, 426 Franklin Ave., Steubenville, OH 43952. Phone 1-(614)-283-1133. Schiappa Memorial Branch Library, Public Library of Steubenville, (Ohio Room), 4141 Mall Dr., Steubenville, OH 43951. Phone 1-(614)-264-6166. Society: Jefferson County Chapter, OGS (contact library for current address). Publishes JEFFERSON COUNTY LINES.

46. KNOX COUNTY

Knox County, authorized/established 1808/1808 from Fairfield County. County seat Mt. Vernon (43050). ONAHRC: OHS in Columbus. Censuses: 1820RIM, 1830RI, 1840RIP, 1850RIMFD, 1860-RIFD, 1870RF, 1880RIF, 1890C, 1900RI, 1810RI, 1920RI.

FHL(FHC) microfilms: administrator (1852-1914), birth (1867-1908), chancery (1805-54), clerk of courts (1808-65), common pleas court (1808-55), death (1867-1908), deed (1808-78), Episcopal (1856-1919), estate (1852-87), executor (1842-1914), guardian (1852-1922), marriage (1808–53, 1860–1912), ministers license, naturalization (1860–1916), plat (1852–1949), Presbyterian (1830–80), supreme court (1810–62), tax (1809–38), veteran (1861–78), will (1808–1911).

OHS microfilms and records: administrator (1852–1914), birth (1867–1908), chancery (1808–54), clerk of courts (1808–62), common pleas court (1816–55), death (1867–1908), estate (1852–87), executor (1852–1914), guardian (1852–1922), marriage (1808–1912), naturalization (1860–1906), supreme court (1810–62), tax (1809–38), will (1808–1911).

DAR volumes: cemetery, marriage. Published volumes: atlas, biography, birth, cemetery, census, city/county directories, family, history, land, marriage, military, will.

Manuscripts in WRHS. For newspapers, see repositories and reference volumes given in Chapter 2, section 30. For genealogical periodical articles, see indexes referred to in Chapter 2, section 19. Libraries: Public Library of Mt. Vernon & Knox County, 201 N. Mulberry St., Mt. Vernon, OH 43050. Phone 1-(614)-392-8671. Faith Lutheran Church Library, 170 Mansfield Ave., Mt. Vernon, OH 43050. Society: Knox County Chapter, OGS (contact library for current address). Publishes KNOX TREE CLIMBER.

47. LAKE COUNTY

Lake County, authorized/established 1840/1840 from Cuyahoga and Geauga Counties. County seat Painesville (44077). ONAHRC: WRHS in Cleveland. Censuses: 1840RIP, 1850RIMFD, 1860RIFD, 1870RF, 1880RIF, 1890C, 1900RI, 1910RI, 1920RI.

FHL(FHC) microfilms: administrator (1840–85), assessor (1849–61), Baptist, birth (1867–1909), board of equalization (1852–1900), bonds (1840–61), cemetery, chancery (1840–53), civil court cases (1853–1909), commissioners (1840–1900), Congregational (1814–18, 1832), criminal (1840–77), death (1867–1909), deed (1839–50), district court (1845–84), inventory (1886–1902), jury (1853–91), marriage (1840–1946), ministers license (1846–85), naturalization (1860–1906), newspapers (1822–46), plat (1852–1951), Presbyterian (1814–70), probate (1840–1903), school (1840–1906), sheriff (1840–83), supreme court (1840–82), tax (1840–72), township (1815–93), will (1853–99).

OHS microfilms and records: administrator (1840–85), Bible, chancery (1840–52), marriage (1840–65), supreme court (1840–52), Western Reserve land (1795–1809), will (1896–99).

DAR volumes: Bible, cemetery, genealogy, infirmary, marriage, mortuary, tax, will. Published volumes: atlas, biography, cemetery, census, church, city/county directories, genealogy, history, inventory of county records, land, marriage, newspaper abstracts, school.

Manuscripts in WRHS. For newspapers, see repositories and reference volumes given in Chapter 2, section 30. For genealogical periodical articles, see indexes referred to in Chapter 2, section 19.

Library: Morley Library, 184 Phelps St., Painesville, OH 44077. Phone 1-(216)-352-3383. Society: Lake County Chapter, OGS (contact library for current address). Publishes LAKE LINES.

---

48. LAWRENCE COUNTY

Lawrence County, author-ized/established 1815/1817 from Gallia and Scioto Counties. County seat Ironton (45638). ONAHRC: OH University in Athens. Censuses: 1820RIM, 1830RI, 1840RIP, 1850RIMFD, 1860RIFD, 1870RF, 1880RIF, 1890C, 1900RI, 1910RI, 1920RI.

FHL(FHC) microfilms: birth (1867-1908), Black (1863), cemetery, chancery (1843-53), childrens home (1874-1951), commissioners (1817-1904), common pleas court (1817-61), county home (1876-1930), death (1867-1908), deed (1818-76), district court (1853-58), jail (1867-1923), marriage (1817-1914), militia (1861-65), military (1861-1919), naturalization (1877-1906), Presbyterian (1828-39), probate (1852-78), quadrennial enumeration (1891-1907), school (1861-80), supreme court (1846-50), tax (1818-38).

DAR volumes: cemetery, genealogy, marriage. Published volumes: atlas, cemetery, census, church, city/county directories, gazetteer, genealogy, history, land, marriage, naturalization, tax.

For newspapers, see repositories and reference volumes given in Chapter 2, section 30. For genealogical periodical articles, see indexes referred to in Chapter 2, section 19. Library: Briggs Lawrence County Public Library, 321 South 4th St., Ironton, OH 45638. Phone 1-(614)-532-1124. Society: Lawrence County Chapter, OGS (contact library for current address). Publishes LAWCO LORE.

---

49. LICKING COUNTY

Licking County, author-ized/established 1808/1808 from Fairfield County. County seat Newark (43055), court house fire in 1875, many records lost. ONAHRC: OHS in Columbus. Censuses: 1820RIM, 1830RI, 1840RIP, 1850RIMFD, 1860RIFD, 1870RF,f 1880RIF, 1890C, 1900RI, 1910RI, 1920RI.

FHL(FHC) microfilms: administrator (1875-1915), birth (1875-1908), cemetery, civil court cases (1875-1917), common pleas court (1813-52), death (1875-1908), deed (1800-1901), executor (1875-1915), guardian (1875-1913), inventory (1875-88), jail (1875-1918), marriage (1808-1933), military (1909-23), naturalization (1867-1906), partition (1816-1912), Presbyterian (1835-1901), probate (1867-88), reconstituted burned probate (1867-75), supreme court (1811-56), tax (1809-40).

OHS microfilms and records: board of health (1853-65), cemetery, chancery (1819-24, 1899-50), commissioners (1855-1904), common pleas court (1814-52), county home (1901-42), jail (1875-1918), marriage (1808–16), military (1909–23), naturalization (1867–1906), Newark (1824–67), supreme court (1814–25, 1839–56), tax (1809–38).

DAR volume: cemetery. Published volumes: atlas, biography, cemetery, census, church, city/county directories, death, family, gazetteer, genealogy, history, inventory of county records, land, marriage, newspaper abstracts, probate, tax, will.

Manuscripts in WRHS. For newspapers, see repositories and reference volumes given in Chapter 2, section 30. For genealogical periodical articles, see indexes referred to in Chapter 2, section 19. Libraries: Newark Public Library, 88 W. Church St., Newark, OH 43055. Phone 1-(614)-345-8972. Licking County Genealogical Society Library, 743 E. Main St., Newark, OH 43055. Phone 1-(614)-345-3571. Society: Licking County Chapter, OGS (contact library for current address). Publishes LICKING LANTERN.

50. LOGAN COUNTY

Logan County, authorized/established 1818/1818 from Champaign County. County seat Bellefontaine (43311). ONAHRC: Wright State University in Dayton. Censuses: 1820RI, 1830RI, 1840RIP, 1850RIMFD, 1860RIFD, 1870RF, 1880RIF, 1890C, 1900RI, 1910RI, 1920RI.

FHL(FHC) microfilms: administrator (1818–1967), birth (1867–1908), Black (1804–57), chancery (1849–57), childrens home (1886–1934), civil court cases (1818–55), common pleas court (1819–94), county home (1850–1978), death (1867–1908), deed (1810–1967), district court (1851–66), Friends (1828–48), guardian (1862–1967), marriage (1818–1966), military (1865–1963), mortgage (1849–52), naturalization (1828–1906), Presbyterian (1828–1952), probate (1852–1967), supreme court (1820–84), tax (1818–38), will (1851–1966).

OHS microfilms and records: Black (1804–57), chancery (1849–57), childrens home (1886–1934), civil court cases (1818–55), common pleas court (1819–94), county home (1850–1978), district court (1851–66), marriage (1818–34), naturalization (1828–84), supreme court (1820–66), tax (1818–38).

DAR volumes: marriage, school. Published volumes: atlas, biography, Black, church, city/county directories, death, family, history, inventory of county records, land, newspaper abstracts, voters, will.

Manuscripts in OHS. For newspapers, see repositories and reference volumes given in Chapter 2, section 30. For genealogical periodical articles, see indexes referred to in Chapter 2, section 19. Libraries: Logan County District Library, Main St. & Sandusky Ave., Bellefontaine, OH 43311. Phone 1-(513)-599-4189. Logan County Genealogical Society Library, 521 E. Columbus Ave., Bellefontaine, OH 43311. Society: Logan County Chapter, OGS (contact library for current address). Publishes BRANCHES AND TWIGS.

51. LORAIN COUNTY

Lorain County, authorized/established 1822/1824 from Cuyahoga, Huron, and Medina Counties. County seat Elyria (44035). ONAHRC: WRHS in Cleveland. Censuses: 1830RI, 1840RIP, 1850RIMFD, 1860RIFD, 1870R, 1880RIF, 1890C, 1900RI, 1810RI, 1920RI.

FHL(FHC) microfilms: Baptist, birth (1867–1908), cemetery, common pleas court (1824–47), death (1867–1908), guardian (1854–1925), marriage (1824–1901), probate (1852–1902), supreme court (1826–47), tax (1824–38), will (1840–1904).

OHS microfilms and records: birth (1867–1908), cemetery, common pleas court (1824–47), death (1867–89), marriage (1824–1901), supreme court (1826–47), tax (1824–38), Western Reserve land (1795–1809).

DAR volumes: Bible, cemetery, court, family, marriage, tax, will. Published volumes: atlas, biography, Black, cemetery, census, church, city/county directories, death, genealogy, history, inventory of county records, marriage, mortuary, will.

Manuscripts in WRHS. For newspapers, see repositories and reference volumes given in Chapter 2, section 30. For genealogical periodical articles, see indexes referred to in Chapter 2, section 19. Library: Elyria Public Library, 320 Washington Ave., Elyria, OH 44035. Phone 1–(216)–323–5747. Society: Lorain County Chapter, OGS (contact library for current address). Publishes THE RESEARCHER.

52. LUCAS COUNTY

Lucas County, authorized/established 1835/1835 from Henry, Sandusky, and Wood Counties. County seat Toledo (43624). ONAHRC: Bowling Green State University. Censuses: 1840RIP, 1850RIMFD, 1860RIFD, 1870R, 1880RIF, 1890C, 1900RI, 1910RI, 1920RI.

FHL(FHC) microfilms: administrator (1859–91), birth (1867–1908), cemetery, chancery (1836–56), civil court cases (1835–1903), clerk of courts (1835–56), common pleas court (1838–53), death (1867–1908), deed (1808–92), district court (1852–55), estate (1852–1959), executor (1859–91), guardian (1859–1970), marriage (1835–1911), Methodist (1894–1959), Presbyterian (1820–1969), probate (1852–90), supreme court (1837–54), tax (1836–38), United Brethren (1873–1901), will (1835–1903).

OHS microfilms and records: Bible, chancery (1836–53), common pleas court (1838–53), marriage (1835–66), supreme court (1837–55), tax (1836–38).

DAR volumes: cemetery, marriage. Published volumes: atlas, Bible, biography, cemetery, city/county directories, history, inventory of county records, marriage, newspaper abstracts, will.

For newspapers, see repositories and reference volumes given in Chapter 2, section 30. For genealogical periodical articles, see indexes referred to in Chapter 2, section 19. Library: Toledo–Lucas County Public Library, 325 Michigan St., Toledo, OH 43624. Phone 1-(419)-255-5255. Society: Lucas County Chapter, OGS (contact library for current address). Publishes FORT INDUSTRY REFLECTIONS.

53. MADISON COUNTY

Madison County, authorized/established 1810/1810 from Franklin County. County seat London (43140). ONAHRC: OHS in Columbus. Censuses: 1820RIM, 1830RI, 1840RIP, 1850RIMFD,d 1860RIFD, 1870R, 1880RIF, 1890C, 1900RI, 1910RI, 1920RI.

FHL(FHC) microfilms: administrator (1869–1904), birth (1867–1908), bonds (1844–1901), cemetery, cemetery deeds (1880–1967), chancery (1841–56), civil court cases (1860–90), commissioners (1810–1903), common pleas court (1810–80), county home (1868–85), death (1888–95), deed (1810–1955), executor (1857–1900), guardian (1857–1932), inventory (1877–1929), jail (1875–1928), land (1852–1964), marriage (1810–1967), military (1865–1967), naturalization (1860–88), Presbyterian (1821–1930), probate (1850–1965), tax (1810–38), veteran (1900–27), will (1810–1967).

OHS microfilms and records: Bible, cemetery, chancery (1841–56), commissioners (1810–1903), common pleas court (1810–80), county home (1868–85), deed (1814–66), jail (1875–1928), marriage (1810–65), military (1865), supreme court (1823–59), tax (1810–38), veteran (1900–27).

DAR volumes: Bible, cemetery, deed, marriage. Published volumes: atlas, biography, birth, cemetery, church, city/county directories, deed, genealogy, history, inventory of county records, land, plat.

For newspapers, see repositories and reference volumes given in Chapter 2, section 30. For genealogical periodical articles, see indexes referred to in Chapter 2, section 19. Library: London Public Library, 20 E. First St., London, OH 43140. Phone 1-(614)-852-9543. Society: Madison County Chapter, OGS (contact library for current address). Publishes MADISONIAN.

54. MAHONING COUNTY

Mahoning County, authorized/established 1846/1846 from Columbiana and Trumbull Counties. County seat Youngstown (44503). ONAHRC: University of Akron. Censuses: 1850RIMFD, 1860RIFD, 1870R, 1880RIF, 1890C, 1900RI, 1810RI, 1920RI.

FHL(FHC) microfilms: administrator (1846–1946), birth (1856–57, 1867–1908), cemetery, civil court cases (1847–67), county home (1855–

59), death (1856–57, 1867–1908), deed (1795–1901), executor (1846–1946), guardian (1846–1946), inventory (1848–86), marriage (1846–1916), military (1861–1909), Presbyterian (1804–86), probate (1852–88), supreme court (1848–51), will (1846–1909).

OHS microfilms and records: city/county directories, civil court cases (1847–67), county home (1855–59), deed (1881–85), military (1861–1909), supreme court (1848–51), Western Reserve land (1795–1809), will (1887–1909).

DAR volumes: Bible, birth, cemetery, church, court, death, family, will. Published volumes: atlas, biography, birth, cemetery, census, church, city/county directories death, family, gazetteer, genealogy, history, land, mail directory, newspaper abstracts, tax, will.

For newspapers, see repositories and reference volumes given in Chapter 2, section 30. For genealogical periodical articles, see indexes referred to in Chapter 2, section 19. Library: Reuben McMillan Free Library Association, Library of Youngstown & Mahoning County, 305 Wick Ave., Youngstown, OH 44503. Phone 1-(216)-744-8636. Society: Mahoning County Chapter, OGS (contact library for current address). Publishes MAHONING MEANDERINGS.

55. MARION COUNTY

Marion County, authorized/established 1820/1824 from Delaware County. County seat Marion (43302). ONAHRC: OHS in Columbus. Censuses: 1830RI, 1840 RIP, 1850RIMFD, 1860RIFD, 1870R, 1880RIF, 1890C, 1900RI, 1810RI, 1920RI.

FHL(FHC) microfilms: Bible, birth (1867–1908), cemetery, commissioners (1824–1904), common pleas court (1824–56), county home (1913–24), death (1867–1908), deed (1821–1954), marriage (1824–1964), military (1865–1970), ministers' license (1861–1976), mortgage (1828–1969), special deeds (1828–70), tax (1824–38), town plats (1821–76).

OHS microfilms and records: Bible, birth (1867–1908), cemetery, chancery (1824–61), commissioners (1824–1904), common pleas court (1824–56), county home (1913–24), death (1867–1908), deed (1821–1954), marriage (1824–1964), military (1865–1970), ministers' license (1861–1976), mortgage (1828–1969), special deeds (1828–70), supreme court (1824–83), tax (1824–38), town plats (1821–76).

DAR volumes: Bible, cemetery, marriage. Published volumes: atlas, biography, cemetery, census, church, city/county directories, court, family, gazetteer, genealogy, history, inventory of county records, land, mortuary, newspaper abstracts, plat.

For newspapers, see repositories and reference volumes given in Chapter 2, section 30. For genealogical periodical articles, see indexes referred to in Chapter 2, section 19. Library: Marion Public Library, 445 E. Church St., Marion, OH 43301. Phone 1-(614)-387-0992. Society:

Marion County Chapter, OGS (contact library for current address). Publishes MARION MEMORIES.

56. MEDINA COUNTY

Medina County, authorized/established 1812/1818 from Portage County. County seat Medina (44256). ONAHRC: WRHS in Cleveland. Censuses: 1820RIM, 1830RI, 1840RIP, 1850RIMFD, 1860RIFD, 1870R, 1880RIF, 1890C, 1900RI, 1910RI, 1920RI.

FHL(FHC) microfilms: birth (1867-1909), common pleas court (1818-52), death (1867-1909), deed (1818-1931), marriage (1818-1965), Presbyterian (1834-83), probate (1818-1949), supreme court (1820-49), tax (1819-38), will (1862-1949).

OHS microfilms and records: cemetery, common pleas court (1818-52), marriage (1818-65), supreme court (1820-49), tax (1819-38), Western Reserve land (1795-1809).

DAR volumes: cemetery, marriage. Published volumes: atlas, biography, census, church, city/county directories, genealogy, history, tax.

For newspapers, see repositories and reference volumes given in Chapter 2, section 30. For genealogical periodical articles, see indexes referred to in Chapter 2, section 19. Library: Medina County District Library, 210 S. Broadway, Medina, OH 44256. Phone 1-(216)-725-0588. Society: Medina County Chapter, OGS (contact library for current address). Publishes MEDINA COUNTY STORY.

57. MEIGS COUNTY

Meigs County, authorized/established 1819/1819 from Athens and Gallia Counties. County seat Pomeroy (45769). ONAHRC: OH University in Athens. Censuses: 1820RIM, 1830RI, 1840RIP, 1850RIMFD, 1860RIFD, 1880RIFM, 1890C, 1900RI, 1910RI, 1920RI.

FHL(FHC) microfilms: administrator (1820-1907), birth (1867-1908), cemetery, chancery (1826-52), common pleas court (1819-54), county home (1871, 1901-81), death (1867-1908), deed (1820-79), district court (1852), executor (1822-1917), inventory (1833-88), marriage (1819-1913), naturalization (1847-62, 1880-1900), pre-county deeds (up to 1819), Presbyterian (1898-99), probate (1824-1972), supreme court (1821-51), tax (1820-38), will (1822-81).

OHS microfilms and records: cemetery, chancery (1826-37, 1846-52), common pleas court (1819-54), county home (1871, 1901-81), district court (1852), marriage (1812-66), naturalization (1847-62), supreme court (1821-51), tax (1820-38).

DAR volumes: cemetery, church, marriage. Published volumes: atlas, census, city/county directories, gazetteer, history, marriage, plat, poll, tax.

Manuscripts in WRHS. For newspapers, see repositories and reference volumes given in Chapter 2, section 30. For genealogical periodical articles, see indexes referred to in Chapter 2, section 19. Libraries: Meigs County Public Library, 216 W. Main, Pomeroy, OH 45769. Phone 1-(614)-992-5813. Chapter Library, Meigs Museum, Butternut St., Pomeroy, OH 45769. Society: Meigs County Chapter, OGS (contact library for current address). Publishes THE MEGA-PHONE.

58. MERCER COUNTY

Mercer County, authorized/established 1820/1824 from Darke County. County seat Celina (45822). ONAHRC: Wright State University in Dayton. Censuses: 1820RIM, 1830RI, 1840RIP, 1850RIMFD, 1860RIFD, 1870R, 1880RIFM, 1890C, 1900RI, 1910RI, 1920RI.

FHL(FHC) microfilms: administrator (1824-92), birth (1867-1908), cemetery, chancery (1838-57), civil court cases (1824-61), common pleas court (1824-71), county home (1888-1938), death (1867-1908), deed (1823-66), estate (1838-51), executor (1824-92), guardian (1824-92), marriage (1838-1916), ministers' license (1870-1966), naturalization (1838-39, 1848-1903), probate (1852-91), supreme court (1825-73), tax (1826-38), will (1825-1902).

OHS microfilms and records: cemetery, chancery (1838-57), civil court cases (1824-61), county home (1888-1938), marriage (1838-80), probate (1824-71), supreme court (1825-73), tax (1826-38).

DAR volumes: cemetery, church, marriage. Published volumes: biography, cemetery, census, church, city/county directories, history, inventory of county records, land, newspaper abstracts.

For newspapers, see repositories and reference volumes given in Chapter 2, section 30. For genealogical periodical articles, see indexes referred to in Chapter 2, section 19. Library: Dwyer-Mercer County District Library, 303 N. Main St., Celina, OH 45822. Phone 1-(419)-586-4442. Society: Mercer County Chapter, OGS (contact library for current address). Publishes MONITOR.

59. MIAMI COUNTY

Miami County, authorized/established 1807/1807 from Montgomery County. County seat Troy (45373). ONAHRC: Wright State University in Dayton. Censuses: 1820RIM, 1830RI, 1840RIP, 1850RIMFD, 1860RIFD, 1870R, 1880RIFM, 1890C, 1900RI, 1910RI, 1920RI.

FHL(FHC) microfilms: administrator (1833-1968), Baptist (1811-44), birth (1853-1908), Black (1804-57), cemetery, chancery (1840-58), childrens home (1879-1939), civil court cases (1807-53), common pleas court (1807-53), county home (1842-1927), death (1867-1908), deed (1807-1902), Friends (1807-1921), guardian (1807-1968), indenture (1880-1904), jail (1882-1920), marriage (1807-1968), militia (1857-65), military (1864-1918), mortgage (1822-1963), naturalization (1860-1906), poll (1817-1902), Presbyterian (1818-70), probate (1855-1968), quadrennial enumeration (1827, 1835), school (1851-1911), supreme court (1807-57), tax (1810-38), will (1807-1902).

OHS microfilms and records: Black (1804-57), cemetery, chancery (1840-58), childrens home (1879-1939), city directories (1875-1907), civil court cases (1807-53), common pleas court (1807-53), county home (1842-1927), Friends (1824-73), indenture (1880-1904), jail (1882-1920), marriage (1807-66), militia (1857-65), military (1861-1918), naturalization (1860-1906), poll (1817-1902), quadrennial enumeration (1827, 1835), school (1851-1911), supreme court (1807-57), tax (1810-38), Tipp City (1851-1978).

DAR volumes: Bible, church, marriage. Published volumes: atlas, Bible, biography, Black, cemetery, church, city/county directories, family, gazetteer, genealogy, history, inventory of county records, land, marriage, newspaper abstracts, will.

For newspapers, see repositories and reference volumes given in Chapter 2, section 30. For genealogical periodical articles, see indexes referred to in Chapter 2, section 19. Library: Troy-Miami County Public Library, 419 W. Main St., Troy, OH 45373. Phone 1-(513)-339-0501. Society: Miami County chapter, OGS (contact library for current address). Publishes GENEALOGICAL AIDS BULLETIN.

60. MONROE COUNTY

Monroe County, authorized/established 1813/1815 from Belmont, Guernsey, and Washington Counties. County seat Woodsfield (43793), court house fires in 1840 and 1867, many records lost. ONAHRC: OH University in Athens. Censuses: 1820RIM, 1830RI, 1840RIP, 1840RIMFD, 1860RIFD, 1870R, 1880RIFM, 1890C, 1900RI, 1910RI, 1920RI.

FHL(FHC) microfilms: birth (1867-1908), cemetery, chancery (1834-56), common pleas court (1818-57), county home (1855-1978), death (1867-1908), deed (1836-1968), Evangelical (1855-86), marriage (1866-1917), Presbyterian (1847-99), supreme court (1820-52), tax (1816-38).

OHS microfilms and records: cemetery, chancery (1834-56), common pleas court (1818-57), county home (1855-1978), district court (1852-65), supreme court (1820-52), tax (1816-58).

DAR volume: cemetery. Published volumes: atlas, cemetery, census, church, city/county directories, family, genealogy, history, inventory of county records, land, marriage, newspaper abstracts, tax.

For newspapers, see repositories and reference volumes given in Chapter 2, section 30. For genealogical periodical articles, see indexes referred to in Chapter 2, section 19. Library: Monroe County District Library, 96 Home Ave., Woodsfield, OH 43793. Phone 1-(614)-472-1954. Society: Monroe County Chapter, OGS (contact library for current address). Publishes THE NAVIGATOR.

61. MONTGOMERY COUNTY

Montgomery County, authorized/established 1803/1803 from Hamilton and Wayne (MI) Counties. County seat Dayton (45202). ONAHRC: Wright State University in Dayton. Censuses: 1820RIM, 1830RI, 1840RIP, 1850-RIMFD, 1860RIFD, 1870R, 1880RIFM, 1890C, 1900RI, 1910RI, 1920RI.

FHL(FHC) microfilms: administrator (1803-94), birth (1867-1910), Black (1804-57), cemetery, chancery (1824-54), circuit court (1885-1912), civil court cases (1803-36), commissioners (1804-1953), common pleas court (1803-1901), county home (1826-1969), court indexes (1857-1901), court minutes (1815-1901), death (1866-1909), deed (1805-1900), district court (1852-83), executor (1803-94), guardian (1803-1900), marriage (1803-1913), military (1865-1917), naturalization (1818-1916), Presbyterian (1817-99), probate (1803-1939), Soldiers' Relief Commission (1867-1921), superior court (1856-87), tax (1798-1809, 1816-50), US Military Home (1867-88), veteran (1884-1902), workhouse (1876-1916), will (1805-1910).

OHS microfilms and records: administrator (1803-94), birth (1867-1910), Black (1804-57), chancery (1824-84), childrens home (1867-1924), circuit court (1885-1912), commissioners (1804-1953), common pleas court (1803-1901), county home (1826-1969), court indexes (1857-1901), court minutes (1815-1901), death (1866-1909), district court (1852-83), Evangelical Lutheran (1809-1933), executor (1803-94), marriage (1803-1913), military (1865-1917), naturalization (1818-1916), probate (1803-1939), Soldiers' Relief Commission (1867-1921), supreme court (1803-53), tax (1806-50), US Military Home (1867-88), veteran (1884-1902), will (1805-1910).

DAR volumes: Bible, cemetery, census, church, deed, marriage, tax. Published volumes: atlas, Bible, biography, birth, cemetery, census, church, city/county directories, death, deed, family, gazetteer, genealogy, history, infirmary, inventory of county records, land, marriage, naturalization, newspaper abstracts, will.

Manuscripts in OHS, WRHS. For newspapers, see repositories and reference volumes given in Chapter 2, section 30. For genealogical periodical articles, see indexes referred to in Chapter 2, section 19. Libraries: Dayton-Montgomery County Public Library, 215 East Third St., Dayton, OH 45202. Phone 1-(513)-227-9500. Wright State University Archives, 3640 Col. Glenn Highway, Dayton, OH 45435.

Phone 1-(513)-837-2091. Wright Memorial Public Library, 1776 Far Hills Ave., Oakwood, OH 45419. Phone 1-(513)-294-7171. Society: Montgomery County Chapter, OGS (contact library for current address). Publishes THE FAMILY TREE.

62. MORGAN COUNTY

Morgan County, authorized/established 1817/1819 from Guernsey, Muskingum, and Washington Counties. County seat McConnelsville (43756). ONAHRC: OH University in Athens. Censuses: 1820RIM, 1830RI, 1840RIP, 1850RIMFD, 1860RIFD, 1870R, 1880-RIFM, 1890C, 1900RI, 1910RI, 1920RI.

FHL(FHC) microfilms: administrator (1821-94), Baptist (1818-1904), birth (1867-1908), common pleas court (1819-60), death (1867-1962), deed (1795-1895), estate (1838-87), executor (1857-92), guardian (1849-94), inventory (1853-88), marriage (1819-1923), militia (1867), naturalization (1861-92), probate (1852-91), tax (1820-49), will (1820-87).

OHS microfilms and records: death (1867-96), marriage (1819-62), tax (1820-38).

DAR volumes: death, marriage. Published volumes: atlas, cemetery, census, church, city/county directories, genealogy, history, land, marriage.

For newspapers, see repositories and reference volumes given in Chapter 2, section 30. For genealogical periodical articles, see indexes referred to in Chapter 2, section 19. Library: Kate Love Simpson Library, 358 E. Main St., McConnelsville, OH 43756. Phone 1-(614)-962-2533. Society: Morgan County Chapter, OGS (contact library for current address). Publishes THE MORGAN LINK.

63. MORROW COUNTY

Morrow County, authorized/established 1848/1848 from Delaware, Knox, Marion, and Richland Counties. County seat Mt. Gilead (43338). ONAHRC: OHS in Columbus. Censuses: 1850RIM, 1860RIMFD, 1870R, 1880RIFM, 1890C, 1900RI, 1910RI, 1920RI.

FHL(FHC) microfilms: birth (1867-1908), chancery (1848-58), common pleas court (1848-56), death (1867-1909), deed (1848-96), Friends (1828-65), guardian (1848-1950), marriage (1848-1926), naturalization (1861-1902), probate (1848-1950), quadrennial enumeration (1875-1907), supreme court (1849-75), will (1848-1903).

OHS microfilms and records: cemetery, chancery (1848-58), common pleas court (1848-56), quadrennial enumeration (1875-1907), supreme court (1849-75).

Published volumes: atlas, cemetery, church, city/county directories, genealogy, history, inventory of county records, land, marriage.

For newspapers, see repositories and reference volumes given in Chapter 2, section 30. For genealogical periodical articles, see indexes referred to in Chapter 2, section 19. Library: Mt. Gilead Free Public Library, 35 East High St., Mt. Gilead, OH 43338. Phone 1-(419)-947-5866. Society: Morrow County Chapter, OGS (contact library for current address). Publishes THE MONUMENT.

64. MUSKINGUM COUNTY

Muskingum County, authorized/established 1804/ 1804 from Fairfield and Washington Counties. County seat Zanesville (43701). ONAHRC: OH University in Athens. Censuses: 1820RIM, 1830RI, 1840RIP, 1850RIMD, 1860-RIFMD, 1870R, 1880RIFM, 1890C, 1900RI, 1910RI, 1920RI.

FHL(FHC) microfilms: administrator (1804-98), birth (1867-1909), cemetery, chancery (1824-52), commissioners (1808-1904), common pleas court (1804-53), county home (1908, 1912), death (1867-1908), deed (1800-1907), Episcopal (1837-1965), executor (1867-1900), guardian (1804-98), jail (1868-1925), marriage (1804-1917), ministers' license (1804-41), naturalization (1816-1905), Presbyterian (1804-1909), probate (1852-87), supreme court (1805-52), tax (1806-38), veteran (1881-1920), votes (1878-92), will (1804-90).

OHS microfilms and records: chancery (1824-52), commissioners (1808-1904), common pleas court (1804-53), county home (1908, 1912), guardian (1804-1901), jail (1868-1925), marriage (1804-97), supreme court (1805-52), tax (1806-38), veteran (1881-1920), votes (1878-92), will (1804-1901).

DAR volumes: Bible, cemetery, church, family, school, tax. Published volumes: atlas, biography, Black, cemetery, church, city/county directories, court, family, gazetteer, genealogy, guardian, history, inventory of county records, land, marriage, mortuary, plat, school, tax, will.

For newspapers, see repositories and reference volumes given in Chapter 2, section 30. For genealogical periodical articles, see indexes referred to in Chapter 2, section 19. Library: John McIntire Library, 220 N. Fifth St., Zanesville, OH 43701. Phone 1-(614)-453-0391. Society: Muskingum County Chapter, OGS (contact library for current address). Publishes THE MUSKINGUM.

65. NOBLE COUNTY

Noble County, authorized/established 1851/1851 from Guernsey, Monroe, Morgan, and Washington Counties. County seat Caldwell (43724). ONAHRC: OH University in Athens.

Censuses: 1860RIFMD, 1870R, 1880RIFM, 1890C, 1900RI, 1910RI, 1920RI.

FHL(FHC) microfilms: administrator (1852–89), birth (1867–1972), chancery (1851–59), common pleas court (1851–57), death (1867–1972), deed (1851–1900), guardian (1852–1904), inventory (1851–88), marriage (1851–1973), military (1861–1913), ministers' license (1860–80), probate (1851–1973), will (1851–95).

OHS microfilms and records: chancery (1851–59), common pleas court (1851–57), marriage (1852–65), military (1861–1913).

DAR volumes: church, death, marriage, mortuary. Published volumes: atlas, biography, cemetery, census, church, city/county directories, gazetteer, inventory of county records, land, marriage, naturalization, will.

For newspapers, see repositories and reference volumes given in Chapter 2, section 30. For genealogical periodical articles, see indexes referred to in Chapter 2, section 19. Library: Caldwell Public Library, Spruce St., Caldwell, OH 43724. Phone 1-(614)-732-4506. Society: Noble County Chapter, OGS (contact library for current address). Publishes NOBLE COUNTY NEWS LETTER.

66. OTTAWA COUNTY

Ottawa County, authorized/established 1840/1840 from Erie, Lucas, and Sandusky Counties. County seat Port Clinton (43452). ONAHRC: Bowling Green State University. Censuses: 1840RIP, 1850RIMF, 1860RIFMD, 1870R, 1880RIFM, 1890C, 1900RI, 1910RI, 1920RI.

FHL(FHC) microfilms: administrator (1876–1909), birth (1867–1908), cemetery, chancery (1841–54), civil court cases (1860–1912), commissioners (1840–85), common pleas court (1840–85), death (1869–1908), deed (1820–1903), Episcopal (1896–1982), guardian (1880–1932), jury (1857–1918), Lutheran (1875–1977), marriage (1840–1930), Methodist (1854–1924), military (1861–1930), naturalization (1851–1903), poll (1847–87), probate (1840–1961), quadrennial enumeration (1899–1907), school (1835–1908), supreme court (1841–72), United Church of Christ (1879–1979), will (1853–1912).

OHS microfilms and records: administrator (1876–1909), birth (1867–1908), common pleas court (1840–58), guardian (1880–1932), marriage (1840–80), military (1865–1912), probate (1835–1915), supreme court (1841–84), will (1889–1912).

Published volumes: atlas, biography, cemetery, church, city/county directories, court, death, history, inventory of county records, newspaper abstracts.

Manuscripts in OHS. For newspapers, see repositories and reference volumes given in Chapter 2, section 30. For genealogical periodical articles, see indexes referred to in Chapter 2, section 19.

193

Library: Ida Rupp Public Library, 310 Madison St., Port Clinton, OH 43452. Phone 1-(419)-732-3211. Society: Ottawa Chapter, OGS (contact library for current address). Publishes MARSHLAND TO HEARTLAND.

---

67. PAULDING COUNTY

Paulding County, author-ized/established 1820/1839 from Darke County. County seat Paulding (45879). ONAHRC: Bowling Green State University. Censuses: 1830RI, 1840RIP, 1850RIMD, 1860RIFMD, 1870R, 1880RIFM, 1890C, 1900RI, 1910Ri, 1920RI.

FHL(FHC) microfilms: administrator (1872-98), birth (1867-1908), Catholic (1868-1983), chancery (1840-66), civil court cases (1852-98), clerk of courts (1839-46), death (1867-1908), deed (1835-1960), executor (1872-91), guardian (1871-91), inventory (1852-90), marriage (1839-1952), military (1862-1928), naturalization (1860-1903), probate (1839-1969), veteran (1862-1972), will (1852-1972).

Published volumes: atlas, gazetteer, history, inventory of county records, marriage, newspaper abstracts.

For newspapers, see repositories and reference volumes given in Chapter 2, section 30. For genealogical periodical articles, see indexes referred to in Chapter 2, section 19. Library: Paulding County Library, 205 S. Main St., Paulding, OH 45879. Phone 1-(419)-399-2032. Society: Paulding County Chapter, OGS (contact library for current address). Publishes PAULDING PATHWAYS.

---

68. PERRY COUNTY

Perry County, authorized/established 1818/1818 from Fairfield, Muskingum, and Washington Counties. County seat New Lexington (43764). ONAHRC: OH University in Athens. Censuses: 1820-RIM, 1830RI, 1840RIP, 1850RIMD, 1860RIFMD, 1870R, 1880RIFM, 1890C, 1900RI, 1910RI, 1920RI.

FHL(FHC) microfilms: administrator (1819-1903), birth (1867-1908), chancery (1821-56), childrens home (1885-1927), civil court cases (1852-1905), clerk of courts (1840-66), commissioners (1818-1902), common pleas court (1818-54), county home (1853-1963), deaf/dumb (1861-78), death (1867-1908), deed (1818-86), Friends (1887-1951), guardian (1848-1910), inventory (1840-87), license (1837-49), marriage (1818-1916), militia (1863), military (1863-1918), naturalization (1859-1906), poll (1822-92), Presbyterian (1855-99), probate (1837-88), quadrennial enumeration (1847-87), school (1864-80), supreme court (1819-52), tax (1819-38), votes (1822-82), will (1817-86).

OHS microfilms and records: cemetery, chancery (1821-56), childrens home (1885-1927), clerk of courts (1840-66), commissioners

(1818–1902), common pleas court (1818–54), county home (1853–1963), deaf/dumb (1861–78), jail (1876–1927), license (1837–49), marriage (1818–78), militia (1863), military (1863–64), poll (1822–92), probate (1837–52), quadrennial enumeration (1847–87), school (1864–80), supreme court (1819–52), tax (1819–38), votes (1822–82).

Published volumes: atlas, biography, cemetery, census, church, city/county directories, death, history, infirmary, inventory of county records, land, marriage, will.

Manuscripts in OHS. For newspapers, see repositories and reference volumes given in Chapter 2, section 30. For genealogical periodical articles, see indexes referred to in Chapter 2, section 19. Library: Perry County District Library, 113 S. Main St., New Lexington, OH 43764. Phone 1-(614)-342-4194. Society: Perry County Chapter, OGS (contact library for current address). Publishes PERRY COUNTY HEIRLINES.

69. PICKAWAY COUNTY

Pickaway County, authorized/established 1810/1810 from Fairfield, Franklin, and Ross Counties. County seat Circleville (43113). ONAHRC: OHS in Columbus. Censuses: 1820RIM, 1830RI, 1840RIP, 1850RIFM, 1860RIFMD, 1870R, 1880RIFM, 1890C, 1900RI, 1910RI, 1920RI.

FHL(FHC) microfilms: birth (1867–1908), cemetery, chancery (1843–57), childrens home (1906–23), commissioners (1810–69), common pleas court (1810–54), county home (1863–1965), death (1867–1908), deed (1810–1916), guardian (1856–86), jail (1861–80), marriage (1810–78), Presbyterian (1879–82), quadrennial enumeration (1863, 1891–99), school (1829–94), supreme court (1810–52), tax (1810–38), will (1810–84).

OHS microfilms and records: cemetery, chancery (1843–57), childrens home (1906–23), commissioners (1810–1969), common pleas court (1810–54), county home (1873–1965), jail (1861–80), marriage (1812–61), quadrennial enumeration (1863, 1891–99), school (1829–94), supreme court (1810–52), tax (1810–38), VA military land grants, will (1808–92).

DAR volumes: Bible, cemetery, marriage, will. Published volumes: atlas, Bible, biography, birth, church, city/county directories, death, family, genealogy, history, inventory of county records, land, marriage, plat.

Manuscripts in OHS, WRHS. For newspapers, see repositories and reference volumes given in Chapter 2, section 30. For genealogical periodical articles, see indexes referred to in Chapter 2, section 19. Library: Pickaway County District Public Library, 165 E. Main St., Circleville, OH 43113. Phone 1-(614)-477-1644. Society: Pickaway County Chapter, OGS (contact library for current address). Publishes THE PICKAWAY QUARTERLY.

70. PIKE COUNTY

Pike County, authorized/established 1815/1815 from Adams, Ross, and Scioto Counties. County seat Waverly (45690).

ONAHRC: OH University in Athens. Censuses: 1820RIM, 1830RI, 1840RIP, 1850RIMD, 1860RIFMD, 1870R, 1880RIFM, 1890C, 1900RI, 1910RI, 1920RI.

FHL(FHC) microfilms: birth (1867-1908), cemetery, chancery (1835-55), childrens home (1882-1957), clerk of courts (1815-1941), commissioners (1815-1905), common pleas court (1815-59), county home (1878-1938), death (1867-1908), deed (1799-1884), district court (1852-74), jail (1873-1929), license (1816-77), Presbyterian (1832-94), supreme court (1815-51), tax (1816-38), will (1817-84).

OHS microfilms and records: chancery (1835-55), childrens home (1882-1957), clerk of courts (1815-1941), commissioners (1815-1905), common pleas court (1815-59), county home (1878-1938), district court (1852-74), jail (1873-1929), license (1816-77), marriage (1815-57), supreme court (1815-51), tax (1816-38).

DAR volumes: court, marriage, will. Published volumes: biography, birth, cemetery, census, city/county directories, court, death, gazetteer, genealogy, history, inventory of county records, land, marriage, plat, tax.

For newspapers, see repositories and reference volumes given in Chapter 2, section 30. For genealogical periodical articles, see indexes referred to in Chapter 2, section 19. Library: Garnet A. Wilson Public Library, 207 North Market St., Waverly, OH 45690. Phone 1-(614)-947-4921. Society: Pike County Chapter, OGS (contact library for current address). Publishes PIKE SPEAKS.

71. PORTAGE COUNTY

Portage County, authorized/established 1808/1808 from Trumbull County. County seat Ravenna (44262).

ONAHRC: University of Akron. Censuses: 1820RIM, 1830RI, 1840RIP, 1850RIMD, 1860RIFMD, 1870R, 1880RIFM, 1890C, 1900RI, 1910RI, 1920RI.

FHL(FHC) microfilms: administrator (1848-89), Baptist (1808-60), birth (1867-1908), cemetery, chancery (1835-53), civil court cases (1809-55), Congregational (1819-99), death (1867-1908), deed (1795-1917), Disciples (1834-63), executor (1874-92), guardian (1819-90), inventory (1862-86), marriage (1808-1917), naturalization (1859-1906), probate (1803-89), supreme court (1823-51), tax (1808-38), will (1823-1918).

OHS microfilms and records: Bible, cemetery, census (1831), chancery (1835-53), civil court cases (1809-55), guardian (1832-84), marriage (1805–65), pioneer, probate (1803–67), supreme court (1823–51), tax (1808–38), Western Reserve land (1795–1809), will (1886–1918). DAR volumes: Bible, census, marriage. Published volumes: atlas, Bible, biography, cemetery, census, church, city/county directories, genealogy, history, inventory of county records, marriage, naturalization, newspaper abstracts, plat, school, tax. Manuscripts in OHS, WRHS. For newspapers, see repositories and reference volumes given in Chapter 2, section 30. For genealogical periodical articles, see indexes referred to in Chapter 2, section 19. Library: Reed Memorial Library, 167 East Main St., Ravenna, OH 44166. Phone 1-(216)-296-2827. Society: Portage County Chapter, OGS (contact library for current address). Publishes PORTAGE PATH TO GENEALOGY.

72. PREBLE COUNTY

Preble County, authorized/established 1808/1808 from Butler and Montgomery Counties. County seat Eaton (45320). ONAHRC: Wright State University in Dayton. Censuses: 1820-RIM, 1830RI, 1840RIP, 1850RIMD, 1860RIFMD, 1870R, 1880RIFM, 1890C, 1900RI, 1910RI, 1920RI.

FHL(FHC) microfilms: administrator (1880–1905), birth (1867–1908), cemetery, chancery (1827–53), childrens home (1884–1946), civil court cases (1808–53), clerk of courts (1808–52), county home (1838–1904), death (1867–1908), deed (1805–1963), executor (1880–1905), Friends (1809–1949), marriage (1808–1903), military (1865–1917), mortgage (1833–86), probate (1858–1901), supreme court (1817–56), tax (1810–38), will (1808–1901).

OHS microfilms and records: cemetery, chancery (1827–53), childrens home (1884–1946), City of Eaton (1872–1976), civil court cases (1808–53), coroner courts (1808–52), county home (1838–1904), supreme court (1817–56), tax (1810–38).

DAR volumes: Bible, cemetery, church, marriage, newspaper. Published volumes: atlas, biography, birth, cemetery, census, church, city/county directories, court, deed, gazetteer, genealogy, history, inventory of county records, land, marriage, naturalization, newspaper abstracts, plat, tax, will. Manuscripts in WRHS. For newspapers, see repositories and reference volumes given in Chapter 2, section 30. For genealogical periodical articles, see indexes referred to in Chapter 2, section 19. Library: Preble County District Library, 301 N. Barron St., Eaton, OH 45320. Phone 1-(513)-456-4250. Society: Preble County Chapter, OGS (contact library for current address). Publishes PREBLE'S PRIDE.

73. PUTNAM COUNTY

Putnam County, authorized/established 1820/1834 from Shelby County. County seat Ottawa (45875), court house fire in 1864, some records lost. ONAHRC: Bowling Green State University. Censuses: 1830RI, 1840RIP, 1850RIMD, 1860RIFMD, 1870R, 1880RIM, 1890C, 1900RI, 1910RI, 1920RI.

FHL(FHC) microfilms: administrator (1882-93), birth (1854-1920), chancery (1850-60), clerk of courts (1835-67), common pleas court (1834-61), county home (1869-1927), death (1867-1920), deed (1830-1951), executor (1882-93), guardian (1880-1943), marriage (1834-1927), Mennonite (1835-1928), military (1861-65), naturalization (1854-1905), Presbyterian (1850-79), probate (1837-1963), tax (1834-8), will (1835-1973).

OHS microfilms and records: chancery (1850-60), clerk of courts (1835-67), common pleas court (1834-61), county home (1869-1927), death (1859-1920), deed (1881-92), guardian (1880-1943), naturalization (1860-1905), tax (1834-8), will (1902-10).

DAR volumes: church, marriage. Published volumes: atlas, biography, cemetery, church, city/county directories, death, gazetteer, genealogy, history, inventory of county records, marriage, newspaper abstracts, plat, school.

Manuscripts in OHS. For newspapers, see repositories and reference volumes given in Chapter 2, section 30. For genealogical periodical articles, see indexes referred to in Chapter 2, section 19. Library: Putnam County District Library, 525 N. Thomas St., Ottawa, OH 45875. Phone 1-(419)-523-3747. Society: Putnam County Chapter, OGS (contact library for current address). Publishes PUTNAM PASTFINDER.

74. RICHLAND COUNTY

Richland County, authorized/established 1808/1813 from Fairfield County. County seat Mansfield (44902). ONAHRC: University of Akron. Censuses: 1820RIM, 1830RI, 1840RIP, 1850RIMD, 1860RIFMD, 1870RM, 1880RIM, 1890C, 1900RI, 1910RI, 1920RI.

FHL(FHC) microfilms: administrator (1813-90), birth (1856-1909), cemetery, chancery (1822-52), childrens home (1880-1917), clerk of courts (1819-53), commissioners (1816-26, 1872-1903), common pleas court (1822-52), death (1890-1908), deed (1814-1927), executor (1849-91), guardian (1846-1905), indenture (1883-1900), inventory (1863-84), marriage (1813-1940), Methodist (1853-1982), naturalization (1852-1906), Presbyterian (1821-1983), probate (1813-1900), Reformed (1831-64), tax (1814-38), will (1816-1903).

OHS microfilms and records: administrator (1813-23), cemetery, chancery (1822-52), childrens home (1880-1917), clerk of courts (1819-53), commissioners (1813-26, 1872-1903), common pleas court (1822-52), indenture (1883-1900), marriage (1813-64), naturalization (1852-1906), tax (1814-38), will (1813-23).

DAR volumes: birth, cemetery, church, death, will. Published volumes: atlas, biography, cemetery, census, church, city/county directories, gazetteer, genealogy, history, inventory of county records, naturalization, newspaper abstracts, plat, school, will.

Manuscripts in OHS. For newspapers, see repositories and reference volumes given in Chapter 2, section 30. For genealogical periodical articles, see indexes referred to in Chapter 2, section 19. Libraries: Mansfield-Richland County Public Library, 43 W. Third St., Mansfield, OH 44902. Phone 1-(419)-524-1041. Marvin Memorial Library, 20 W. Whitney Ave., Shelby, OH 44875. Phone 1-(419)-347-5576. Societies: Richland County Chapter, OGS (contact library for current address). Publishes PASTFINDER. Richland-Shelby Chapter, OGS (contact library for current address). Publishes SHELBY SPIRIT.

75. ROSS COUNTY

Ross County, authorized/established 17979/1798 from Adams and Washington Counties. County seat Chillicothe (45601). ONAHRC: OH University in Athens. Censuses: 1820RIM, 1830RI, 1840RIP, 1850RIMFD, 1860RIFMD, 1870RM, 1880RIM, 1890C, 1900RI, 1910RI, 1820RI.

FHL(FHC) microfilms: administrator (1849-96), birth (1867-1908), Black (1804-55), cemetery, chancery (1824-52), commissioners (1809-46, 1861-1904), common pleas court (1798-1870), death (1867-1908), deed (1797-1925), estray (1805-23, 1862-1918), executor (1849-96), Friends (1871-1948), guardian (1849-89), jail (1881-1910), jury (1875-93), justices (1830-55), marriage (1798-1910), military (1862-1918), naturalization (1851-1906), New Jerusalem (1838-79), notaries (1858-86), Presbyterian (1804-98), supreme court (1803-47), tax (1800-38), tavern license (1815-39), will (1797-1879), witness (1803-29, 1852-9).

OHS microfilms and records: Black (1804-55) , cemetery, commissioners (1809-46, 1861-1904), common pleas court (1798-1870), estate (1798-1903), jail (1881-1910), marriage (1798-1890), military (1861-1918), supreme court (1805-43), tax (1800-38), will (1797-1845).

DAR volumes: cemetery, church, estate, family, genealogy, marriage, will. Published volumes: atlas, Bible, Black, cemetery, church, city/county directories, family, genealogy, history, inventory of county records, land, marriage, newspaper abstracts, will.

Manuscripts in OHS, WRHS. For newspapers, see repositories and reference volumes given in Chapter 2, section 30. For genealogical periodical articles, see indexes referred to in Chapter 2, section 19. Libraries: Chillicothe & Ross County Public Library, 140-146 Paint St., Chillicothe OH 45601. McKell Library, 30 W. Fifth, Chillicothe, OH 45601. Society: Ross County Chapter, OGS (contact library for current address). Publishes THE RCGS NEWSLETTER.

---

76. SANDUSKY COUNTY

Sandusky County, authorized/established 1820/1820 from Huron County. County seat Fremont (43420). ONAHRC: Bowling Green State University. Censuses: 1820RIM, 1830RI, 1840RIP, 1850RIMFD, 1860RIFMD, 1870RM, 1880RIM, 1890C, 1900RI, 1910RI, 1920RI.

FHL(FHC) microfilms: administrator (1820-88), birth (1867-1916), cemetery, chancery (1826-56), common pleas court (1820-61), county home (1882-1936), death (1867-1916), deed (1822-1902), district court (1852-56), executor (1852-86), guardian (1852-1901), marriage (1820-1967), Methodist (1822-95), military (1865- 1937), naturalization (1830-1912), probate (1820-1965), probate packets, supreme court (1823-57), will (1959).

OHS microfilms and records: administrator (1820-42), cemetery, chancery (1845-56), common pleas court (1820-56), county home (1882-1936), deed (1822-1902), district court (1852-56), marriage (1820-70), military (1865-1937), naturalization (1830-1912), probate (1852-1910), supreme court (1823-57), tax (1823-38).

DAR volumes: cemetery, marriage. Published volumes: atlas, biography, cemetery, church, gazetteer, genealogy, history, inventory of county records, newspaper abstracts, plat.

Manuscripts in OHS. For newspapers, see repositories and reference volumes given in Chapter 2, section 30. For genealogical periodical articles, see indexes referred to in Chapter 2, section 19. Libraries: Birchard Public Library of Sandusky County, 423 Croghan St., Fremont, OH 43420. Phone 1-(419)-334-7101. Rutherford B. Hayes Library, 1337 Hayes Ave., Fremont, OH 43420. Phone 1-(419)-332-2081. Society: Sandusky County Chapter, OGS (contact library for current address). Publishes KITH 'N KIN.

---

77. SCIOTO COUNTY

Scioto County, authorized/established 1803/1803 from Adams County. County seat Portsmouth (45662). ONAHRC: OH University in Athens. Censuses: 1820RIM, 1830RI, 1840RIP, 1850RIMFD, 1860RIFMD, 1870RM, 1880RIM, 1890C, 1900RI, 1910RI, 1920RI.

FHL(FHC) microfilms: birth (1856-1908), chancery (1839-55), commissioners (1812-1906), common pleas court (1810-57), county home

(1871–96, 1909–12), death (1856–1908), deed (1803–76), marriage (1804–1911), military (1900), naturalization (1859–1900), supreme court (1809–57), tax (1806–38), will (1810–76).

OHS microfilms and records: commissioners (1812–1906), common pleas court (1810–57), county home (1871–96, 1909–12), marriage (1804–65), military (1900), supreme court (1809–57), tax (1806–38).

DAR volumes: cemetery, marriage. Published volumes: biography, cemetery, census, city/county directories, court, gazetteer, history, inventory of county records, land, marriage, plat, tax.

Manuscripts in OHS. For newspapers, see repositories and reference volumes given in Chapter 2, section 30. For genealogical periodical articles, see indexes referred to in Chapter 2, section 19. Library: Portsmouth Public Library, 1220 Gallia St., Portsmouth, OH 45662. Phone 1-(614)–354–5688. Society: Scioto County Chapter, OGS (contact library for current address). Publishes SCIOTO COUNTY CHAPTER NEWSLETTER.

78. SENECA COUNTY

Seneca County, authorized/established 1820/1824 from Huron County. County seat Tiffin (44883), court house fire in 1841, some records lost. ONAHRC: Bowling Green State University. Censuses: 1830RI, 1840RIP, 1850RIMFD, 1860RIMD, 1870RFMD, 1880RIM. 1890C, 1900RI, 1910RI, 1920RI.

FHL(FHC) microfilms: birth (1867–1909), bond (1849–69), cemetery, chancery (1824–58), civil court cases (1852–1912), clerk of courts (1825–1914), commissioners (1841–61), common pleas court (1834–54), county home (1881–1966), death (1867–1908), deed (1821–1902), district court (1851–77), Evangelical (1842–1914), land entry (1821–1926), marriage (1841–1951), Methodist (1834–1983), naturalization (1852–1930), Presbyterian (1828–1930), probate (1852–87), quadrennial enumeration (1899–1903), reform school (1885–86), Reformed (1843–1960), supreme court (1825–55), tax (1826–38), United Church of Christ (1833–1983), veteran (1885–1944), will (1828–1964).

OHS microfilms and records: cemetery, chancery (1824–58), clerk of courts (1825–1914), common pleas court (1834–54), county home (1881–1966), deed (1821–1926), district court (1851–77), land entry (1821–1926), marriage (1841–67), military (1865–1951), probate (1853–1912), supreme court (1825–55), tax (1826–38), will (1901–10).

DAR volumes: cemetery, history, marriage. Published volumes: atlas, Bible, biography, cemetery, church, city/county directories, gazetteer, history, inventory of county records, newspaper abstracts, plat.

Manuscripts in OHS, Hayes Library. For newspapers, see repositories and reference volumes given in Chapter 2, section 30. For genealogical periodical articles, see indexes referred to in Chapter 2, section 19. Library: Tiffin-Seneca County Public Library, 77 Jefferson St., Tiffin, OH 44883. Phone 1-(419)-447-3751. Society: Seneca County Chapter, OGS (contact library for current address). Publishes SENECA SEARCHERS.

---

79. SHELBY COUNTY

Shelby County, authorized/established 1819/1819 from Miami County. County seat Sidney (45365). ONAHRC: Wright State University in Dayton. Censuses: 1820RIM, 1830RI, 1840RIP, 1850RIMFD, 1860RIMD, 1870RFM, 1880RIM, 1890C, 1900RI, 1910RI, 1920RI.

FHL(FHC) microfilms: administrator (1851-1911), birth (1851-58, 1867-1908), chancery (1839-57), childrens home (1896-1921), circuit court (1885-1912), civil court cases (1819-54), clerk of courts (1818-57), county home (1866-1947), criminal cases (1819-1914), death (1857-58, 1867-1904), deed (1819-1966), district court (1857-87), executor (1851-1911), guardian (1851-1919), jail (1879-1923), marriage (1824-1904), military (1863-1917), mortgage (1835-1908), naturalization (1843-1905), poll (1819-74), probate (1852-1901), quadrennial enumeration (1819-75), supreme court (1820-59), tax (1820-38), tavern license (1887-1947), will (1825-1902).

OHS microfilms and records: birth (1857-58), cemetery, chancery (1839-57), childrens home (1896-1921), circuit court (1888-1912), civil court cases (1819-54), clerk of courts (1818-57), county home (1866-1947), criminal cases (1819-), death (1857-58), district court (1857-87), jail (1879-1923), marriage (1825-65), military (1863-65, 1885-86), naturalization (1843-61), poll (1819-74), quadrennial enumeration (1819-75), supreme court (1820-59), tax (1820-38), tavern license (1887-1947).

DAR volumes: Bible, cemetery, marriage. Published volumes: atlas, biography, cemetery, church, city/county directories, history, inventory of county records, land, marriage, naturalization, newspaper abstracts.

For newspapers, see repositories and reference volumes given in Chapter 2, section 30. For genealogical periodical articles, see indexes referred to in Chapter 2, section 19. Libraries: Amos Memorial Public Library, 230 E. North St., Sidney, OH 45365. Phone 1-(513)-492-8354. Marvin Memorial Library, 29 W. Whitney Ave., Shelby, OH 44875. Phone 1-(519)-347-5576. Society: Richland-Shelby Chapter, OGS (contact library for current address). Publishes SHELBY SPIRIT.

---

80. STARK COUNTY

Stark County, authorized/established 1808/1809 from Columbiana County. County seat Canton (44702). ONAHRC: University of Akron. Censuses: 1920-RIM, 1830RI, 1840RIP, 1850RIMFD,

1860RIMD, 1870RFM, 1880RIM, 1890C, 1900RI, 1910RI, 1920RI.

FHL(FHC) microfilms: administrator (1810-90), Associate Reformed (1865-81), birth (1867-1908), common pleas court (1809-66), death (1867-1908), deed (1809-1906), guardian (1816-91), inventory (1880-86), land (1809-1906), marriage (1809-1972), military (1865), naturalization (1861-1903), poll (1858-76), Presbyterian (1826-96), Reformed (1897-1934), school (1862), supreme court (1810-68), tax (1810-38), will (1811-1943).

OHS microfilms and records: Bible, birth, cemetery, church, common pleas court (1810-66), early settlers, marriage (1808-65), military (1865), poll (1858-76), school (1862), supreme court (1834-68), tax (1810-38), will (1809-90).

DAR volumes: Bible, cemetery, church, family, history, marriage, will. Published volumes: atlas, Bible, biography, cemetery, census, church, city/county directories, genealogy, history, inventory of county records, land, marriage.

For newspapers, see repositories and reference volumes given in Chapter 2, section 30. For genealogical periodical articles, see indexes referred to in Chapter 2, section 19. Library: Stark County district Library, 715 Market Ave., North Canton, OH 44702. Phone 1-(216)-452-0665. Societies: Stark County Chapter, OGS (contact library for current address). Publishes TREE CLIMBER. Alliance Chapter, OGS (contact library for current address). Publishes TAGS NEWSLETTER.

81. SUMMIT COUNTY

Summit County, authorized/established 1840/1840 from Medina, Portage, and Stark Counties. County seat Akron (44308). ONAHRC: University of Akron. Censuses: 1840RIP, 1850-RIMFD, 1860RIMD, 1870RFM, 1880RIM, 1890C, 1900RI, 1910RI, 1920RI.

FHL(FHC) microfilms: administrator (1846-1944), birth (1866-1908), common pleas court (1840-70), death (1870-1908), deed (1840-1914), estate (1841-1944), guardian (1840-86), Jewish (1865-1968), marriage (1840-1916), militia (1857-65), naturalization (1859-1906), Presbyterian (1809-1938), probate (1852-86), supreme court (1842-51), United Church of Christ (1817-1967), will (1839-1909).

OHS microfilms and records: Bible, cemetery, clerk of courts (1840-70), common pleas court (1840-52), marriage (1840-65), militia (1857-65), naturalization (1859-1906), supreme court (1842-51), Western Reserve land (1795-1809), will (1887-1909).

DAR volumes: Bible, cemetery, marriage, will. Published volumes: atlas, biography, cemetery, census, church, city/county directories, death, family, genealogy, history, inventory of county records, land, marriage, school, tax, will.

For newspapers, see repositories and reference volumes given in Chapter 2, section 30. For genealogical periodical articles, see indexes referred to in Chapter 2, section 19. Libraries: Akron-Summit County Public Library, 55 S. Main St., Akron, OH 44326. Phone 1-(216)-762-7621. Family History Library, 106 East Howe Rd., Tallmadge, OH 44278. Society: Summit County Chapter, OGS (contact library for current address). Publishes THE HIGHPOINT.

82. TRUMBULL COUNTY

Trumbull County, authorized/established 1800/1800 from Jefferson and Wayne (MI) Counties. County seat Warren (44481), court house fire in 1895, some records lost. ONAHRC: WRHS in Cleveland. Censuses: 1820RIM, 1830RI, 1840RIP, 1850RIMFD, 1860RIMD, 1870RFM, 1880RIM, 1890C, 1900RI, 1920RI.

FHL(FHC) microfilms: administrator (1853-63, 1882-93), appraisal (1882-90), Baptist (1820-27), birth (1867-1908), cemetery, commissioners (1837-1908), Congregational (1817-69), death (1867-1908), deed (1795-1845), executor (1853-86), guardian (1839-99), indenture (1824-69), inventory (1853-90), land sales petitions (1852-87), marriage (1803-1916), military (1861-1919), Presbyterian (1817-69), probate (1803-87), school (1831-1913), supreme court (1807-41), tax (1806-38), Western Reserve Land (1795-1809), will (1841-86).

OHS microfilms and records: birth, cemetery, commissioners (1837-1908), death, indenture (1824-69), marriage (1803-65), military (1861-1919), pioneer women, school (1831-1913), tax (1806-38), War of 1812, will (1803-50).

DAR volumes: court, history, marriage. Published volumes: atlas, Bible, biography, birth, cemetery, census, church, court, death, deed, family, genealogy, history, inventory of county records, land, marriage, naturalization, newspaper abstracts, will.

For newspapers, see repositories and reference volumes given in Chapter 2, section 30. For genealogical periodical articles, see indexes referred to in Chapter 2, section 19. Library: Warren-Trumbull County Public Library, 444 Mahoning Avenue, NW, Warren, OH 44483. Phone 1-(216)-399-8807. Society: Trumbull County Chapter, OGS (contact library for current address). Publishes ANCESTOR TRAILS.

83. TUSCARAWAS COUNTY

Tuscarawas County, authorized/established 1808/1808 from Muskingum County. County seat New Philadelphia (44663). ONAHRC: University of Akron. Censuses: 1820RIM, 1830RI, 1840RIP, 1850RIMFD, 1860RIMD, 1870RFM, 1880RIM, 1890C, 1900RI, 1910RI, 1920RI.

FHL(FHC) microfilms: administrator (1817–1978), appearance (1852–1970), birth (1867–1908), commissioners (1808–1901), common pleas court (1808–70), death (1867–1908), executor (1854–93), guardian (1832–1977), jail (1904–29), law record (1808–54), marriage (1808–1978), naturalization (1854–1906), probate (1808–1938), supreme court (1827–52), tax (1810–38), will (1809–1909).

OHS microfilms and records: administrator (1817–1978), appearance (1852–1970), birth (1867–1966), commissioners (1808–1901), common pleas court (1808–70), county home (1862–1912), death (1867–1966), guardian (1832–1977), law record (1808–54), marriage (1808–1978), naturalization (1854–1906), probate (1808–1938), supreme court (1827–52), tax (1810–38), will (1809–53).

DAR volume: will. Published volumes: atlas, biography, cemetery, census, church, city/county directories, gazetteer, history, inventory of county records, land, marriage, will.

For newspapers, see repositories and reference volumes given in Chapter 2, section 30. For genealogical periodical articles, see indexes referred to in Chapter 2, section 19. Library: Tuscarawas County Public Library, 121 Fair Avenue, NW, New Philadelphia, OH 44663. Phone 1-(216)-364-4474. Society: Tuscarawas County Chapter, OGS (contact library for current address). Publishes PIONEER FOOTPRINTS.

84. UNION COUNTY

Union County, authorized/established 1820/1820 from Delaware, Franklin, Logan, and Madison Counties. ONAHRC: OHS in Columbus. Censuses: 1820RIM, 1830RI, 1840RIP, 1850RIMFD, 1860RIMD, 1870RFM, 1880RIM, 1890C, 1900RI, 1910RI, 1920RI.

FHL(FHC) microfilms: administrator (1820–52, 1870–1907), birth (1867–1909), childrens home (1884–1907), commissioners (1820–1900), common pleas court (1820–55), death (1867–1903), deed (1811–1954), district court (1820–78), executor (1861–1903), guardian (1855–1906), land sale (1820–43), marriage (1820–1904), military (1861–99), mortgage (1851–1901), naturalization (1860–1906), Presbyterian (1821–98), probate (1852–1901), supreme court (1820–78), tax (1820–38), will (1852–1903).

OHS microfilms and records: childrens home (1884–1907), commissioners (1820–1900), common pleas court (1820–55), district court (1820–78), land sale (1820–43), marriage (1820–65), supreme court (1820–78), tax (1820–38).

DAR volumes: cemetery, death, marriage. Published volumes: atlas, Bible, cemetery, church, court, death, gazetteer, genealogy, history, inventory of county records, land, newspaper abstracts, plat.

Manuscripts in OHS. For newspapers, see repositories and reference volumes given in Chapter 2, section 30. For genealogical periodical articles, see indexes referred to in Chapter 2, section 19.

Library: Marysville Public Library, 231 S. Plum St., Marysville, OH 43040. Phone 1-(513)-642-1876. Society: Union County Chapter, OGS (contact library for current address). Publishes UNION ECHOES.

85. VAN WERT COUNTY

Van Wert County, authorized/established 1820/1837 from Darke County. ONAHRC: Bowling Green State University. Censuses: 1830RI, 1840RIP, 1850RIMFD, 1860RIMD, 1870RFM, 1880RIM, 1890C, 1900RI, 1820RI.

FHL(FHC) microfilms: administrator (1862-1903), birth (1867-1908), clerk of courts (1837-1912), common pleas court (1837-92), coroner (1880-1939), death (1867-1908), deed (1838-86), district court (1842-84), divorce (1902-25), estate (1839-1933), guardian (1873-96), jail (1873-96), land entry (1824-64), land sales (1829-83), marriage (1840-1951), military (1865-1953), naturalization (1852-1905), probate (1852-1910), supreme court (1843-75), tax (1833), will (1840-1911).

OHS microfilms and records: common pleas court (1837-56), deed (1838-86), guardian (1873-96), jail (1874-1912), marriage (1840-65, 1891-99), military (1865-1953).

DAR volume: marriage. Published volumes: atlas, biography, cemetery, census, church, genealogy, history, inventory of county records, land, marriage, newspaper abstracts, plat, will.

For newspapers, see repositories and reference volumes given in Chapter 2, section 30. For genealogical periodical articles, see indexes referred to in Chapter 2, section 19. Library: Brumback Library, 215 W. Main St., Van Wert, OH 45891. Phone 1-(419)-238-2168. Society: Van Wert Chapter, OGS (contact library for current address). Publishes THE VAN WERT CONNECTION.

86. VINTON COUNTY

Vinton County, authorized/established 1850/1850 from Athens, Gallia, Hocking, Jackson, and Ross Counties. County seat McArthur (45651). ONAHRC: OH University in Athens. Censuses: 1850RIMFD, 1860RIMD, 1870RFM, 1880RIM, 1890C, 1900RI, 1910RI, 1920RI.

FHL(FHC) microfilms: birth (1867-1962), church, commissioners (1850-1908), death (1867-1952), deed (1850-76), marriage (1850-1914), naturalization (1877-1926), probate (1852-80), school (1850-63), will (1853-76.

OHS microfilms and records: cemetery, commissioners (1850-1908), marriage (1850-65), school (1850-63).

DAR volumes: cemetery, marriage. Published volumes: atlas, biography, cemetery, census, church, Civil War, history, inventory of county records, land, marriage.

For newspapers, see repositories and reference volumes given in Chapter 2, section 30. For genealogical periodical articles, see indexes referred to in Chapter 2, section 19. Library: Herbert Wescoat Memorial Library, 122 W. Main St., McArthur, OH 45651. Phone 1-(614)-596-5691. Society: Vinton County Chapter, OGS (contact library for current address). Publishes VINTON COUNTY HERITAGE.

87. WARREN COUNTY

Warren County, authorized/established 1803/1803 from Hamilton County. County seat Lebanon (45036). ONAHRC: University of Cincinnati. Censuses: 1820RIM, 1830RI, 1840RIP, 1850RIMFD, 1860RIMD, 1870RFM, 1880RIM, 1890C, 1900RI, 1910RI, 1820RI.

FHL(FHC) microfilms: administrator (1865–81), apprentice (1824–67), Baptist (1820–46), birth (1867–1908), chancery (1824–51), childrens home (1875–1952), civil court cases (1803–52), commissioners (1803–1901), common pleas court (1803–70), death (1867–1908), deed (1795–1910), estate (1803–1970), executor (1865–81), Friends (1790–1963), guardian (1860–90), indenture (1824–67), marriage (1803–1924), naturalization (1856–1906), Presbyterian (1837–1901), probate (1844–86), probate bonds (1803–65), Shakers (1837–84, 1902–11), supreme court (1803–75), tax (1806–38), United Society (1801–1911), will (1804–95).

OHS microfilms and records: apprentice (1824–67), Bible, cemetery, chancery (1824–51), childrens home (1874–1952), civil court cases (1803–52), common pleas court (1803–70), indenture (1824–67), supreme court (1803–75), tax (1806–38).

DAR volumes: Bible, cemetery, family, marriage. Published volumes: apprentice, atlas, Bible, cemetery, church, court, family, gazetteer, genealogy, history, land, marriage, probate, will.

For newspapers, see repositories and reference volumes given in Chapter 2, section 30. For genealogical periodical articles, see indexes referred to in Chapter 2, section 19. Libraries: Lebanon Public Library, 101 S. Broadway, Lebanon, OH 45036. Phone 1-(513)-932-2665. Warren County Genealogical Society Library, 300 E. Silver St., Lebanon, OH 45036. Phone 1-(513)-933-1144. Society: Warren County Chapter, OGS (contact library for current address). Publishes WARREN COUNTY NEWSLETTER and HEIRLINE.

88. WASHINGTON COUNTY

Washington County, authorized/established 1788/1788 as an original county. County seat Marietta (45750). ONAHRC: OH University in Athens. Censuses: 1800RI, 1810RI, 1820RIM, 1830RI, 1840RIP, 1850RIMFD, 1860RIMD, 1870RFM, 1880RIFM, 1890C, 1900RI, 1910RI, 1920RI.

FHL(FHC) microfilms: administrator (1803-1949), Baptist, birth (1867-1914), civil court cases (1795-1825), Civil War (1860-70), commissioners (1797-1902), common pleas court (1790-1848), Congregational (1840-88), county home (1836-1920), death (1867-1908), deed (1788-1900), executor (1808-1949), guardian (1803-1949), jail (1868-1927), marriage (1789-1918), military (1816-1914), naturalization (1859-1905), poll (1802-1908), Presbyterian (1810-), probate (1789-1886), quadrennial enumeration (1887-1911), quarter sessions (1800-02), supreme court (1808-09, 1818-41), surveyor (1805-73), tax (1800, 1801-50), will (1853-1889).

OHS microfilms and records: Civil War (1860-70), commissioners (1797-1902), common pleas court (1790-1848), county home (1836-1920), jail (1868-1927), marriage (1789-1864), military (1861-1914), poll (1802-1908), quadrennial enumeration (1887-1911), quarter sessions (1800-02), supreme court (1808-09, 1818-41), tax (1800, 1808-38), will (1790-1860).

DAR volumes: Bible, cemetery, church, court, death, family, marriage, newspaper abstracts, probate, will. Published volumes: atlas, Bible, biography, Black, cemetery, census, church, court, death, family, gazetteer, genealogy, history, inventory of county records, land, marriage, naturalization, newspaper abstracts, plat, probate, school, tax, will.

For newspapers, see repositories and reference volumes given in Chapter 2, section 30. For genealogical periodical articles, see indexes referred to in Chapter 2, section 19. Library: Washington County Public Library, 615 Fifth St., Marietta, OH 45750. Phone 1-(614)-373-1057. Society: Washington County Chapter, OGS (contact library for current address). Publishes WASHINGTON.

89. WAYNE COUNTY

Wayne County, authorized/established 1808/1812 from Columbiana County. County seat Wooster (44691). ONAHRC: University of Akron. Censuses: 1820RIM, 1830RI, 1840RIP, 1850RIMFD, 1860RIMD, 1870RFM, 1880RIFM, 1890C, 1900RI, 1910RI, 1920RI.

FHL(FHC) microfilms: administrator (1844-70, 1880-89), appraisal (1831-44), appearance (1812-52), birth (1867-1908), chancery (1817-49), civil court cases (1837-88), common pleas court (1817-74), death (1867-1908), deed (1813-1914), district court (1849-89), guardian (1849-96), marriage (1813-1934), Mennonite (1822-1940), ministers' licenses (1819-56), naturalization (1861-1903), Presbyterian (1816-99), probate (1808-1950), Reformed (1883-88), religious incorporations (1819-56), supreme court (1813-52), tax (1814-38).

OHS microfilms and records: appearance (1812-52), Bible, cemetery, chancery (1817-49), common pleas court (1817-74), marriage (1812-64), supreme court (1813-52), tax (1814-38).

208

DAR volumes: Bible, cemetery, church, family, marriage, population. Published volumes: atlas, biography, Black, cemetery, census, church, estate, family, guardian, history, inventory of county records, marriage, mortuary, naturalization, tax, will.

For newspapers, see repositories and reference volumes given in Chapter 2, section 30. For genealogical periodical articles, see indexes referred to in Chapter 2, section 19. Library: Wayne County Public Library, 304 N. Market St., Wooster, OH 44691. Phone 1-(216)-262-0916. Society: Wayne County Chapter, OGS ((contact library for current address). Publishes WAYNE COUNTY HISTORICAL SOCIETY.

90. WILLIAMS COUNTY

Williams County, authorized/established 1820/1824 from Darke County. County seat Bryan (43506). ONAHRC: Bowling Green State University. Censuses: 1830RI, 1840RIP, 1850RIMFD, 1860RIMD, 1870RFM, 1880RIFM, 1890C, 1900RI, 1910RI, 1920RI.

FHL(FHC) microfilms: administrator (1845-93), birth (1867-1941), chancery (1841-56), civil court cases (1859-87), common pleas court (1824-78), county home (1874-1955), death (1867-1941), deed (1824-1964), Episcopal (1870-), executor (1856-87), guardian (1856-87), infirmary (1874-1955), inventory (1856-88), Lutheran (1862-), marriage (1824-1918), military (1859-1972), naturalization (1836-42, 1860-1929), Presbyterian (1872-), probate (1825-1972), real estate (1852-86), supreme court (1833-60), tax (1827-50), will (1827-1911).

OHS microfilms and records: chancery (1841-56), civil court cases (1859-87), common pleas court (1824-78), county home (1874-1955), deed (1881-86), naturalization (1836-42, 1860-1929), supreme court (1833-60), tax (1827-38).

Published volumes: atlas, biography, census, family, gazetteer, history, inventory of county records, marriage, newspaper abstracts.

For newspapers, see repositories and reference volumes given in Chapter 2, section 30. For genealogical periodical articles, see indexes referred to in Chapter 2, section 19. Library: Williams County Public Library, 107 East High St., Bryan, OH 43506. Phone 1-(419)-636-6734. Society: Williams County Chapter, OGS (contact library for current address). Publishes OHIO'S LAST FRONTIER.

91. WOOD COUNTY

Wood County, authorized/established 1820/1820 from Logan County. County seat Bowling Green (43402). ONAHRC: Bowling Green State University. Censuses: 1830RI, 1840RIP, 1850RIMFD, 1860-RIMD, 1870RFM, 1880RIFM, 1890C, 1900RI, 1910RI, 1920RI.

FHL(FHC) microfilms: administrator (1820-85), appearance (1826-99), birth (1867-1909), cemetery, common pleas court (1823-56), death (1867-1908), deed (1820-1912), district court (1841-76), guardian (1852-88), infirmary (1868-1915), Lutheran (1800-1983), marriage (1820-1929), Methodist (1881-1967), military (1865-1941), mortgage (1838-81), naturalization (1859-1906), poll (1821-73), Presbyterian (1823-1982), probate (1820-1960), quadrennial enumeration (1842, 1855-60, 1895-99), supreme court (1825-76), tax (1822-43), will (1899-1910).

OHS microfilms and records: administrator (1821-85), cemetery, common pleas court (1823-56), coroner (1841-76), guardian (1852-85), marriage (1820-65), military (1865-1937), supreme court (1825-76), tax (1822-38), will (1899-1910).

DAR volumes: cemetery, marriage. Published volumes: atlas, biography, cemetery, census, church, estate, genealogy, guardian, history, inventory of county records, newspaper abstracts, will.

For newspapers, see repositories and reference volumes given in Chapter 2, section 30. For genealogical periodical articles, see indexes referred to in Chapter 2, section 19. Library: Wood County District Library, 251 N. Main St., Bowling Green, OH 43402. Phone 1-(419)-352-5104. Society: Wood County Chapter, OGS (contact library for current address). Publishes NEWSLETTER.

92. WYANDOT COUNTY

Wyandot County, authorized/established 1845/1845 from Crawford, Hancock, Hardin, and Marion Counties. county seat Upper Sandusky (43351). ONAHRC: Bowling Green State University. Censuses: 1850RIMFD, 1860RID, 1870RFM, 1880RIFM, 1890C, 1900RI, 1910RI, 1920RI.

FHL(FHC) microfilms: administrator (1845-1903), birth (1867-1940), common pleas court (1845-1919), death (1867-1908), deed (1826-1946), estate (1845-1906), executor (1860-95), guardian (1860-1920), inventory (1845-88), marriage (1845-1951), military (1862-1924), mortgage (1845-88), naturalization (1860-1905), probate (1845-1952), Universalist (1870-1912), will (1845-1911).

OHS microfilms and records: cemetery, deed (1826-70), marriage (1845-65), probate (1852-89), will (1901-06).

DAR volume: cemetery. Published volumes: atlas, Bible, biography, cemetery, census, city/county directories, deed, history, inventory of county records, naturalization newspaper abstracts, plat.

For newspapers, see repositories and reference volumes given in Chapter 2, section 30. For genealogical periodical articles, see indexes referred to in Chapter 2, section 19. Libraries: Wyandot County Historical Society Library, 130 S. 7th St., Upper Sandusky, OH 43351. Phone 1-(419)-294-3857. Upper Sandusky Community Library, 301 N. Sandusky, Upper Sandusky, OH 433512. Phone 1-(419)-294-1345.

<u>Society</u>: Wyandot County Chapter, OGS (contact library for current address). Publishes WYANDOT TRACERS.

Abbreviations

ACPL	Allen County Public Library
C	1890 Union pension census
CH	County court houses
D	Death or mortality censuses
DAR	Daughters of the American Revolution
F	Farm and ranch censuses
FHC	Family History Center
FHL	Family History Library
LGL	Large genealogical libraries
LL	Local libraries
LR	Local repositories
M	Manufactures censuses
NA	National Archives
NARB	National Archives Regional Branches
OGS	Ohio Genealogical Society
OHS	Ohio Historical Society
ONAHRC	Ohio Network of American History Research Centers
P	1840 Revolutionary War veteran census
PLC	Public Library of Cincinnati
R	Regular censuses
RL	Regional libraries
SLO	State Library of Ohio
T	Tax substitutes for censuses
WPA	Works Progress Administration
WRHS	Western Reserve Historical Society

Books by George K. Schweitzer

CIVIL WAR GENEALOGY. A 78-paged book of 316 sources for tracing your Civil War ancestor. Chapters include [I]: The Civil War, [II]: The Archives, [III]: National Publications, [IV]: State Publications, [V]: Local Sources, [VI]: Military Unit Histories, [VII]: Civil War Events.

GEORGIA GENEALOGICAL RESEARCH. A 235-paged book containing 1303 sources for tracing your GA ancestor along with detailed instructions. Chapters include [I]: GA Background, [II]: Types of Records, [III]: Record Locations, [IV]: Research Procedure and County Listings (detailed listing of records available for each of the 159 GA counties).

GERMAN GENEALOGICAL RESEARCH. A 252-paged book containing 1924 sources for tracing your German ancestor along with detailed instructions. Chapters include [I]: German Background, [II]: Germans to America, [III]: Bridging the Atlantic, [IV]: Types of German Records, [V]: German Record Repositories, [VI]: The German Language.

HANDBOOK OF GENEALOGICAL SOURCES. A 217-paged book describing all major and many minor sources of genealogical information with precise and detailed instructions for obtaining data from them. 129 sections going from adoptions, archives, atlases---down through gazetteers, group theory, guardianships---to War of 1812, ward maps, wills, and WPA records.

KENTUCKY GENEALOGICAL RESEARCH. A 154-paged book containing 1191 sources for tracing your KY ancestor along with detailed instructions. Chapters include [I]: KY Background, [II]: Types of Records, [III]: Record Locations, [IV]: Research Procedure and County Listings (detailed listing of records available for each of the 120 KY counties).

MARYLAND GENEALOGICAL RESEARCH. A 208-paged book containing 1176 sources for tracing your MD ancestor along with detailed instructions. Chapters include [I]: MD Background, [II]: Types of Records, [III]: Record Locations, [IV]: Research Procedure and County Listings (detailed listing of records available for each of the 23 MD counties and for Baltimore City).

MASSACHUSETTS GENEALOGICAL RESEARCH. A 279-paged book containing 1709 sources for tracing your MA ancestor along with detailed instructions. Chapters include [I]: MA Background, [II]: Types of Records, [III]: Record Locations, [IV]: Research Procedure and County-Town-City Listings (detailed listing of records available for each of the 14 MA counties and the 351 cities-towns).

NEW YORK GENEALOGICAL RESEARCH. A 240-paged book containing 1426 sources for tracing your NY ancestor along with detailed instructions. Chapters include [I]: NY Background, [II]: Types of Records, [III]: Record Locations, [IV]: Research Procedure and NY City Record Listings (detailed listing of records available for the 5 counties of NY City), [V]: Record Listings for Other Counties (detailed listing of records available for each of the other 57 NY counties).

NORTH CAROLINA GENEALOGICAL RESEARCH. A 172-paged book containing 1233 sources for tracing your NC ancestor along with detailed instructions. Chapters include [I]: NC Background, [II]: Types of Records, [III]: Record Locations, [IV]: Research Procedure and County Listings (detailed listing of records available for each of the 100 NC counties).

OHIO GENEALOGICAL RESEARCH. A 212-paged book containing 1241 sources for tracing your OH ancestor along with detailed instructions. Chapters include [I]: OH Background, [II]: Types of Records, [III]: Record Locations, [IV]: Research Procedure and County Listings (detailed listing of records available for each of the 88 OH counties).

PENNSYLVANIA GENEALOGICAL RESEARCH. A 225-paged book containing 1309 sources for tracing your PA ancestor along with detailed instructions. Chapters include [I]: PA Background, [II]: Types of Records, [III]: Record Locations, [IV]: Research Procedure and County Listings (detailed listing of records available for each of the 67 PA counties).

REVOLUTIONARY WAR GENEALOGY. A 110-paged book containing 407 sources for tracing your Revolutionary War ancestor. Chapters include [I]: Revolutionary War History, [II]: The Archives, [III]: National Publications, [IV]: State Publications, [V]: Local Sources, [VI]: Military Unit Histories, [VII]: Sites and Museums.

SOUTH CAROLINA GENEALOGICAL RESEARCH. A 190-paged book containing 1107 sources for tracing your SC ancestor along with detailed instructions. Chapters include [I]: SC Background, [II]: Types of Records, [III]: Record Locations, [IV]: Research Procedure and County Listings (detailed listing of records available for each of the 47 SC counties and districts).

TENNESSEE GENEALOGICAL RESEARCH. A 136-paged book containing 1073 sources for tracing your TN ancestor along with detailed instructions. Chapters include [I]: TN Background, [II]: Types of Records, [III]: Record Locations, [IV]: Research Procedure and County Listings (detailed listing of records available for each of the 96 TN counties).

VIRGINIA GENEALOGICAL RESEARCH. A 187-paged book containing 1273 sources for tracing your VA ancestor along with detailed instructions. Chapters include [I]: VA Background, [II]: Types of Records, [III]: Record Locations, [IV]: Research Procedure and County Listings (detailed listing of records available for each of the 100 VA counties and 41 major cities).

WAR OF 1812 GENEALOGY. A 75-paged book of 289 sources for tracing your War of 1812 ancestor. Chapters include [I]: History of the War, [II]: Service Records, [III]: Post-War Records, [IV]: Publications, [V]: Local Sources, [VI]: Sites and Events, [VII]: Sources for British and Canadian Participants.

All of the above books may be ordered from Dr. Geo. K. Schweitzer, 407 Ascot Court, Knoxville, TN 37923-5807. Send a long SASE for a FREE descriptive leaflet and prices.